Moving With Words & Actions

Physical Literacy for Preschool and Primary Children

Meeting the National Standards & Grade-Level Outcomes

Rhonda L. Clements, EdD

Manhattanville College

Sharon L. Schneider, MS

Hofstra University

SHAPE America

SOCIETY OF HEALTH AND PHYSICAL EDUCATORS®

health. moves. minds.

Human Kinetics

Library-of-Congress Cataloging-in-Publication

Names: Clements, Rhonda L., author. | Schneider, Sharon L., author.
Title: Moving with words & actions : physical literacy for preschool and
  primary children / Rhonda L. Clements, Sharon L. Schneider.
Other titles: Moving with words and actions
Description: Champaign, IL : Human Kinetics, 2017. | Includes bibliographical
  references.
Identifiers: LCCN 2017018111 (print) | LCCN 2017034474 (ebook) | ISBN
  9781492548621 (e-book) | ISBN 9781492547907 (print)
Subjects: LCSH: Movement education. | Physical education and training--Study
  and teaching (Preschool) | Physical education and training--Study and
  teaching (Elementary)
Classification: LCC GV452 (ebook) | LCC GV452 .C57 2017 (print) | DDC
  372.86--dc23
LC record available at https://lccn.loc.gov/2017018111

ISBN: 978-1-4925-4790-7 (print)

Copyright © 2017 by SHAPE America – Society of Health and Physical Educators

Suggested citation: Clements, R.L., and Schneider, S.L. 2017. *Moving with words & actions: Physical literacy for preschool and primary children*. Reston, VA: SHAPE America; Champaign, IL: Human Kinetics.

The web addresses cited in this text were current as of May 2017, unless otherwise noted.

Acquisitions Editor: Ray Vallese; **SHAPE America Editor:** Joe McGavin; **Developmental Editor:** Jacqueline Eaton Blakley; **Senior Managing Editor:** Amy Stahl; **Copyeditor:** Annette Pierce; **Graphic Designer:** Angela K. Snyder; **Cover Designer:** Keri Evans; **Photograph (cover):** Mark Bowden/Getty Images/iStockphoto; **Senior Art Manager:** Kelly Hendren; **Illustrations:** © Rhonda L. Clements and Sharon L. Schneider; **Printer:** Sheridan Books

Printed in the United States of America

10 9 8 7 6 5 4 3 2 1

The paper in this book is certified under a sustainable forestry program.

Human Kinetics
Website: www.HumanKinetics.com

United States: Human Kinetics
P.O. Box 5076
Champaign, IL 61825-5076
800-747-4457
e-mail: info@hkusa.com

Canada: Human Kinetics
475 Devonshire Road Unit 100
Windsor, ON N8Y 2L5
800-465-7301 (in Canada only)
e-mail: info@hkcanada.com

Europe: Human Kinetics
107 Bradford Road
Stanningley
Leeds LS28 6AT, United Kingdom
+44 (0) 113 255 5665
e-mail: hk@hkeurope.com

For information about Human Kinetics' coverage in other areas of the world, please visit our website: www.HumanKinetics.com

E7041

"Movement, imagination and play are keys to a happy childhood."

Sharon Schneider

"To be someone, you must become someone."

Rhonda Clements

Contents

Chapter 9 Moving With Words & Actions in Language Arts. . . . 207

Preface

With the rate of childhood obesity increasing and beginning at an earlier age in many parts of the world, opportunities for planned physical activity and unstructured physical play are needed now more than ever. This book's content supports SHAPE America's National Standards for K-12 Physical Education (published in 2013), which stress that the goal of physical education is to develop physically literate individuals who have the knowledge, skills, and confidence to enjoy a lifetime of healthful physical activity. This goal is also critical for teachers of young children who are searching for age-appropriate content, for a better understanding of how to plan and implement comprehensive lessons, and for suggestions of ways to assess a lesson's success. *Moving With Words & Actions* addresses the teacher's desire to implement activities that can awaken children's love for lifelong physical activity. It also confronts the problem of childhood obesity by providing the tools needed to increase the young child's level of physical activity and movement competency.

We selected the title *Moving With Words & Actions: Physical Literacy for Preschool and Primary Children* for this book because words are the key stimuli for engaging children in active movement. The use of words to entice children to move is presented according to topics that the child can relate to readily, such as those found in his or her immediate environment and those that reflect the body's parts and capabilities as well as the child's academic learning. With the great emphasis on language arts and literacy skills, as seen in the areas of math literacy, English literacy, computer literacy, and science literacy, it seems most appropriate that the title of this book reinforce the fact that words and actions work together in lesson plans that enrich children's knowledge of their expanding world, their understanding of themselves and others, and their ability to move competently and confidently within it. The title *Moving With Words & Actions* makes this point clear as you select from a variety of lesson plans that contain as many as 30 action words.

Literacy development in children is directly related to language development. Physical literacy is directly related to children's ability to move efficiently and effectively to complete age-appropriate movement tasks. Just as young children use words to become more language-literate, their understanding and demonstration of action words can help them become more physically literate. This is seen as the young child begins to learn that every movement that he or she performs has a word to describe that action. The term "physically literate" makes use of children's fascination with new words, their delight in moving actively with peers, and their strong urge to participate cooperatively in learning tasks made up of group physical activities that emphasize action words. The outcome is a solid first step toward the child's becoming a physically literate learner who later will move with a high level of competence and confidence in multiple environments throughout an active life. This book links physical literacy with words so that you will have ample activities to foster and enhance this concept.

Organization and Content

Whether employed in childcare centers or programs or in public or private elementary schools, teachers of preschool and primary children have a responsibility to promote children's physical literacy development based on the most current theories, professional knowledge, and research. This book is organized so that its lesson plans are associated with National Standards and respected guidelines. In addition, all lesson plans were field-tested according to best practices. It also is organized with the understanding that readers' professional training and their levels of experience with young children might vary. Therefore, the book is divided into two distinct parts.

Part I emphasizes *setting the standard* with age-appropriate content, instruction, and assessment. Chapter 1 begins by offering strong evidence of the importance that words play in the lives of young children. SHAPE America's National Standards for K-12 Physical Education are identified, along with a discussion of how physical literacy applies to the young child. The chapter continues with a comprehensive listing of more than 90 locomotor and nonlocomotor skills. Because not all young children are able to understand the meaning of some action words immediately, each skill is defined and placed in a sentence structure that you can use when introducing or reinforcing new physical skills to your students. This invaluable content is followed by a listing of movement concepts and an explanation of their importance in expanding the young child's knowledge of the body. The chapter ends with information related to key manipulative skills and several learning tasks that do not require advanced training to teach.

Chapter 2 provides great insight into creating and implementing lessons plans. Concrete information that reaffirms the importance of behavioral objectives and what constitutes an appropriate learning task, that uses knowledge about students to inform teaching, that highlights the two primary instructional strategies for this age group, and that simplifies one's understanding of academic language is especially meaningful. Chapter 3 identifies five additional teaching practices that are certain to interest student teachers when creating preservice lessons or demonstration lessons for employment opportunities. The goal of this chapter is to make the most of every lesson. Part I is completed by chapter 4, in which we identify three assessment techniques that coincide with contemporary practices in physical education and in the early childhood setting.

Part II of *Moving With Words & Actions* presents more than 70 lessons that address the content areas associated most closely with the young child's body, home, community, language, and knowledge of the world. Chapter 5 provides content knowledge for enhanced physical literacy regarding the body's physical nature. All lesson plans examine different body parts and the ways in which they move. The chapter also emphasizes the child's awareness of healthy foods and their benefits. Chapter 6 addresses children's understanding of their local communities through learning tasks that highlight the roles of community helpers and settings that are familiar to most young children. Chapter 7 draws on the fact that children are fascinated by the movement of living creatures in their home environments and other parts of the world. The lesson plans in this chapter help children gain an appreciation of these creatures as they imitate their movements, behaviors, and characteristics. Chapter 8 fills a large void in the use of movement to reinforce math and science content for young children. Action rhymes, riddles, and a variety of games serve as innovative learning tasks for teaching this environmental and numerical content. Chapter 9 elaborates and expands on children's language arts and movement vocabulary, beginning with alphabet challenges, action poems, movement riddles, and more than 15 movement narratives that are certain to stimulate children's love for moderate to vigorous movement.

Audience

Moving With Words & Actions provides more than 70 lesson plans that can satisfy young children's urge for movement and increase their physical literacy while also expanding their understanding of words, movements, and academic concepts. The book represents an indispensable resource for anyone responsible for teaching children ages 3 through 8: physical educators, classroom teachers, daycare and preschool specialists, movement specialists, community group leaders, home school groups, afterschool specialists, and special education teachers.

Teacher trainers in physical education will find original movement content presented in a manner that they can modify easily to fit lesson plan formats for teacher certification such as the nationally recognized Educational Teacher Performance Assessment (edTPA). All content is designed to meet SHAPE America's National Standards for K-12 Physical Education (2013). Also, teacher trainers in early childhood and elementary school education will be able to adapt the activities to fit their profession's basic lesson plans as they discover two instructional strategies used commonly by physical education teachers in schoolyards or limited spaces. Teachers working within an inclusive setting or in a self-contained classroom can adapt the learning tasks easily to meet the requirements found in individualized education programs and 504 accommodation plans. Also, recess, lunchtime, and afterschool specialists will find the contents of this book dynamic and appropriate because of the noncompetitive nature of the activities. Most important, the majority of the learning tasks in this book do not require equipment or a specialized setting, and they complement existing curricula. The contents of this book serve as an excellent resource for practitioners in search of innovative activities that blend physical activity with academic concepts for developing physically literate children.

Unique Features and Benefits

Each lesson plan provides children with new understandings about how the body functions, moves, and grows in healthy ways. The child's movement vocabulary is guaranteed to be enhanced after participating in just a few of the lessons. This emphasis on words and their impact on learning enrich children's physical literacy greatly. This is possible also because, unlike most resources that focus on only one movement activity per lesson, each lesson in this book contains no fewer than three learning tasks that involve moderate to vigorous activity. These lessons are aimed at the needs and interests of the individual child, partners, and the whole class. You can use the lessons immediately because they require little, if any, equipment. Most important, each lesson has been field-tested with young children for its appropriateness, and each addresses one or more of the National Standards through one or more of SHAPE America's Grade-Level Outcomes for K-12 Physical Education, which were published in 2013 and describe what children should know and be able to do in each grade. These features in each of the more than 70 lesson plans offer a positive first step in providing teachers of young children the ability to plan, practice instructional strategies, and employ suggested means to assess learning.

Acknowledgments

The authors would like to extend their sincere gratitude to the school administrators, faculty, staff, and children of the following early childhood learning centers and elementary schools, whose feedback and knowledge greatly enhanced the contents of this book.

- Educational Alliance, New York, New York
- Farmingdale School District Universal Pre-K Program, Farmingdale, New York, in partnership with Hofstra University's Early Childhood Education Program
- Monsignor Boyle Head Start, Bronx, New York
- Quick Start Day Care Center, St. Albans, New York
- Silver Lake Head Start, Staten Island, New York
- The Earl C. McGraw School, Hampden, Maine
- Regional School Unit 22, Hampden, Maine
- The Growing Tree North Extended Day Nursery School, Roslyn Heights, New York
- The Growing Tree Nursery School, Roslyn, New York
- Wyandanch Head Start, Wyandanch, New York

Sincere appreciation to students at Hofstra University's School of Education majoring in early childhood and childhood teacher education programs and the graduate students from Manhattanville College majoring in physical education and sport pedagogy, who have also contributed their ideas and field testing to this book's content. We also recognize the imagination and field-testing talents of our former students and current professionals: Gayle L. Horowitz, Andrea Lee, and Jennifer Joyce. We would like to acknowledge Mutaz Bakri, from Umm Alqura University, Mecca Saudi Arabia, who has participated in a cultural exchange in order to apply the teaching principles to his home country.

We would like to identify the following professionals who provided their insightful expertise: Joe McGavin, book publication manager, SHAPE America; Ray Vallese, acquisitions editor, Human Kinetics; Jacqueline Blakley, developmental editor, Human Kinetics; G.H.C. Illustrations; June Alpert, MS, RD, CDN, nutritionist; Arlene H. Jurofsky, MS, environmental specialist; Frances Cruz, IT specialist, Manhattanville College; Emily Eng, principal of Transfiguration School and assessment specialist; Andrea S. Libresco, EdD, and Rosebud S. Elijah, PhD, codirectors of graduate early childhood and childhood education programs, Hofstra University; Paula Steinberg, MS, research, training and curriculum development for special populations; Mary E. McDonald, PhD, BCBA, Hofstra University, applied behavior analysis and autism specialist; Cantor Todd Rosner, religious leader and child specialist; Amy Rady, EdD, chair of the Department of Fitness, Exercise, and Sports at the New Jersey City University; and Patricia Vardin, EdD, chair of the Department of Early Childhood Education, Manhattanville College.

Finally, we would like to express our love to our family members, Sylvia J. Giallombardo; Jay Schneider; Marcy, Sas, Yosi and Ronen Ovadia; Scott, Krysten, Ella, and Ralph Schneider; for their reassurance during the long hours and involvement that this book required.

SHAPE America thanks the following members for reviewing the content of this book: Ali Brian, PhD, Louisiana Tech University; Jeffrey S. Gehris, PhD, Temple University; Michael Tenoschok, EdD, Georgia Department of Education; Ingrid Johnson, PhD, Grand Valley State University; and Casandra Waller, EdS, Escambia County (FL) School District.

PART I

Setting the Standard With Age-Appropriate Content, Instruction, and Assessment

CHAPTER 1

Selecting Age-Appropriate Content

This chapter introduces the relationship between word knowledge and movement in a young child's learning process, as well as addressing the need to select age-appropriate content. This content focuses on the power of words in a young child's life, the importance of physical literacy, and SHAPE America's National Standards for K-12 Physical Education. It also identifies the use of SHAPE America's *Active Start* physical activity guidelines for young children and Head Start's Early Learning Outcomes Framework as a foundation for selecting the correct content. Laban's four movement concepts and the young child's physical locomotor, nonlocomotor, and manipulative skills are of key importance. The chapter also contains guidelines to help you select the most appropriate content for a particular child's age and maturation level.

The Power of Words

Most educators agree that words play a powerful role in a young child's learning. One of the most impressive examples of such learning comes from the life story of Helen Keller, who could neither see nor hear yet learned from her American teacher, Anne Sullivan, that all objects and living things have names that identify them, and that these names consist of different letters. Sullivan repeatedly used her finger to spell the word "doll" into Helen's palm after having Helen feel the shape and texture of her doll. After several trials in which Sullivan used familiar objects such as a coffee mug and then brushing water onto Helen's hand and spelling the word "water" into her other hand, Helen's learning took a wondrous leap forward. With repeated trials and exposure to different items in her immediate environment, Helen recognized the words for what they represent. From then on, she used words to communicate her needs, thoughts, and actions to the many people whose lives she enhanced over her lifetime.

In a similar way, words are the key that young children use to open the door to language, communication, and the understanding of concepts. Words are the means by which children process information through the cognitive domain. Not only do children learn that words are used to represent names of objects and living things, but they also learn that words help them to describe situations and events and to talk about their feelings. As children get older, they realize that words create the lyrics to their favorite songs and describe the actions in their favorite storybooks.

In this book's lesson plans, *action words* describe how we can move our body in different ways. In the simplest sense, these words expose children to ways in which they can move from one space to another space beyond simply walking or running. Action words also can encourage children to stay in a limited space and move individual body parts beyond basic bending and stretching actions. With this emphasis on moving in a variety of creative and skillful ways, the action words take on an educative purpose and are referred to as the child's **movement vocabulary**. The teaching process results in children increasing their ability to move more effectively while also becoming more knowledgeable about words and their meaning. This body–mind connection is the basis of *physical literacy* and you can expand it even more when you introduce learning tasks based on topics that reflect the child's interests, environment, and physical capabilities.

Moving With Words & Actions uses carefully designed lesson plans that incorporate age-appropriate words grouped into five distinctive topics to expand children's physical abilities. Beginning in chapter 5, lesson plans introduce words that spark children's interest in their body parts and systems, muscle actions, and body expressions, as well as in healthy foods. Lesson plans in chapter 6 introduce words that expand children's awareness of the environment beyond that of their home settings, including words that challenge children to copy the actions common to people who work and help in their community. Lesson plans in chapter 7 focus on living creatures, using words associated with the movements and behaviors of animals living on the ground and in the water and air. The lesson plans in chapter 8 introduce words found in the realm of science and math. This includes science movements reflecting substances, surfaces and textures, power sources, wave actions, and wind patterns among others. Chapter 8 also introduces movements that coincide with words related to basic math concepts; children move according to words and numbers that rhyme, form geometric shapes with their bodies, and perform movements that require a simple understanding of words related to measurement.

Chapter 9 aims to improve young children's literacy and language arts skills through *movement narratives* as they become enchanted with words. The narratives are unique fairytale-like stories designed to capture children's interest while enlarging their movement vocabulary. These learning tasks foster a new awareness of how the child can demonstrate words physically so that they come to life. This use of words is critical to developing a physically literate learner. It also is one way that young children can experience the joy of words and movement together and discover, as Helen Keller did, that words can be part of a powerful learning experience.

Physical Literacy and National Standards

From birth, children have a natural desire to explore and experience new challenges. For the youngest child, learning occurs through play as parents introduce the child to the immediate environment. As children reach age 3, their yearning to explore and experience new things still exists, and parents and other adults must guide their exploration of the world beyond the home. This includes teaching basic concepts reflecting the child's body, physical development, word usage or vocabulary, community setting, and expanded environment.

When discussed as a whole, teachers of physical education and early childhood specialists use the term "physical literacy," which takes into account the child's total learning process (Roetert & Jeffries, 2014). SHAPE America incorporates the term physical literacy as part of the goal of physical education (2014, p. 4) and cites its definition as "the ability to move with competence and confidence in a wide variety of physical activities in multiple environments" (Mandigo, Francis, Lodewyk & Lopez, 2012, p. 28; Whitehead, 2001). Each of the lesson plans in this book address one or more of SHAPE America's National Standards for K-12 Physical Education, which are as follows:

- **Standard 1.** The physically literate individual demonstrates competency in a variety of motor skills and movement patterns.
- **Standard 2.** The physically literate individual applies knowledge of concepts, principles, strategies and tactics related to movement and performance.
- **Standard 3.** The physically literate individual demonstrates the knowledge and skills to achieve and maintain a health-enhancing level of physical activity and fitness.
- **Standard 4.** The physically literate individual exhibits responsible personal and social behavior that respects self and others.
- **Standard 5.** The physically literate individual recognizes the value of physical activity for health, enjoyment, challenge, self-expression and/or social interaction.

Guidelines and Frameworks

Active Start: A Statement of Physical Activity Guidelines for Children From Birth to Age 5 (NASPE, now known as SHAPE America - Society of Health and Physical Educators, 2009) has been instrumental in providing teachers who work with young children with a clearer understanding of the importance of daily physical activity. The following identifies *Active Start*'s five guidelines for preschool-age children:

- **Guideline 1.** Preschoolers should accumulate at least 60 minutes of structured physical activity each day.
- **Guideline 2.** Preschoolers should engage in at least 60 minutes—and up to several hours—of unstructured physical activity each day, and should not be sedentary for more than 60 minutes at a time, except when sleeping.
- **Guideline 3.** Preschoolers should be encouraged to develop competence in fundamental motor skills that will serve as the building blocks for future motor skillfulness and physical activity.
- **Guideline 4.** Preschoolers should have access to indoor and outdoor areas that meet or exceed recommended safety standards for performing large-muscle activities.
- **Guideline 5.** Caregivers and parents in charge of preschoolers' health and well-being are responsible for understanding the importance of physical activity and for promoting movement skills by providing opportunities for structured and unstructured physical activity.

Moving With Words & Actions complements *Active Start's* Guideline 5 by providing caregivers and teachers with many structured physical activity lessons. The lesson plans are especially helpful for new teachers and caregivers who have limited or no experience in teaching fundamental motor skills. It is critical that these skills be taught correctly so that they serve as the foundation for motor skillfulness. Furthermore, the task of engaging children actively in structured games and movement experiences for 60 minutes each day can be challenging unless you have ample content from which to draw. Many of the learning tasks in *Moving With Words & Actions* also can follow children onto the playground, where they can explore several of the movement activities in a fun and unstructured way without unnecessary fear about safety.

Another important guideline in the form of a national framework is *Head Start Early Learning Outcomes Framework: Ages Birth to Five* (2015). This information was first introduced in 2000 as a guide to curriculum planning and assessing the progress of developing children ages 3 through 5. Its new design is to provide a direction in preparing children to enter kindergarten in five domains categorized by (1) approaches to learning, (2) social and emotional development, (3) language and literacy, (4) cognition, and (5) perceptual, motor, and physical development.

The learning tasks contained in *Moving With Words & Actions* can help Head Start coordinators as they strive to prepare lessons that meet each domain. For example, when preparing a lesson within the domain of language and literacy, the narratives included in this resource, such as Fairy Tale Actions (see chapter 9), coincide directly with the outcomes in that domain. In the domain perceptual, motor, and physical development, the focus is on increasing the child's locomotor and nonlocomotor skills, specifically his or her proficiency of control and balance in walking, climbing, running, jumping, hopping, skipping, marching, and galloping. Because all of the learning tasks in *Moving With Words & Actions* include many of these locomotor skills, Head Start coordinators will find the tasks appealing.

Movement Concepts as Age-Appropriate Content

Cultivating an understanding of SHAPE America's National Standards for K-12 Physical Education as well as NASPE's Active Start guidelines (2009), and Head Start's Early Learning Outcomes Framework: Ages Birth to Five (2015) is the first step in selecting content that coincides with the young child's age and stage of development. The content used most often for this age group is attributed to Laban's four *movement concepts*. Over the years, Laban's theories have been translated into a user-friendly resource that is respected by professionals in dance and gymnastics, a variety of sport experts, and physical education teachers working with young children and children in early-elementary school.

Laban was born in 1879 in Austria at a time when theorists were applying mathematical principles to movement involving physics. After many years, Laban's fascination with movement enabled him to develop a comprehensive system of dance notation that allowed him to record movement in written form. In the early 1950s, progressive leaders in physical education translated Laban's theories into four questions that focused on "basic movement" in the areas of dance, mime, theatre, and physical education. In the early 1980s, those four questions and the concepts that emerged became the primary basis for lessons in the early-elementary grades in physical education. Soon after, they also became the foundation for early childhood physical education lessons along with the child's first introduction to basic motor skill activities (Clements, 1988; Clements, 2016).

Each lesson plan in *Moving With Words & Actions* contains at least one movement concept aimed at increasing children's physical skills and their understanding of the body. *National Standards & Grade-Level Outcomes for K-12 Physical Education* (SHAPE America, 2014) defines movement concepts as "the application of knowledge and concepts related to skillful performance of movement and fitness activities, such as spatial awareness, effort, tactics, strategies and principles related to movement efficiency and health-enhancing fitness" (p. 117). The four basic movement questions and their inherent movement concepts that are most appropriate for young children are as follows:

1. **What is the body capable of doing?**

   ◆ **Body awareness:** Knowing the names and locations of various body parts and exploring the movement possibilities of the body.

   ◆ **Body image:** A more realistic conception of his or her body. Body image is acquired after gaining a better understanding of different size relationships, movement possibilities, and perception of physical extremities.

   ◆ **Body management:** The **Awareness** and movement capabilities as the child learns to manage the body in a variety of situations and learns that different body parts are responsible for gross- and small-motor movements.

2. **Where does the body move?**

   ◆ **Spatial awareness:** The awareness of and ability to move through space. This is acquired when the child experiences and understands how much space the body requires when it is in different positions, how to avoid fixed objects when moving around, and how to fit under and move the body over different types of surfaces.

   ◆ **Self-space:** The area within the child's reach where he or she can be alone and can't touch other people or objects.

   ◆ **General space:** All area beyond the child's reach.

   ◆ **Direction:** The child's awareness of the line along which the body or body parts move: sideward, left, right, upward, downward, forward, backward, diagonal.

   ◆ **Range:** The child's awareness of the distance of objects in relation to the body: near or far, narrow or wide, long or short, above or below.

   ◆ **Level:** The child's awareness of and ability to move in horizontal planes at various levels: low, medium, high.

   ◆ **Pathway:** The child's awareness of the route the body takes to move through space: diagonal, straight, twisted, angular, zigzag, curved, and circular.

3. **How does the body move?**

   ◆ **Speed and time:** The child's awareness of and ability to move the whole or parts of the body quickly or slowly. This is movement associated with speed: quick or slow, sudden or sustained.

   ◆ **Force:** The child's awareness of and ability to use different degrees of muscle tension and strength for more efficient and expressive movement. This movement is associated with effort, weight, and energy: strong or weak, heavy or light, hard or soft, harsh or gentle.

   ◆ **Flow:** The child's awareness and ability to link movements sequentially. Free flow is fluent, uncontrolled movement. Bound flow is movement capable of being controlled, restrained, or momentarily stopped.

4. **With whom or with what can the body move?**

- ◆ **Relationships with people:** The awareness of and ability to move in relation to others: interacting with a partner, small group, or whole class. Sample relationships include side to side, leading, following, surrounding, mirroring and matching, unison and contrast among, meeting and parting, rising and sinking, passing, and linking.

- ◆ **Relationships with objects:** The awareness of and ability to move in relation to an object or piece of equipment. Sample relationships include behind and in front, between, among, alongside, over and under, near and far, along, and through.

A Young Child's Physical Skills

With this conceptual understanding, physical education teachers working with children ages 3 through 8 and early childhood specialists can emphasize movement as the foundation of physical education and physical literacy. The term *physical literacy* encompasses Laban's four concepts mentioned earlier, as well as manipulative skills and a large variety of locomotor and nonlocomotor skills. The following locomotor and nonlocomotor skills (also referred to as *traveling skills* and *nontraveling skills* by many dance teachers and as *movement patterns* by other physical education specialists) are the foundation of the child's *movement vocabulary*. These skills are described here with a brief definition and a short sentence that you can use to help young children and English language learners better understand the meaning of the word.

Locomotor Movement Skills

Advancing: Moving forward or ahead. Example: The soldier kept *advancing* to the front of the line.

Charging: Rushing at something with force. Example: The elephants are *charging* through the jungle, stomping on trees and scaring other animals.

Climbing: Moving upward using both the hands and feet. Example: I saw the girl *climbing* to the top of the tree.

Crawling: Moving slowly with arms, hands, knees, stomach, and legs along the floor. Example: The baby was *crawling* on the floor to reach his bottle.

Creeping: Moving slowly, close to the ground. Example: *Creeping* along the floor, the little mouse looked for some cheese.

Darting: Moving suddenly and swiftly in short, quick movements. Example: The frog's tongue kept *darting* out to catch the fly.

Dashing: Moving with sudden speed. Example: When the sudden rainstorm came, the girl found herself *dashing* to her house.

Exploring: Traveling throughout an unfamiliar space for purposes of discovering. Example: The sailor used a submarine for *exploring* the ocean floor.

Flying: Moving through the air with wings. Example: The birds are *flying* south for the winter.

Galloping: Moving forward with a slide step, keeping one foot in front. Example: The horses made a lot of noise while *galloping* to the barn.

Hiding: Moving out of sight. Example: The twins were *hiding* in their rooms.

Hopping: Stepping with one foot and landing on one foot. Example: The girl tried *hopping* on one foot when she played hopscotch.

Jumping: Taking off with both feet and landing on two feet. Example: Have you ever tried *jumping* over a mud puddle.

Leaping: Stretching one leg forward and landing on that foot. Example: The ballerina smiled while *leaping* high into the air.

Marching: Walking with regular, long, even steps. Example: The firefighters are *marching* in today's parade.

Pouncing: Jumping down suddenly to seize an object or thing. Example: The lion cubs were *pouncing* on each other.

Rolling: Turning over and over. Example: The snowball grew while *rolling* down the hill.

Running: Moving faster than a walk. Example: The tiny mouse tried *running* away as quickly as it could.

Rushing: Moving or acting quickly. Example: The boy was *rushing* to the movie.

Scampering: Moving quickly using small steps. Example: The squirrel *scampered* about gathering nuts.

Scattering: Separating and going in many directions. Example: When the wind blew the leaves, they were *scattered* over the yard.

Scuffling: Scraping or dragging the feet. Example: The little girl *scuffled* her feet in the sand.

Scurrying: Moving lightly and quickly. Example: The mouse *scurried* into the hole.

Searching: Looking for an object, person, or thing. Example: The boy *searched* in his pockets for his money.

Shuffling: Walking using small steps and keeping the feet and knees together. Example: While walking home, the boy *shuffled* his feet and buried his hands deep in his pockets.

Skating: Gliding along ice. Example: The children *skated* on the frozen pond.

Sliding: Moving smoothly over a surface. Example: The baseball player *slid* safely into third base.

Slithering: Moving the entire body along the ground. Example: The snake *slithered* under the rock.

Sneaking: Moving in a sly or secret way. Example: The children *sneaked* a cookie from the cookie jar.

Soaring: Rising, flying, or gliding high in the air. Example: The birds *soared* high in the sky near the top of the mountain.

Strolling: Walking in a slow, relaxed way. Example: The children *strolled* along the beach to watch the sunset.

Strutting: Walking in a swaggering or proud manner. Example: The peacock *strutted* to show off his colorful feathers.

Surrounding: Being on all sides, encircling. Example: A fence *surrounded* the schoolyard.

Swimming: Moving through water using the whole body. Example: The children went *swimming* in the pool.

Tiptoeing: Walking softly on the tips of the toes. Example: The girl *tiptoed* out of the room so she wouldn't wake up her grandfather.

Tramping: Walking with a heavy step. Example: The children *tramped* through the deep snow into the house.

Trudging: Walking slowly or with effort. Example: The children were so tired from their long walk that they *trudged* the last few blocks home.

Waddling: Swaying from side to side using short steps. Example: Both penguins and ducks *waddled* at the zoo.

Walking: Moving on feet at a steady pace. Example: The girl's mother *walked* with her friends to stay healthy.

Wandering: Moving without a destination or purpose. Example: The boy *wandered* through the forest.

Nonlocomotor Movement Skills

Arching: Forming a curved structure. Example: The cat *arched* its back.

Balancing: Being in a steady, stable position. Example: The boy *balanced* a bean bag on his elbow.

Bending: Becoming curved or crooked. Example: The girl *bent* over to tie her sneaker.

Bobbing: Quickly moving up and down. Example: The boat *bobbed* up and down in the water.

Bouncing: Coming back or up after hitting the surface. Example: The girl *bounced* up and down on the mattress.

Bursting: Breaking open suddenly and violently. Example: The fireworks *burst* with a flash in the sky.

Clapping: Striking hands together noisily and quickly. Example: The people *clapped* their hands as loudly as they could.

Collapsing: Falling down suddenly or caving in. Example: The child *collapsed* on her bed and went right to sleep.

Crumbling: Breaking or falling into small pieces. Example: The cookie *crumbled* into small pieces.

Crunching: Grinding or crushing loudly. Example: The fallen leaves *crunched* under the boy's boots.

Curling: Moving in a round shape. Example: The boy tucked in his chin, *curled* his body, and did a forward roll.

Dangling: Hanging loosely. Example: The lady's long earrings *dangled* from her ears.

Deflating: Collapsing by letting air out. Example: The car tire *deflated* after it ran over a nail.

Dodging: Avoiding by moving quickly from side to side. Example: The boy *dodged* back and forth so the chaser couldn't tag him.

Ducking: Lowering the head or body quickly. Example: The children *ducked* their heads so they wouldn't hit the tree branch.

Expanding: Becoming or making larger. Example: When the runners inhaled deeply, their lungs *expanded*.

Fluttering: Flapping the wings quickly, but not flying. Example: The fly's wings *fluttered*, but it could not escape the spider's web.

Freezing: Becoming motionless or fixed. Example: The boy *froze* in place with his hand in the cookie jar when he heard his mom open the door.

Grabbing: Seizing suddenly, snatching. Example: The child *grabbed* the ball from her friend's hand.

Hanging: Being attached by the upper end only; fastening something from above only, without support from below. Example: The picture was *hanging* on the wall.

Holding: Keeping something in the arms or hands. Example: The girl *held* the ball close to her body.

Hovering: Staying in one place in the air. Example: The helicopter *hovered* over the ground.

Inflating: Expanding by filling with air. Example: The boy huffed, puffed, and *inflated* all the beach balls.

Jerking: Moving with sudden, sharp movements. Example: The pony *jerked* the reins from the rider's hands.

Kneeling: Lowering onto a bent knee. Example: The boy *kneeled* down to find the ball under the chair.

Leaning: Slanting from an upward position and supporting one's weight. Example: The children *leaned* into the strong wind.

Lying down: Being in a flat, resting position. Example: The campers *lay down* in their sleeping bags.

Lifting: Raising upward. Example: The girl *lifted* her trophy for all to see.

Melting: Lessening or fading away gradually, dissolving. Example: The butter *melted* in the frying pan.

Pressing: Applying steady force against. Example: The boy *pressed* the elevator button to go to the next floor.

Pulling: Tugging toward oneself. Example: The children *pulled* at the tug-of-war rope.

Pushing: Pressing away from oneself. Example: The snowplow *pushed* the snow.

Reaching: Stretching out or extending. Example: The boy *reached* his arm out to help his friend.

Rising: Getting up from lying, sitting, or kneeling. Example: The girl *raised* her body to get out of bed.

Shaking: Moving with short, quick movements. Example: The man *shook* his arm to get the blood moving.

Shivering: Shaking out of control. Example: The girl was so cold from being out in the snow that she *shivered* and jumped up and down

Shrinking: Decreasing in size. Example: The hamburger was cooked too long and *shrank* to a small patty.

Shuddering: Trembling or shivering suddenly. Example: The boy *shuddered* and became frightened by the make-believe ghost.

Sinking: Moving to a lower level. Example: The rock *sank* to the bottom of the pool.

Spinning: Rotating at a high speed. Example: The wheel on the truck *spun* around and around.

Squeezing: Pressing together with force. Example: The girl *squeezed* her mother's hand.

Stamping: Placing a foot down heavily and noisily with the weight evenly on the flat foot. The foot remains in this position. Example: Dinosaurs *stamped* their big feet and made the earth shake.

Standing: Staying in an upright position. Example: The soldier *stood* very still and tall.

Stomping: Placing a foot down heavily with the weight evenly on the flat foot, then quickly lifting the foot up. Example: The little girl *stomped* on one foot to shake off the snow.

Stretching: Becoming a greater length or width. Example: The basketball player *stretched* up high to try to touch the basketball rim.

Swaying: Moving back and forth. Example: The trees *swayed* in the strong wind.

Swinging: Moving back and forth by turning on a hinge. Example: Monkeys enjoy *swinging* on vines from tree to tree.

Toppling: Falling over. Example: The child's toy blocks *toppled* over.

Trembling: Shaking from fear or cold. Example: The boy's body *trembled* when he was out in the cold snow.

Tugging: Pulling strongly. Example: The little girl *tugged* with great force to pull on her boots.

Turning: Moving around a center, rotating. Example: The mother *turned* the door knob.

Twirling: Moving the whole or parts of the body in a circular motion. Example: The ballerina *twirled* in three circles.

Twisting: Rotating an individual body part around another body part. Example: The baker *twisted* the dough into the shape of a pretzel.

Vibrating: Moving back and forth quickly. Example: The airplane flew so low over our home that all the walls *vibrated*.

Whirling: Spinning quickly. Example: The dancers held their arms out as they *whirled* around to the music.

Wiggling: Moving parts or the whole body in a swaying motion. Example: The worm *wiggled* its whole body.

Wobbling: Moving from side to side in a shaky manner. Example: The bicycle *wobbled* back and forth as it went down the street.

Manipulative Skills

Just as early childhood teachers use small objects (e.g., math tiles, blocks, clay, and puzzles) to increase the young child's fine motor skills, physical education teachers also strive to increase children's manipulative skills. Another age-appropriate content area that is important to young children's development is manipulative or object-control skills involving items such as balls and bean bags. *National Standards & Grade-Level Outcomes for K-12 Physical Education* defines manipulative skills as "skills that require controlling or manipulating objects such as kicking, striking, throwing, catching and dribbling" (SHAPE America, 2014, p. 117). While this book does not include lessons aimed specifically at teaching manipulative skills, it does offer the following suggested learning tasks for each age level and instructional cues for ball skills to assist teachers who have ample equipment.

Learning Tasks for PreK-Kindergarten (Rolling at the Side of the Body)

With the ball on the floor or ground: Ask the child to make shapes over the ball (e.g., bridge, triangle, wide), run around the ball a specific number of times, perform locomotor skills around the ball, or spin the ball with the fingertips and hands and then run around until it stops.

While standing: Roll the ball in different shapes, along lines on the floor using the fingertips, or in the shape of the first letter of the child's first name.

While sitting: Lift legs and roll the ball under them, or roll the ball around the body.

While standing: Roll the ball around the legs, or roll the ball and then run and stop the ball.

Partner: Act as human bowling pins by taking turns rolling the ball through a partner's legs. Or stand 10-12 feet (3-3.6 m) from a partner and roll the ball, trying to contact the partner's body so that it collapses to the floor. Exchange roles.

Learning Tasks for Grade 1 (Rolling and Fielding)

While standing: Roll the ball for distance then run and stop the ball, roll to a partner while the partner moves his or her body to the right or left several feet (.5-1 m) in order to field the ball.

While on one knee: Roll the ball around the body, roll it back and forth under the arch made by one knee.

Partner: Roll the ball to a stationary partner and take a step back every time the partner receives the ball.

Learning Tasks for Grade 2 (Two-Hand Bounce and Catch)

While standing: Use two hands to bounce and catch the ball for all of these. Bounce and catch the ball. Bounce the ball, clap, and then catch the ball. Bounce the ball, turn around, and then catch it. Bounce the ball in a circle shape or a box shape. Bounce the ball along the lines on the floor.

Partner: Follow the leader (partners take turns being the leader, such as one partner performing a bounce and catch skill throughout the playing area while his or her partner follows the same path and skill).

Learning Tasks for Grade 3 (Toss and Throw)

While standing: Toss the ball upward and let it land on different body parts. Toss the ball upward while walking. Reach back between the legs and toss the ball up in front of the body. Toss the ball high, clap, and then catch it. Toss the ball over the head, turn around, and then catch it.

Partner: One partner is the post and remains stationary. The other child stands 10 to 15 feet (3-4.5 m) away and tosses the ball to the post. The child who tossed the ball immediately runs around the post and returns to his or her original spot, catches the tossed ball from the post, repeats the action 10 times, and then exchange roles.

Use the following instructional cues for fundamental ball skills.

Teaching Tossing and Throwing

- ■ Your elbow should lead.
- ■ Bend the elbow.
- ■ Step forward with the foot opposite your throwing arm. Or bring your throwing arm back and the opposite foot points forward.
- ■ Keep your throwing arm close to your ear.

- Stretch your body forward.
- Throw like a baseball pitcher.

Teaching Catching and Fielding

- Keep your arms in front of the body.
- Hug the ball as you catch it.
- Move to catch the ball.
- Bend your knees so that you can move quickly to the ball.
- Place one foot in front of the other and be ready to move quickly.

Considerations for Content

While some children in preschool and kindergarten will demonstrate the ability to perform most or all locomotor and nonlocomotor skills as well as many manipulative skills, you should recognize differences in maturation levels and realize that not every child's ability will coincide with his or her age. Table 1.1 shows physical skills that children of different ages typically are able to perform.

TABLE 1.1 Physical Skills for Children From Birth Through Age 5

6-12 months	1-2 years	2-3 years	3-4 years	5 years
Patting	Clapping	Marching	Hopping	Strutting
Reaching	Grabbing	Tramping	Bouncing	Sneaking
Grasping	Squeezing	Shuffling	Tossing	Tiptoeing
Releasing	Pressing	Running	Galloping	Surrounding
Stretching	Arching	Climbing	Darting	Charging
Creeping	Stamping	Sliding	Dashing	Scurrying
Crawling	Pushing	Rushing	Dodging	Scattering
Walking	Pulling	Waddling	Flying	Tagging
Balancing	Jerking	Holding	Trudging	Chasing
Shaking	Rising	Rolling	Soaring	Prancing
Pulling	Falling	Balancing	Slithering	Skating
Pointing	Walking	Collapsing	Plodding	Tumbling
Rolling	Swaying	Turning	Wandering	Dangling
	Jumping	Twisting	Springing	Swinging
	Rolling	Jumping	Jumping	Jumping
	Kicking	Exploring	Searching	Skipping
	Balancing	Hiding	Scampering	Leaping
	Shaking		Tossing	Throwing
	Climbing		Fielding	Catching
			Striking	Striking

Clements, R. "Integrating Physical Play Throughout the Prekindergarten Program." Illinois Resource Center Summer Institute, 1998.

Remember to select content that matches the child's current functioning level. If a physical skill is too easy, the child might not attempt it because of boredom. If the activity has no grounding in past experience, the child might not know how to approach the physical skill and won't make an attempt. That's why we provide an example sentence for each locomotor and nonlocomotor skill to further foster the child's understanding of the word. Thus, in early childhood, children build on what they already know, and the more precise the match is between a child's age and stage of development when first being introduced to new content, the more likely he or she is to succeed.

Summary

Overall, you can feel more assured that your lessons are age appropriate for young learners if you consider standards and guidelines early within the selection process of the content, and the content reflect words and physical skills that enhance the child's understanding and ability to move in a variety of ways. All content should be engaging and appropriate so that children can find success and build on the goal of becoming a physically literate learner.

CHAPTER 2

Creating and Implementing Lesson Plans

From an education standpoint, physically literate learning starts with thoughtful planning to introduce young children to a variety of movement skills. A *lesson plan* aimed at physical literacy for young children is a step-by-step written account of what you would like to happen during a class session. It should specify what you are trying to accomplish and how you intend to accomplish it and should list the materials needed to complete the lesson.

The preparation of written lesson plans is one of the best ways to crystallize your thinking. It provides a format for action that you can review before the actual teaching takes place to increase the likelihood that you will remember key objectives, learning tasks, and props or materials that engage the children. It also provides a source of reference during teaching. Less experienced teachers usually find it difficult to keep several things in mind and convey important information while managing a group of young children who have curious minds.

A well-prepared lesson plan helps a less experienced teacher overcome feelings of insecurity and nervousness. It also helps the teacher to be definite and specific rather than being indefinite and vague. Feelings of frustration often occur when a teacher depends solely on memory and tries to wing it. A written plan prevents wandering and inappropriate improvisation during the class session and provides a means for determining whether the objectives actually were met.

In this chapter, you will learn the key parts of an effective lesson plan, including determining the lesson's central focus, selecting behavioral objectives, planning learning tasks, making smooth transitions between learning tasks, and identifying student characteristics that influence your preparation.

Selecting Behavioral Objectives

As a rule, all lesson plans contain objectives to work toward while presenting the lesson's content. These are called *behavioral objectives* because each focuses on a behavioral domain that humans use when learning or practicing new content. The domains for physical educators and preschool and classroom teachers who teach movement skills include the cognitive, affective, and psychomotor. Effective teachers create lesson objectives that reflect all three domains to best tap young children's learning potential.

Some action words (verbs) reflect one domain better than another. You can use these verbs to create a lesson plan objective that focuses on one of the three domains.

Cognitive domain objectives are intended to increase children's knowledge of objects and things, as well as their ability to remember and apply that knowledge. In the lesson plans presented in *Moving With Words & Actions,* the primary cognitive focus is to convey simple facts related to the body, nutrition, the roles of community helpers, the environment, living creatures, language arts, and math skills, so that children will be able to meet the *cognitive objectives* of the lessons. We use verbs in the lesson plans to describe the cognitive objective, specifying the action that each child must display to show that he or she has met the objective. For example, if an objective states "The child will *identify,*" the verb used to describe how children will meet the objective is *identify.* Other verbs you can use to develop cognitive objectives for your lessons include *name, label, discuss, talk about, describe, define, explain, compare, respond verbally, recall, remember, match, illustrate, draw, underline, critique, repeat, differentiate,* and *point to.*

You can address *affective domain objectives,* which refer to the child's feelings, by having children interact with peers in a partner learning task or in a small- or large-group learning task. These objectives stress the importance of children's interacting in a friendly and respectful manner with other children to ensure a positive learning experience. It's important to create affective domain objectives that you or a school administrator can observe easily. The affective domain focus should be on responsible personal and social behavior that respects self and others, rules and etiquette, and safety. The following verbs might be useful when creating an affective domain objective for physical education: *negotiate, show appreciation, accept others, depend on others, contribute, resolve, express an interest, exhibit, assist, share, volunteer, interact,* and *remain on task.*

Typically, *psychomotor domain objectives* focus on the physical skill that you are trying to teach in the lesson. In the older-elementary grades, psychomotor objectives can be relatively complex and generally consist of three parts to ensure effective instruction. The first part is referred to as the "behavior," or the actual physical skill that you want the child to perform. The second part of the objective is the "criteria." This element focuses on a specific number of times that the child should demonstrate or perform the skill at an acceptable level. The third part refers to the "condition," which is the learning environment or game situation in which the child performs the skill during the lesson.

Although teachers working with children in preschool and primary grades also maintain high expectations for skill performance, they place much less emphasis on children's attaining a mastery level in any given skill. That's because, often, their students are being introduced to the skill for the first time. Here are some verbs used commonly to create psychomotor domain objectives: *manipulate, perform, demonstrate, imitate, develop, exhibit, explore,* and *create.*

Determining the Central Focus

The *central focus* of a lesson plan is simply a statement that summarizes what you want to achieve within the lesson. For example, when teaching older students the sport of basketball, the central focus could be performing basic basketball skills in a modified game. When teaching basketball, this focus keeps you on task throughout the planning process. With preschool children, the lesson's central focus most often includes movement patterns (e.g., locomotor and nonlocomotor skills that serve as building blocks to more skillful movements) and basic movement concepts (such as body awareness, spatial awareness, time, force, or flow and relationship concepts) used in modified games and activities. It also can include emerging health-enhancing fitness concepts about the body, such as increased flexibility through age-appropriate bending and twisting activities. The central focus captures the overall skills, content, and activities that shape the lesson for better planning.

Planning Learning Tasks (Ages 3-8)

Each lesson plan in this book contains three learning tasks. Learning tasks can be basic in nature when working with young children, but all in this book are purposefully planned to include an activity, discussion, and other modes of participation that engage children in the learning process. After introducing the central focus, or purpose, of the day's lesson to the children (e.g., *The purpose of today's lesson is to use our bodies to explore many shapes.*), you introduce Learning Task 1, an individual activity that prepares bodies for movement. Learning Task 2 is a partner activity that helps children practice the movement skill, and it can include a series of movement challenges in which children are in their self-space and interact with classmates. Learning Task 3 is a whole-group learning task in which children can practice the physical skill (psychomotor domain objective), interact with classmates and be motivated to participate again (affective domain objective), and reflect on what they have learned (cognitive domain objective) by responding to meaningful questions.

Making Smooth Transitions Between Learning Tasks

To implement learning tasks effectively so that children are fully engaged and involved in all three domains of learning during your lesson, use class management and organizing techniques that maintain the flow of the lesson.

One important technique is the use of start and stop signals. On any given day, children use their senses to look or listen for indicators that signal them to start or stop activities. Children listen to the voices of older siblings and adults in charge. They respond to spoken cues and sounds to move to another activity, lunch, and recess; to return to the classroom; and to pack up to go home. They look for traffic and hand signals to cross the street safely. They listen for automobile horns. Each day is filled with stimuli and forms of signals to indicate expected methods of behavior and response.

In the gymnasium, classroom, or play space, children also have come to expect signals and sounds to assist them in the transition from one activity to the next. So, it's effective to use signals for starting and stopping and while making transitions from individual tasks (Learning Activity 1) to partner tasks (Learning Activity 2) to whole-group tasks (Learning Activity 3). For example, children generally start activities at the initiation of the teacher's signal. You can communicate through sound, sight, or touch. Flickering lights, verbal cues, sounds, gentle touches, cue cards, music, or body movements easily convey the message that you are ready to begin the activity. Verbal cues can be as simple as asking, "Are you ready? And [pause] go!" or "After I say three, we will start. Are you ready? One, two, three, and [pause] go!" You also can raise your arm and explain to the children, "When I lower my arm and my hand touches my side, you can start. Are you ready?" The key is to ensure that the children understand the starting signal and are focused on being ready to participate.

You also might use music as stop and start signals. For example, "When the music begins, you will start to move, and when the music stops, you must stop quickly." Other ending signals could include, "When the music stops, freeze wherever you are," "Stay frozen in the exact body position you are in," "Apply your brakes," or "Pose for a photo." (You can use an imaginary camera to take the photo.) You could also use green, red, and yellow construction paper to symbolize a traffic light; different hand claps; a favorite phrase; or a short whistle.

It's just as important for you to have a signal to stop or end a learning task. Children need to know when to stop. When using music in the background, children should know to stop when you turn the music off. Some children respond to the command "stop" when spoken in a louder voice, a low-pitched voice, a softer voice, or an exaggerated "aaaannd [pause] stop!"

Effective instruction when implementing a learning task requires concrete direction. Telling 3-year-old children to "line up" is too vague for their comprehension. Instead, use the following directions to help children position their bodies to begin the learning task (see figure 2.1).

- **Form a behind-line.** Children stand behind one another, with eyes looking at the back of the head of the classmate in front of them.
- **Make a side-by-side line with your bodies.** Children stand shoulder to shoulder. It is best to specify where you want the children to stand, (e.g., against the back wall or standing on the white line). If pushing or crowding occurs, ask the children to "stretch the line and make it longer."
- **Find your own self-space in the playing area.** You also can refer to self-space as personal space, as in figure 2.1, where each child can stand or sit without being touched and without touching someone else or an object.
- **Work with two classmates to create a triangle shape.** To form a triangle, groups of three children face inward.
- **Circle with the teacher.** When you have the children organized in a circle formation, you should become part of the circle, not stand in the center of the circle, from which some children would face your back.
- **Stand one body-length apart.** When you need space between partners in a learning task, ask the children to space themselves one body-length apart, either by lying on the ground or by standing with arms outstretched to the side of the body as a form of measurement.

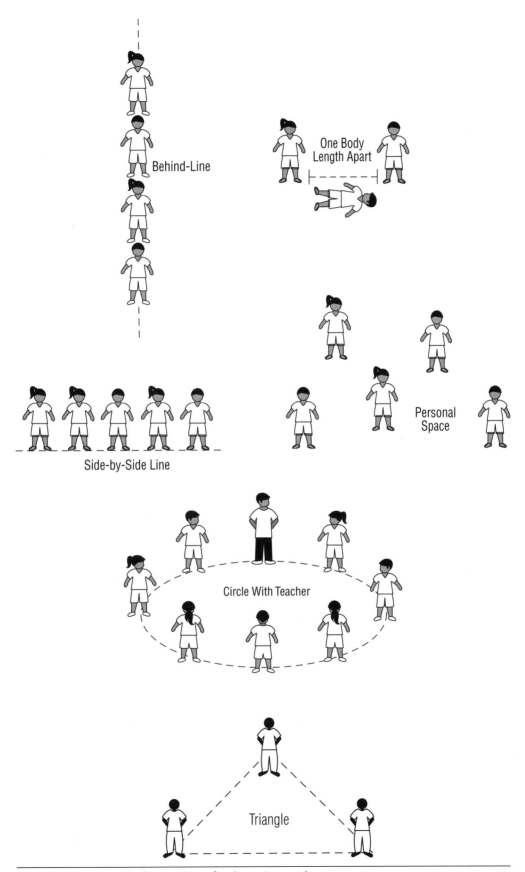

FIGURE 2.1 Sample formations for learning tasks.

Creative Ways to Form Groups

The task of grouping very young children can be quite challenging. Many children will not have encountered this request before, which can frustrate them. You have many options for helping children become part of a larger group. When choosing a method, keep in mind that some younger children are timid about approaching other children. And with their boundless energy and excitement for play, young children tend to forget the assigned numbers or colors you might use to group older children. In addition, you should be sensitive to children who are consistently unable to find a partner; avoid the "last one chosen" stigma. Try some of the following proven techniques for forming groups.

Finding a Partner

- Ask children to find someone who has the same color hair, eyes, or clothing.
- Invite children to find someone who likes the same flavor of ice cream.
- Tell them to find someone who has the same number of syllables in his or her first name.
- Say, "When I say 'go,' please find a partner."
- Play music and have children smile and greet one another while moving throughout the playing area. When the music stops, those who last greeted each another become partners.
- Request that each child find a partner who was born in the same season.
- Ask children to circulate and find a partner. Any child who does not have a partner is considered lost and moves to you, who is in charge of the lost and found department. You then pair lost children. In the case of only one lost child, he or she selects which group to join.

Creating Small Groups

- Ask partners to join another set of partners to make a group of four.
- Distribute a deck of playing cards. Groups of four are formed by students who have the same number. Flash cards also provide opportunities for finding others with the same picture, color, number, or letter.
- In classrooms where children sit at colored tables, children can be divided by tables.
- Write the names of each child on a craft stick or slip of paper and store them in a container. Pull four sticks or slips of paper from the container to form a group.

Creating Two Large Groups

- Place pom-poms of two different colors in a container or lunch bag. Each child selects a pom-pom. Other items such as colored plastic jacks, colored craft sticks, stickers, or small plastic figurines work well.
- Using a side-by-side line, ask the children to take either a giant step forward or a giant step back. Children who moved forward are in the first group, and those who stepped back are in the second group.
- Each child decides quietly whether to be a cow that says "moo" or a cat that says "meow." Children walk throughout the playing area making their animal sounds. Once all the animals find each other, the cows go to one side of the playing area, and the cats move to the opposite side.

- Ask children to close their eyes and either raise their hands or keep their hands to the side.
- The teacher creates a zip line by moving quickly through the children while saying the magic word, "zzzzip." The children on each side of the zip line form a group.

Please keep in mind that most learning tasks do not require an exact number of children within each group.

Structuring the Learning Environment to Be Physically Safe

Implementing a lesson aimed at increased physical literacy for young children requires preparation and forethought to ensure maximum participation with a minimum of risk.

Clothing

- Please check that all sneakers are tied and on the proper feet.
- When possible, ask girls who are wearing a dress or skirt to slip on a pair of shorts to prepare for movement.
- Hooded sweatshirts can pose a choking danger for children.
- Be aware of dangling jewelry such as necklaces and bracelets.

Preparing the Playing Area

- In the classroom, push all chairs under the desks, remove books and small obstacles from the floor and place them on tables or desks, and move larger obstacles to the sides of the room.
- Outside, check to make certain that the playing area is safe and free of debris, broken glass, and other harmful objects. Note whether any child has allergies to bees or grass. The child's medical records should contain the procedures to follow for ensuring the child's safety, including avoiding allergens.
- Clearly mark and explain boundaries and start and finish lines. Children should understand their limits.

Playing Safely

- For any chase-and-flee activity (i.e., tag-style game), remind children about proper or gentle touches.
- Children must listen to your directions and be respectful of the rules and of each other.
- Arrange for proper spacing between groups. Children should not run toward or into each other.
- If children do not follow direction during an activity, stop the activity and review your expectations.
- Analyze the activity for possible safety problems. If you observe a risk of injury, stop the play and fix the problem.
- Enforce rules about materials and equipment and inspect them before their use.
- Keep pens, pencils, gum, lollipops, food, and drinks out the playing area.

■ Closely monitor children identified with medical conditions (e.g., asthma, diabetes) during their participation and immediately after the session. Those children's medical records should contain the procedures for ensuring the children's safety.

■ Whenever possible, keep a first aid kit readily available.

Knowledge of Students to Inform Teaching

To ensure student learning, you must not only know your content and its related objectives and pedagogy, but also have knowledge of the students to whom you wish to teach that content. This understanding was missing in earlier times, before the realization that students in kindergarten through grade 12 learn best through active engagement in their individual ways. This awareness is sometimes referred to as *knowledge of students to inform teaching*, and many early childhood professionals have adopted this thinking for their lesson planning (Stanford Center for Assessment, Learning, & Equity [SCALE], 2016). They recognize that effective teachers take into account many factors that can influence the success of a lesson, such as a child's limited English ability, or differences in travel experiences, or even how much sleep a child had before coming to class. Therefore, the following lists identify characteristics of preschool and kindergarten students you should consider when planning age-appropriate lessons. This will increase the likelihood that your students will be able to participate more fully in the lessons.

What Young Children Can Remember

■ Colors, shapes, letters, and figures described in movement tasks
■ Objects associated with a particular setting
■ The names of story characters
■ Past experiences to yield new movement patterns
■ The names of locomotor and nonlocomotor skills

How Young Children Can Practice Creative Thinking

■ Pretending to move like an object or thing
■ Imagining that the body is manipulating an object to complete a task
■ Visualizing items that cannot be seen
■ Discovering a novel way to move
■ Following an imaginary pathway

How Young Children Like to Solve Simple Problems

■ Recognizing how things are different and alike
■ Working out a movement response
■ Finding ways to improve the movement response
■ Using the body to show how different objects feel when touched
■ Discovering how to link movements

Young Children's Beginning Language Development

■ Identifying the names of the body parts
■ Demonstrating the meaning of words to a poem, song, or story
■ Discussing facts related to objects or things

▪ Assuming the language of an imaginary character
▪ Making wants known
▪ Conveying words that express emotion

How Young Children Understand Themselves

▪ Using specific body parts to show how they feel
▪ Using specific body parts in the development of a game
▪ Realizing they have the ability to control the speed with which their body moves
▪ Learning the roles of people who influence their life
▪ Realizing that the body can perform movements related to specific animals

How Young Children Can Interact With Peers

▪ Switching roles with a classmate
▪ Manipulating a partner's body to move in specific ways
▪ Working with classmates to form a large object with their bodies
▪ Demonstrating cooperation with classmates

Personal Community and Cultural Awareness

Present-day lesson planning stresses the need for teachers to take into account children's everyday experiences, community settings, and cultural backgrounds. This aspect of teacher preparation is fundamental to the educational process. An understanding of community assets also opens the door to teaching children how their home environment differs from other home settings. This is possible when the child is introduced to the actions and behaviors common to community facilities and settings. The following learning task is one example for children in grades 1 and 2:

Explain to the children that the first great builders were from a place called Egypt and they created large stone temples. Today's builders are called architects, who use steel, glass, plastics, bricks, concrete, wood, and other materials to make their designs. Encourage the children to perform the following actions:

- Show me that you can *make* a wide, flat shape to represent the base or foundation of a large building.
- Who can *make* an arch shape with his or her body? A rounded dome shape?
- How can you *stand* tall like the columns that hold up a roof?
- *Raise* your hands over your head to make a church steeple that points to the sky. Can you make a box shape like a Jewish synagogue or temple? Who can make the tall tower shape found in Muslim mosques?
- Can you *turn* your body to *make* the twisted spiral shapes seen at the tops of large city skyscrapers?

Following the construction of buildings, you can explain that outdoor paint colors often are chosen based on the location and culture of a neighborhood. For example, buildings in the desert might be painted in sandy colors or, if in the woods, darker colors are used to blend in with trees. Other times, cultures select their favorite colors; for example, Eastern cultures like red, which represents good fortune. Irish people consider green to bring good luck. House painters use paint buckets and brushes to make buildings more beautiful. Challenge children to demonstrate the following actions. *Note:* action words, or verbs, are highlighted in italics.

- Can you *step* into a pair of overalls? *Pull* on gloves to protect your hands and *slip* on a small cap to cover your hair.
- Before we paint the outside of the house, let's *throw* a large tarp or drop cloth over the bushes and outdoor chairs. Now use a make-believe scraper to remove the old paint.
- *Open* the bucket and *mix* the paint with a circular motion. *Dip* your brush into the bucket and *paint* the walls a bright sunny color.
- *Discover* how to use up-and-down strokes. Try using a paint roller for long, smooth strokes. Paint long lines outside the door and windows.
- Finish the paint job by showing me how you can *climb* up a ladder to reach the highest peak of the building. Now *stretch* and *paint*.

Instructional Strategies

In selecting the appropriate instructional strategy for presenting the content, it is imperative that the strategy match the child's interests and abilities and foster a love for physical activity. This book uses two similar instructional strategies for sparking children's interest in learning new skills: the *imitative approach* and the *movement exploration approach*.

Using the Imitative Approach

The word "imitative" has a Latin origin (imitari), meaning to make a copy of and likeness. The English adopted the term at the end of the 16th century and used it to describe a behavior or quality to emulate that all children and adults possess. This belief stems from the basic premise that humans are imitative creatures with similar interests, forms of communication, and ways of moving. We all engage in an endless change of behavior patterns that make us eat alike, dress alike, act alike, and play and move in similar ways. Concerning young children, Friedrich Froebel, internationally recognized German pedagogue best known for founding the kindergarten movement in 1837 said, "What the child imitates, he begins to understand" (Section 36, p. 42, 1887). Effective teachers use a young child's urge to imitate the verbal and physical behaviors of his or her parents and siblings. These teachers then become models for the child's further development.

Providing a model for children to imitate as they overhear words has long been recognized as one way children acquire identity and language (Bandura, 1977; Erikson, 1963/1993; Piaget, 1962; Singer, 1973; Skinner, 1974). The value of imitation is also apparent in many abstract forms of communication, including dance or rhythms, music, and movement. For example, dance professionals use an imitative approach when they prompt a child to follow the words and movements of an action poem or song. They also use the imitative approach when they ask children to repeat simple rhythmical beats using handheld instruments such as drums, tambourines, and Lummi sticks or when they prompt children to duplicate the slapping, clapping, and pounding actions common to hand-clapping chants. In addition, music provides opportunities to imitate the different types of sounds and moods you have selected.

Physical educators, early childhood specialists, and classroom teachers can find great success when using the imitative approach to introduce basic movement skills and concepts appropriate to the child's level of readiness. For example, a preschool child's movement vocabulary is greatly expanded each time the teacher conveys the proper name of a physical skill such as galloping and then demonstrates the movements for the child to copy. A typical teacher delivery might be, "Make believe you are a herd of wild horses and follow me as we gallop forward."

In the simplest sense, you can challenge preschool children to mimic sayings such as busy as a bee, light as a feather, cold as ice, stiff as a board, and sly as a fox. Children can use their bodies to portray a variety of feelings and expressions, such as acting fearless, frightened, angry, and gloomy. Other examples include demonstrating action words and assuming the body gestures and facial expressions of storybook characters in movement narratives that are included in this book.

Using Expressive Feeling Words
I can use my body to show how I feel . . .

A: adorable, adventurous, afraid, angry, anxious, ashamed, amazed, awkward

B: bashful, beautiful, bold, bored, brave, baffled

C: carefree, cautious, clumsy, confident, crazy, curious, cute, confused, cranky, cheery

D: daring, depressed, disgusted, droopy, delighted, disappointed

E: ecstatic, embarrassed, enraged, evil, exhausted, enthusiastic, excited

F: fearless, fierce, floppy, friendly, frightened, frustrated, furious

G: gloomy, greedy, guilty, gorgeous, grimy, gruesome, grumbly, grumpy, giggly

H: happy, heavy, heroic, hopeful, hot, huge, helpless, horrified

I: interested, icky

J: jealous, jolly, jumpy, joyful

K: kind, kooky

L: lazy, light, lovely, likeable

M: mad, mighty, mischievous, moody, mopey

N: nervous, nice, noisy

O: overwhelmed, old

P: playful, proud, powerful

Q: quiet, queasy

R: rowdy, restless, relaxed

S: sad, shy, silly, skinny, shocked, sly, small, smiley, surprised, sleepy, slimy, successful, sorrowful, scared

T: tense, timid, tiny, tired, tearful

U: ugly, unhappy

V: vigorous, victorious

W: wicked, wise, worried, weepy, weird

X, Y, Z: yucky, youthful, zippy

Your behavior can also encourage preschool children to mimic novel ways of moving, such as duplicating the common movements of animals or to follow your locomotive skills along imaginary pathways or to reproduce a combination of movements after observing your performance. In each learning task, display enthusiasm and great facial expression to spark the child's continued involvement.

Teachers who favor the imitative approach when working with young children recognize the importance of fostering the child's imagination. They realize that many preschool children become easily frustrated and develop anxiety that inhibits further participation unless a model is available to duplicate or copy. This is especially true if a child has no concept of how to perform a physical task. When working with 3- and 4-year-old children, use carefully selected cues and prompts that are appropriate to the child's stage of development. Among others, typical teacher deliveries might include the following phrases:

- *Imagine* your foot is a pencil and you are drawing a picture on the floor.
- *What if* your hand were a paint brush? Make long and squiggly marks.
- *Make believe* you are a kangaroo jumping along a path.
- *Create* the shape of an orange with your body.
- *Build* a tunnel with your legs.
- *Pretend* you are a soap bubble floating high in the sky until you pop!

The challenge is to select content that has meaning or is relevant to the child. For example, if the child has no conception or mental image of how to "pretend to be a spaceship blasting," or "make believe you are paddling a canoe," discussion or desired action must take place. Furthermore, asking a child to "pretend to be a football player," or "make believe that you are a basketball player," will only have meaning to a child if he or she has been exposed to that character's movements.

Common imitative prompts that encourage the child to copy, follow, repeat, mirror, echo, or shadow the teacher's movements or verbal suggestion include the following:

- Make believe . . .
- Pretend . . .
- Create . . .
- Make up . . .
- Suppose . . .
- Imagine you are . . .
- Act as if . . .
- Move like . . .
- Copy me . . .
- Follow me . . .
- Build . . .
- My turn . . . Now your turn.
- Invent a new way . . .
- Show how . . .
- Show me . . .

Teachers who favor the imitative approach with preschool children are inclined to believe that imitative experiences do not stifle a child's ability for creativity and self-expression because all humans need a foundation from which to pull creative thoughts, ideas, and knowledge. Imitation serves as the foundation on which higher-order thinking skills can be constructed. They also see the importance of planning tasks that present challenges within the child's range of ability, and they capitalize on the child's interests. Another benefit to this approach is that young children are not hampered by their lack of vocabulary and inability to follow verbal directions because the greatest emphasis is on the use of sight.

It's important to remember that a 2-year-old child has a vocabulary of approximately 200 words. Between ages 3 and 4, children typically will more than quadruple their vocabulary from about 1,000 to more than 4,000 words, acquiring new words at the astonishing rate of about 9 per day. However, it isn't until a child is at least 6 years old, with a vocabulary of 8,000 to 14,000 words, that he or she should be expected to comprehend the complex directions that teachers typically use. Therefore, using the imitative approach with preschool children can serve as a means for learning, as 3-year-olds can carry out a sequence of only one simple direction, and 4-year-olds are able to hold only two ideas or directions at a time (e.g., "Eduardo, please pick up the ball, and put it into the storage bin."). It also provides a foundation for greater movement challenges taught through movement exploration.

Using the Movement Exploration Approach

Assuming that most children have acquired a variety of new movement concepts and locomotor skills through the use of the imitative approach, it is now time to capitalize on the children's past experiences that form the structure into which they can assimilate new learning. Children ages 5 through 8 can greatly benefit from the teacher's use of the movement exploration approach as a means to learn additional locomotor and nonlocomotor skills and more classroom concepts. From a theoretical standpoint, the teacher plays a critical role in expanding the child's awareness of and ability to perform movement skills, even though they do not serve as a model for the child to imitate because, ultimately, older children must perform the cognitive operations to construct meaning.

Your role as teacher is to ask a series of planned movement questions that challenge children to explore a variety of movement possibilities. For example, if the central focus of the lesson is to increase the child's awareness of different types of shapes and of shapes that the body can make, you can ask questions about objects that are common to the child's cognitive awareness. These could include asking, "Who can show me a round apple shape with his or her body?" Or, "Is it possible to make a twisted pretzel shape using your body?" Children at this age also are able to make comparisons between their body parts and those of other living creatures. For example, "Crickets hear with their legs. Can you point to the body part that *we* use to hear sound?" When exploring the different speeds that the body can move, you can base questions on images of speed boats, jet airplanes, and race cars as well as the movements of snails and turtles. When teaching the child where the body can move through space, the questions can focus on moving at a high level, where birds fly, or a low level, where ants crawl. In most instances, you can use descriptive words within each question to encourage the child to rely on previously learned knowledge and experiences.

At this stage, it's more important that children respond physically in a variety of creative ways and situations than it is that they develop advanced skills for movement efficiency. For example, the skill of jumping, which emphasizes taking off and landing with balance, also can address the following:

- Expression of a feeling (*Show me how much fun jumping up and down can be.*)
- Spatial awareness (*Who can use all of their muscles to jump like a frog from one lily pad to another lily pad in the big pond?*)
- Moving over or around objects (*Can you jump over the box? Now around the box?*)
- Physical fitness (*Let's see whether our hearts beat faster when we continue to jump up and down.*)
- Socialization (*Is it possible to jump up high and high-five your partner's hand?*)

In these sample movement exploration prompts, the need to execute the jump at maximum efficiency is not as important as the need for the child to obtain a greater understanding of how the jump can be used in different situations and in creative ways.

Therefore, movement exploration is a means for a child to use the skills acquired in preschool and elaborate on them by organizing and processing the information in the form of multiple movement responses. This approach also ensures active participation, provides opportunities for creative thinking with classmates, increases the child's responsibility in following directions, and fosters the child's self-esteem with feelings reflecting "I can do it!"

Common movement exploration prompts that encourage children to respond in multiple ways include the following:

- Can you . . . ?
- Determine the best way to . . .
- Discover different ways to . . .
- Explore other ways . . .
- Find another way to . . .
- How many different body parts . . . ?
- How would you . . . ?
- How do you . . . ?
- How can you . . . ?
- How else would you . . . ?
- How many ways . . . ?
- Is it possible...?
- In how many ways . . . ?
- See how many different ways . . .
- See if you can . . .
- Show me a different way to . . .
- Who can . . . ?
- What does a . . . ?
- In what ways can you . . . ?
- What kinds of things . . . ?
- Try changing . . .
- Try to find another . . .
- Try it again another way.

Planning Supports for Children With Special Needs

When every child is taught in the least restrictive learning environment, every child can relate to the joy experienced when actively moving. The combination of using imitative learning and movement exploration permits more children to succeed through their natural ability to copy, imitate, and follow the teacher or through their desire to be expressive and respond in a variety of ways. You can use each learning task in a variety of play spaces regardless of size, shape, or setting. However, we suggest strongly that all teachers familiarize themselves with each child's individualized education plan (IEP) or 504 accommodation plan to ensure that individually required accommodations are made before any lesson is implemented. Discussions with parents and medical professionals may also be indicated. Sample teaching considerations for inclusion are as follows:

Teaching Children With Visual Impairment

■ Use brightly colored props and materials as well as wall and floor markings to assist in identifying segments of the playing area and boundaries.

■ Use clear and succinct wording in your directions.

■ Use sound (e.g., music, whistle) to indicate transitions and changes within the activity.

■ Provide a partner who can assist a child with visual impairment in following directions and movement.

■ Offer gentle physical guidance to help the child performing nonlocomotor and locomotor skills.

■ Consider using toys and dolls with moveable body parts to demonstrate and allow the child to feel various movement concepts.

Teaching Children With Hearing Impairment

■ Position yourself near and child's face to better facilitate lip reading and sign language.

■ Arrange lighting so it's on you, and not shining in the child's eyes.

■ Use visual aids such as cue cards, hand signals, and facial expressions.

■ Signify the beginning and ending of learning tasks by flickering of lights.

■ Be aware of balance limitations caused by the child's hearing loss.

■ Allow the child with hearing impairment to work with a partner.

■ Use the imitative approach, which allows the child to follow posed movement phrases such as "copy me," "follow me," "my turn," "now it's your turn".

Teaching Children With Physical Challenges

■ Consider greater space requirements for children who use wheelchairs.

■ Consider modifying the distance traveled while performing a locomotor skill.

■ Consider using props that are lighter weight or in varied shapes to permit easier gripping and manipulation.

■ Immediately following the lesson, allow time to adjust apparatuses such as braces, crutches, wheelchairs, and prosthetics.

■ Understand the implications of the challenges each child faces and their impact on the learning task.

■ Be aware of physical signs or verbal cues indicating the child is experiencing the onset of difficulties symptomatic of the health impairment.

■ Recognize the onset of fatigue and the need to modify the next movement challenge to be less physically demanding.

Teaching Children With Emotional Disturbance

■ Use clear and consistent rules with this population, and state expectations and consequences.

■ Provide activities that encourage the child to express feelings and emotions.

■ Use music to provide an additional prop to enhance self-expression and increase participation levels.

■ Use a progression of learning experiences, beginning with the most simple and progressing to the more complex.

■ Use individual learning tasks for children who need to avoid physical contact.

■ Whenever possible, remove distractions and unnecessary obstacles and equipment from the playing area.

Teaching Children With Learning Disabilities

- Use short or concise instructions you can repeat as necessary.
- Prepare to rephrase the instructions.
- Use positive reinforcement as a key to successful participation.
- Plan the focus and direction of activities, keeping distractions to a minimum.
- Always strive to be consistent in class management, behavior, and stating expectations.
- Focus on achievements regardless of how small and use words of encouragement.

Teaching Children With Autism Spectrum Disorder (ASD)

- Follow posted class rules and established routines consistently.
- Use wall and floor markings (e.g., floor lines or spots, cones, footprints, arrows, pictures, words, and enter and exit signs for the learning task) to clearly identify pathways, segments of the playing area, boundaries, and transitions from one area to the next after completing a task.
- Use concise instructions along with visual cues such as pointing to a picture of a child stretching his or her body into a wide shape or demonstrating the skill using exaggerated body gestures.
- Use visual cues as another form of communication. These may include gestures, photos, videos, apps, charts, diagrams, and words showing a simple sequence of events in the form of a picture story.
- Give children individual floor markers to help prevent drifting and bumping into others.
- Establish and identify a small and quieter space for a child with ASD to take a break and regroup as needed.
- Inform the child what is expected and where to go next after the learning task has concluded (e.g., "First we practice jumping and then . . .").
- Because a child with ASD might have difficulty communicating verbally, watch for signs that he or she is trying to communicate (e.g., behavior, gestures, body language, and facial expression).
- Use a personal visual schedule attached to the wall by Velcro to show the order of the learning tasks so that the child knows which activity to work on in the lesson.

Finally, when striving for inclusion, administer all learning tasks with a smile and patience and an understanding of the unique challenges each child faces. This applies to all children, especially those who require the self-esteem building that is prevalent in children with special needs.

Providing Differentiated Instruction

One of the greatest challenges teachers face is treating each child as an individual even though classes are full of children with various learning styles and instructional preferences. The most common way to meet this challenge is finding ways to help each young child aspire to his or her potential through a technique known as *differentiated instruction*. Differentiated instruction, or differentiating instruction, is a planned technique used to increase the likelihood that a child (or small group of children) will find success and build on this success in future lessons. To do so, teachers strive to take the child's cognitive, social, and physical strengths and interests into account when planning the lesson. By differentiating instruction, children are set up for success and are taught to their strengths. Effective teachers address the needs of individual children identified with specific disabilities by adapting or modifying the existing learning tasks or environment. In contrast, differentiated instruction modifies the content, learning tasks, or environment or all three to meet the needs of all diverse learners.

The following examples are just a few of the many ways you can differentiate instruction for young children.

- Appeal to the child's different senses.
- Get to know the child's background, which helps to identify his or her strengths, areas that need improvement, and special interests.
- Change the boundaries of the playing space (make it smaller or larger depending on the learning task) and remove unnecessary obstacles that distract the child.
- Implement multiple levels of questioning and give the child immediate feedback about his or her performance.
- Decrease or increase the distance to the target or goal.
- Modify a learning task, let the child work at his or her own pace, or decrease the number of challenges.
- Slow the pace of the lesson.
- Provide rest periods during vigorous, physical learning tasks.

Academic Language

In recent years, the concept of *academic language* has drawn a great deal of attention in the field of education as a whole. Academic language is the oral and written language used for academic purposes. This addition to the lesson plan is very general and also includes nonverbal language used for academic purposes. In physical education, its importance is based on the need for children not only to perform physical skills, but also to express their understanding of the skills and concepts in a linguistic manner. This aspect helps children become more engaged in learning the content. The lesson plans in *Moving With Words & Actions* address academic language according to the following three elements, which also are used by classroom teachers when they create lessons.

- **Language function** refers to the learning outcome or outcomes or verbs selected for the lesson. Common language functions in early childhood physical education include, but are not limited to, *interpreting* the best way to solve a movement problem (e.g., jumping over or crawling under), *describing* how to perform a particular movement, such as hopping on one foot and using the arms to maintain one's balance, *explaining* how to perform a movement, and *critiquing* a classmate's performance. Many teachers find it helpful to complete this element of the lesson by stating, "The child uses language to . . ." or "uses language to interpret, describe, and so on." These phrases can help a new teacher remain focused on the language function and are part of each lesson in *Moving With Words & Actions*.
- **Vocabulary** refers to words or concepts that are specific to a particular discipline. In early childhood, many words and concepts enrich the child's understanding of his or her body or ability to move in a variety of ways.

These can be described or defined for the child and also put in a sentence. Each lesson plan in *Moving With Words & Actions* has no fewer than five vocabulary words that either are common to the physical education profession or the classroom content area.

■ **Syntax or discourse:** On some rare occasions, physical education teachers working with children in the older-elementary grades use syntax. Syntax can be a set of symbols when focusing on math calculations or sport diagrams outlining offensive and defensive systems. Discourse, which is a verbal interchange of communication, is more common in lessons for younger children. Teachers most often engage in discourse with their students at the end of the lesson.

Summary

You can modify or expand the contents of this chapter to fit the needs of a particular school's program. You may already be following a format that has been mandated by your school's administration. In this case, the content can still be helpful when training new colleagues that have not yet been introduced to the value of lesson planning. In either situation, young children benefit from caring individuals who find the time to enrich their program with sequential lessons aimed at creating a more physically literate learner.

CHAPTER 3

Making the Most of Every Lesson

This chapter is aimed at helping you enhance the more than 70 lesson plans contained in this book. All lessons are designed to meet the interests and needs of young children of varying abilities, and they take place in a cooperative learning environment free from competition and use little or no equipment. In addition, all activities can take place in a variety of settings both indoors and outside. Even in the smallest setting, effective preschool teachers can rearrange chairs and tables creatively to provide adequate space for movement. Of course, while that is a positive feature of the lesson plans for preschool teachers, physical education teachers often have the use of a multipurpose room or gymnasium. Regardless, all teachers can benefit from each lesson.

To show how you can make the most of each lesson plan in this book, in this chapter we'll look deeper into a sample lesson plan, Body Shapes and Creations, which we chose because it was a favorite among teachers and children during the field-testing process for this book. Looking at this sample lesson plan will give you an overview of the lesson plan for immediate use. In this chapter we will also identify additional considerations for teachers desiring a more comprehensive program. You can implement these considerations in all 70 lesson plans.

A Typical Lesson Plan: Body Shapes and Creations

Most teachers agree that the **central focus** is the key element in any lesson plan. The central focus of the sample lesson plan reinforces that the body can form different shapes and poses. Explicit in this focus, the teacher then expands this understanding by creating three **behavioral objectives**. The *cognitive objective* is directed toward each student's identifying and describing a variety of shapes that his or her body can make. In the *affective objective*, classmates interact in a friendly and respectful manner while molding and shaping their partner's body into familiar objects or things. In the *psychomotor objective*, the student manipulates and molds four or five classmates' bodies into one large connected shape and then describes the group pose to other classmates who have done the same. Then all groups come together to create a whole-group imaginary art gallery called Creative Body Gallery.

■ To visualize this sample lesson plan, in **Learning Task 1**, the children are scattered throughout general space. Begin by asking the children to see whether they can *curl* their bodies and create an egg or oval shaped statue. Explain that when you clap your hands, the children must discover a way to make a statue in a box or square shape. Follow this by asking the children, "Who can show me what a silly statue might look like?" followed by asking, "Is it possible to change your body to create a very tall statue shape?" Finally, ask "How many body parts can you *wiggle* or *shake* to *relax* your muscles? Can you show me?"

■ In **Learning Task 2**, ask the children to explain how they can use Play-Doh to make different shapes and objects (e.g., by *bending, stretching, rolling,* and *twisting*). Encourage them to move quickly and select a partner (e.g., "Who can find a partner that has the same color shirt or pants that you are wearing?"). Suggest that one child pretend to be a large can of Play-Doh. The other partner pretends to be a sculptor and "molds" the Play-Doh into familiar shapes such as round, triangle, box, wide, long, and narrow. A child can also mold his or her partner's body into an object such as a tree, table, chair, or rocket. At the end of Learning Task 2, the sculptor identifies and describes the partner's Play-Doh body shape and they exchange roles after three to four minutes.

LESSONS

BODY SHAPES AND CREATIONS

National Standards Addressed

- **Standard 1.** The physically literate individual demonstrates competency in a variety of motor skills and movement patterns.
- **Standard 4.** The physically literate individual exhibits responsible personal and social behavior that respects self and others.

Instructional Materials/Props

Lively music, a can of Play-Doh or modeling clay (optional), posters showing different shapes (optional), photographs of statues in the community, state, and nation (optional), device to play music, a whistle for safety

Central Focus

To reinforce that the body can form different shapes and poses.

Objectives

- **Cognitive:** The child will identify and describe a variety of shapes that his or her body can make.
- **Affective:** The child will interact in a friendly and respectful manner while molding and shaping their partner's body into familiar objects or things.
- **Psychomotor:** The child will manipulate and mold four or five classmates' bodies into one large connected shape and then describes the group pose to other classmates who have done the same. Then all groups come together to create a whole-group imaginary art gallery called Creative Body Gallery.

Component of Health-Related Fitness

Flexibility

Learning Task 1: Preparing Our Bodies to Move

Class organization: Children are scattered throughout general space

Challenge the children to perform the following actions:

- Can you *curl* your body and create an egg or oval shaped statue?
- When I clap my hands, discover a way to make a box or square shape statue.
- Who can show me what a silly statue might look like?
- Is it possible to change your body to create a very tall statue shape?
- How many body parts can you *wiggle* or *shake* to *relax* our muscles? Can you show me?

Learning Task 2: Partner Challenge

Class organization: Partners are scattered in self-spaces.

Present the following: A sculptor is a person who uses materials to mold and shape in order to create an object or thing.

Ask the children to explain how they can use Play-Doh to make different shapes and objects (e.g., by *bending, stretching, rolling,* and *twisting*).

■ In **Learning Task 3**, Creative Body Gallery, divide the children into groups of five or six. One child from each group assumes the role of sculptor, while the remainder of the children in each group imagine they are molding clay or Play-Doh. The children acting as sculptors mold their group members' bodies into a large shape. Following this, one group at a time displays its creation for the remaining classmates and discuss the shapes they formed. For a greater challenge, ask two children to connect the group shapes to create an imaginary whole-group body gallery.

■ For an additional learning task, explain that museums often contain different types of statues. Encourage children to move vigorously around the playing area when music begins. When the music stops, call out, "frozen statue." All children freeze, holding their statue pose until the music begins again. The next time the music stops, call out "rounded or circle statue," and the children respond. Follow the action with the words "tall statue," "tiny statue," and "giant statue." With each trial, you may vary the type of locomotor skills that the children perform (e.g., *jump, gallop,* or *skip*).

> - Encourage them to move quickly and select a partner (e.g., Who can find a partner that has the same color shirt or pants that you are wearing?).
> - Suggest that one child pretend to be a large can of Play-Doh. The other partner pretends to be a sculptor and "molds" the Play-Doh into familiar shapes such as round, triangle, box, wide, long, and narrow. A child can also mold his or her partner's body into an object such as a tree, table, chair, or rocket. At the end of the learning task, the sculptor identifies and describes the partner's Play-Doh body shape and they exchange roles after three to four minutes.
>
> **Learning Task 3: Gallery**
>
> **Class organization:** Children are scattered in identified groups
>
> Present the following: *A gallery is a place that displays of art for people to view.*
> - **Creative Body Gallery:** Divide the children into groups of five or six. One child from each group assumes the role of sculptor, while the remainder of the children in each group imagine they are molding clay or Play-Doh. The children acting as sculptors mold their group member's bodies into a large shape. Following this, one group at a time displays its creation for the remaining classmates and discuss the shapes they formed. For a greater challenge, ask two children to connect the group shapes to create an imaginary whole-group body gallery.
> - **Fun Frozen Statue Shapes:** Children are encouraged to vigorously move about the playing area when the music begins. When the music stops, you would call out, "Frozen Statue." All children freeze holding their pose until the music begins again. The next time the music is stopped, you would call out, "rounded or circle statue." The action is followed by the words, "tall statue," "tiny statue," and "giant statue." With each trial, you may choose to vary the type of locomotor skills that the children would perform (e.g., jump, gallop, or skip).
>
> **Assessment Questions**
> 1. What kinds of shapes did we make today (e.g., narrow, tall, short, wide, box, circle)?
> 2. Which body parts were the easiest to bend into different poses?
> 3. Who can tell me how your body shape will change as you grow older?
>
> **Academic Language Demands**
> - **Language function:** Uses language in this lesson plan to identify and describe shapes and objects that the body can make and offer opportunities for both partners to critique each other's imaginative pose each child created while in the role of sculptor.
> - **Vocabulary:** Specific shapes the body can make (e.g., box, circle, square, oval, rectangle) while posing or while stretching (to become a greater width or length), and the word sculptor is defined as a person who uses materials to mold and shape in order to create an object or thing. The word gallery is defined as a place that displays pieces of art for people to view, and a museum is identified as a building that contains exhibits for people to study or learn about.
> - **Syntax or discourse:** A verbal interchange focusing on the understanding that our body can change into many shapes in order to complete different physical tasks over time as we grow and become stronger and better movers.

At the end of the lesson, ask the children the following **assessment** questions: "What kinds of shapes did we make today (e.g., narrow, tall, short, wide, box, circle)?" followed by, "Which body parts were the easiest to bend into different poses?" and "Who can tell me how your body shape will change as you grow older?"

To meet the academic language demands, beginning with the *language function,* use language in this lesson plan to *identify* and *describe* shapes and objects that the body can make and offer opportunities for both partners to *critique* the imaginative pose each child created while in the role of sculptor. The *vocabulary* most prevalent in the lesson plan focuses on specific shapes the body can make (e.g., box, circle, square, oval, rectangle) while posing or while stretching (to become a greater width or length), and the word *sculptor* is defined as a person who uses materials to mold and shape in order to create an object or thing. The word *gallery* is defined as a place that displays pieces of art for people to view, and a *museum* is identified as a building that contains exhibits for people to study or learn about. The *discourse* is the verbal interchange focusing on the understanding that our body can form many shapes in order to complete different physical tasks over time as we grow and become stronger and better movers.

Overall, the **component of health-related fitness** that the lesson plan emphasizes is flexibility, and the **National Standards** most addressed include **Standard 1** ("The physically literate individual demonstrates competency in a variety of motor skills and movement patterns.") and **Standard 4** ("The physically literate individual exhibits responsible personal and social behavior that respects self and others.").

Making Lesson Plans More Purposeful

The second part of this chapter addresses ways to make lesson plans more purposeful. This section provides elements to consider that can enhance the dynamics of your lesson plans, even for young children. Among others, these considerations include unique uses of instructional materials, special safety considerations, provisions for special needs, the importance of students' prior knowledge, motivating physically literate learners, instructional cues and prompts, state education standards, and using references and research as a solid foundation.

Instructional Materials and Props

When selecting **instructional materials or props** for the lesson plan, these can include but are not limited to physical education equipment, charts (e.g., vocabulary wall charts), posters, music, books, safety supplies, materials for children with special needs, computer, and a video camera. For the sample lesson plan Body Shapes and Creations, instructional materials and props selected include lively music to encourage active stretching, a device to play music, a whistle for safety, a can of modeling clay or Play-Doh to motivate the child, and posters illustrating statues and shapes. Photographs of statues found in the local community, state, and nation can also be included.

The word "prop" is a common term that early childhood educators use to refer to materials or equipment that can add a sense of realism to learning tasks for both the teacher and the children. Children are instantly more motivated to become physically active when props are included in the lesson. With a little thought, you can easily spark children's imagination, reinforce already-learned concepts, and enhance the learning of new content. This could be as simple as using a storybook with pictures, small plastic animals or figurines, or still pictures of common objects. You can conduct learning tasks using props in the classroom, the multipurpose room, the gymnasium, and outdoors. Sample props and equipment are listed here.

Equipment

- Bean bags (available in colors, numbers, letters, and animal shapes or can be homemade)
- Hoops
- Jump ropes
- Tumbling mats
- Cones

- Floor spots
- Frisbees
- Burlap sacks
- Beach balls
- Balloons

Classroom Items

- Animal figures
- Carpet squares
- Chairs
- Chalk
- Classroom blocks
- Card table
- Desk
- Books
- Finger and hand puppets
- Wooden blocks
- Pictures

Household Items

- Cardboard boxes
- Shoe boxes
- Paper plates
- Paper hats
- Paper bags
- Bowls
- Sponges
- Old tube socks
- Pillows
- Bed sheets
- Blankets
- Newspaper
- Paper towel cylinders
- Gift wrap cylinders
- Toilet paper cylinders
- Aluminum foil
- Plastic bottles (empty and clean)
- Water hose
- Mattress
- Mirrors
- Maps
- Plastic buckets
- Bubble wrap
- Bicycle inner tubes
- Stuffed animals

- Pinwheel
- Flash cards (animals, colors, letters, numbers)
- Dress-up clothing
- Masks
- Hats

Music Supplies

- Recorded music and music player
- Sound effects
- Homemade rhythm instruments

Art Supplies

- Art paper
- Construction paper
- Crepe paper
- Styrofoam
- Dowel rods
- Craft sticks
- String
- Tape
- Clay
- Ribbon

Community Items

- Tires
- Planks of lumber
- Ladder
- Barrels
- PVC pipe
- Rain gutters
- Saw horse
- Cable spools
- Packing crates
- Road signs
- Traffic signals
- Travel posters

Outdoor Items

- Cut grass
- Bags of leaves
- Branches
- Rocks
- Sand
- Bales of hay
- Dirt pile
- Tree stumps
- Tree cookies (cross sections of tree trunks that teachers use to illustrate how trees grow)
- Water

Special Safety Considerations

Chapter 2 identifies a comprehensive list of **safety considerations** when structuring the learning environment. When implementing the lesson plans in this book, consider including written reminders and suggestions such as checking to make sure all sneakers are tied, asking children to take off hoodies and scarves, and removing obstacles in the playing area. A particular class may need to be reminded of safety rules or start and stop signals for active participation.

Provisions for Special Needs

It is important that you check for any special accommodations that you might need to provide for allowing children with special needs to participate in each lesson. For example, if a child in your class has a hearing impairment, position yourself so that you face the child, and use visual cues while asking the child to create the body shapes in Learning Task 1. For additional support, have a buddy work with the child in his or her self-space. In Learning Task 3, you might flicker the lights to signify when the music stops and use visual aids (e.g., cue cards with words and pictures and a physical demonstration) for each new challenge. In addition, an English-speaking student can work alongside an English-language learner in the class. Chapter 2 provides a comprehensive list of additional provisions.

Students' Prior Knowledge

This lesson plan element refers to content knowledge, skills, life experiences, and any previous understanding that will help children succeed while participating in the learning tasks. Before you implement the Body Shapes and Creations lesson, for example, children will have been taught to move to their self-spaces and should have some basic knowledge of shapes in order to address the teacher's questions. It's also important for the children to have acquired some understanding of balance (i.e., to be in a steady, stable position). It also helps if they know that they can relate to other children for longer periods of time, which will influence the success of the partner and whole-group learning tasks. Effective teachers realize that socially, children at this age like being challenged, doing things well, and being admired for their accomplishments. This admiration is exhibited through the teacher's use of praise to motivate physically literate learners.

An understanding of children's prior knowledge is also critical to determining which age or grade level the lesson is best suited to. In the sample lesson, the central focus is aimed at preschool and kindergarten students because most children in grades 1 and 2 already realize that they can mold their bodies into a variety of shapes. When we field-tested this lesson, however, one teacher working with a second-grade class welcomed the implementation of this lesson because she had many English-language learners within the class, and the partner work within the lesson was very helpful in meeting her curriculum objectives. Likewise, a teacher working with children in grade 1 identified this lesson as being an effective way for him to teach cooperation to a group of children who had not shown a willingness to be supportive to each other's ideas during class participation. In these two cases the teacher's understanding of his or her student's prior knowledge and knowing how classmates typically interacted with each other was very helpful in determining if the lesson would be appropriate for a particulate grade level. Effective teachers should always add this element to their planning process when selecting or creating lesson tasks for the physically literate learner.

Health-Enhancing Components of Physical Activity

One of the most important aspects of becoming a physically literate individual is *being physically fit*. Physical education teachers are specially trained to implement lessons that include one or more obvious health-related fitness components to address this ongoing goal. These include **cardiorespiratory endurance**, which is the ability of the child's heart, lungs, blood vessels, and major muscle groups to persist in vigorous movement such as participating in a chase and flee game. Teaching young children that the heart is a muscle that needs to be exercised to become stronger is a good first step for preschool children. Of course, the long-term benefit of being able to participate in vigorous movement is that it might prevent or reduce the likelihood of cardiovascular disease in later life. Therefore, most physical educators agree that cardiorespiratory endurance is the most important component of physical fitness that can be instilled in young children. **Flexibility** is the range of motion of the muscles and joints. Each time the child is challenged to move his or her skeletal muscles beyond their normal resting length, the child's flexibility is enhanced. Creative stretches involving twisting, turning, and fun bending activities, such as those in our sample lesson contribute to this component.

Muscular strength is the ability to use muscles to exert force against resistance. While muscular strength is less emphasized for ages 3 to 8, it is helpful that children participate in lessons that convey the need for strong muscles. Young children also benefit from participating in learning tasks that teach the child simple facts about their muscles: for example, that the muscles in our legs can be made short or long to help the body move. The development of muscular strength will reduce the incidence of injury during game play and sport participation in later years.

Muscular endurance is the ability of skeletal muscle to exert force (not necessarily maximal for the young child) over an extended period of time. The child is introduced to muscular endurance through the varying speed of movement and in activities associated with power.

The final health-enhancing component is **body composition**. Knowledge of this concept is beyond the young child's understanding and is not common to resources aimed at this age level. However, teachers should understand that body composition is the relationship of percentage of body fat to lean body weight (muscle, bone, cartilage, and vital organs). Unfortunately, being overfat or overweight usually does start in childhood, and it has a limiting effect on the other components of fitness. Therefore, the learning tasks in this resource that are aimed at increasing the child's understanding of good eating can indirectly serve as a wonderful means to introduce this component to children and their parents. Knowledge of these health-enhancing fitness components should be a part of every lesson. This consideration should help motivate each child to become more physically active and ultimately more physically fit.

Motivating Physically Literate Learners

Physical literacy recognizes even the smallest achievement, and you can incorporate this element by using a variety of encouraging words aimed at the child's increased learning. The delivery is in your smile and the expressive way you speak. Children appreciate kind words and knowing that they have been noticed for their good work and extra effort. To help increase the child's level of self-esteem and motivation, develop a repertoire of encouraging words and phrases that extend beyond "good job." These words also serve as a foundation for the in-depth specific feedback that teachers commonly use when they introduce more advanced skills and concepts. In the sample Body Shapes and Creations lesson, you could compliment the student by saying, "In my eyes, your silly statue is a winner." In the partner activity, you could comment, "I wish I had my camera," when referring to the partner Play-Doh creation, and praise the children while performing in the whole-group Creative Body Gallery learning task by saying, "Your group effort is terrific." Comments such as these inspire greater creativity in future lessons. The following suggested expressions are intended to help you motivate.

Individual Learning Tasks

- "I see great progress."
- "You did it!"
- "I'm so proud of you!"
- "Let me shake your hand."
- "Congratulations, kiddo!"
- "You've got it now!"
- "Good for you."
- "You should really feel proud of yourself."
- "You really are very good at that."
- "I admire your talent."
- "You made that look easy."
- "See what you can accomplish if you try."
- "How do you feel now?"
- "I knew you could do it."
- "I'm so proud of you for trying."
- "In my eyes, you are a winner."
- "I appreciate your help."
- "I like the way you thought of that."
- "I admire your determination."

- "You almost have it."
- "I can tell you're trying very hard."
- "With a little practice, look what you can do."

Partner Learning Tasks

- "You've taken a big step in the process."
- "I can tell you've both been practicing."
- "You can do it!"
- "Wow! The dynamic duo!"
- "Great going!"
- "Way to go!"
- "Wonderful!"
- "Well done!"
- "Perfect!"
- "I wish I had my camera."
- "I like that."
- "Very nice!"
- "Wow!"
- "Absolutely perfect!"
- "Now that's what I call perfect."
- "I admire your skills."
- "I'm impressed!"
- "Together you can make it happen."
- "You're getting better each time."
- "You made that look easy."
- "Much better."
- "Nice try!"
- "You two are terrific."
- "Thank you!"
- "I like how you share."
- "What a great idea!"

Whole-Group Learning Tasks

- "Great comparison!"
- "Super duper!"
- "Fantastic!"
- "Excellent!"
- "Outstanding!"
- "Amazing!"
- "That's incredible!"
- "Outrageous!"
- "Magnificent!"
- "Awesome!"
- "Tremendous!"

- "Marvelous!"
- "Remarkable!"
- "Yes!"
- "Good thinking!"
- "You almost have it!"
- "I love it!"
- "This is great!"
- "You have really outdone yourselves."
- "That's the best ever!"
- "Now that's what I call creative thinking."
- "That's more like it."
- "Your group effort is terrific."
- "That's the way!"
- "This is what I call group effort."

Instructional Cues and Prompts

Effective teachers not only select age-appropriate content, but they also offer **instructional cues or prompts** that assist children during the learning process. These cues and prompts help children to stay on task and focus on key points of the skill or movement. In the sample Body Shapes and Creations lesson, instructional cues play an important role. For example, in Learning Task 1, use cues specifically to expand on the child's understanding of different body parts that form shapes (e.g., "Bending our body means to become curved or crooked," and "You can use many different body parts to create a silly shape," and "Stretch way up on your toes to make a tall shape," and "Wiggling helps keep our muscles from being stiff.")

In Learning Task 2, the instructional cues focus on partner interactions. For example, you can reinforce the roles of each partner by saying, "Gently mold and shape your partner's body. Never pull," and "You should remain very still in the shape that your partner, who is pretending to be a sculptor, has formed." In Learning Task 3, the instructional cues focus on students cooperating and a child or two in the role of sculptor creating a large-group, make-believe art gallery. Your cues might be "Think about many creative shapes, such as a triangle, box, circle, and oval that can be combined to make a large object," and "Everyone needs to stand still and hold their poses for the sculpture."

You will likely have much less trouble providing instructional cues for locomotor skills. The following are the most common for young children.

Instructional Cues for Walking

- As you walk, gently swing your arms back and forth next to your body.
- Keep your head up while walking and your eyes looking forward ahead so that you do not bump into objects and other children.
- Walk like you normally do and try to keep your head level without bobbing up and down.
- Hold your stomach in while you walk.
- Your heel is the first part of your foot to touch the ground.

Instructional Cues for Running

- Keep your head up while running and your eyes looking forward so that you do not bump into other children.
- Push off with the front part of your foot.
- Bend your arms and swing them back and forth close to the sides of your body.
- Lift your knees while you run.
- If you want to run fast, you must bend your knees and lift them more.

Instructional Cues for Jumping

- Bend your knees and ankles before taking off for a jump.
- Swing your arms back and then forward as fast as you can.
- Land with your knees bent.
- Land lightly on your toes and the balls of your feet.

Instructional Cues for Hopping

- Keep your head and chest up.
- Use your arms for balance when you hop.
- Hop on one foot.
- Bend your knee as you land lightly on your toes and the ball of your foot.
- If you want to hop higher, you must swing your arms up.

Instructional Cues for Galloping

- Keep your head and chest up.
- Keep one foot in front of your body.
- Step forward with one foot and bring the other foot to it.
- Move forward, keeping the same leg in front.
- Let your arms relax and allow them to swing forward and back freely.

Instructional Cues for Sliding

- Move one foot to the side and quickly move the other foot to it.
- Slide your feet along the floor.
- Lead with the same foot.
- Remember that your body is moving sideways.
- Try not to bounce.

Instructional Cues for Skipping (Age 5 and Older)

- Keep your head and chest upright.
- Lift your knees when you skip.
- Swing your arms back and forth at your side.
- Step, hop. Step, hop. Step, hop.

Instructional Cues for Leaping (Grade 3)

- Take off from one foot and land on the other.
- Strive for height and graceful flight.

- Land lightly and relaxed.
- Use your arms to help you leap.
- Push off and reach.

State Education Standards

In addition to national standards, most teachers have an understanding of their respective state physical education learning standards. For example, in our sample Body Shapes and Creations lesson, physical education teachers living in the state of New York would identify New York State Physical Education Learning Standard 2 as closely coinciding with the objectives of the lesson.

_____1: Personal Health and Fitness

Students will have the necessary knowledge and skills to establish and maintain physical fitness, participate in physical activity, and maintain personal health. Students will perform basic motor and manipulative skills. They will attain competency in a variety of physical activities and proficiency in a few select complex motor and sports activities. Students will design personal fitness programs to improve cardiorespiratory endurance, flexibility, muscular strength, endurance, and body composition.

__X__2: A Safe and Healthy Environment

Students will demonstrate responsible personal and social behavior while engaged in physical activity. They will understand that physical activity provides the opportunity for enjoyment, challenge, self-expression, and communication. Students will be able to identify safety hazards and react effectively to ensure a safe and positive experience for all participants.

_____3: Resource Management

Students will be aware of and able to access opportunities available to them within their community to engage in physical activity. They will be informed consumers and be able to evaluate facilities and programs. Students will also be aware of some career options in the field of physical education and sports.

Summary

The considerations in this chapter are intended to assist you in enriching the young child's movement experience for every lesson. Effective teachers take the time to locate instructional materials and props, provide for an inclusive environment, take into account the student's prior knowledge, implement at least one primary health-enhancing component of physical activity, and utilize state standards to guide their decision making. You can find your state's physical education standards on SHAPE America's website, www.shapeamerica.org. Integrating your state's standards with the lesson-planning guidelines in this chapter will improve your ability to develop physically literate learners.

CHAPTER 4

Assessing Children's Ability to Move With Words & Actions

For many years, the preferred assessment tools for children in the older-elementary grades in the United States was a written test focusing on rules and a sport-related skills test. This was expanded to include several forms of authentic or self-assessment tools such as logs or journals to determine whether learning had occurred. SHAPE America's *PE Metrics*™ offers assessments based on the National Standards for K-12 Physical Education.

PE Metrics contains a wealth of information to help teachers determine which criteria to use when observing children executing physical skills. For example, *PE Metrics* includes rubrics for assessing children's skill levels in hopping, running, sliding, underhand catching and throwing, striking, and weight transfer. These rubrics identify those children who need additional practice or remediation and help you recognize performances demonstrated in good form with consistency of action. *PE Metrics* is of tremendous value for teachers who have not created their own assessment tools but want to collect individual performance data and then transfer the information onto assessment scoresheets for the class as a whole.

Likewise, early childhood classroom teachers and teacher trainers can find numerous textbooks that identify a variety of strategies for assessing the cognitive and social behaviors of children ages 3 to 8 years. Most resources identify examples of generally accepted assessment criteria (e.g., the child's ability to solve simple math problems involving blocks) and discuss the advantages and disadvantages of each strategy when assessing the extent to which learning has occurred. The focus of early childhood assessment is to determine whether children have reached an identified goal by a particular age so that teachers can analyze the results and use them to inform their planning for greater program effectiveness. Therefore, it is important that all assessment focus on the child's progress toward goals and objectives that are educationally and developmentally significant (Beaty, 2014; Copple & Bredekamp, 2010; McAfee, Leong, & Bodrova, 2015; Van Horn, Nourot, Scales, & Alward, 2015; Warner & Sower, 2005).

Less attention has been given to assessing the movement and motor competency of 3- and 4- year-old children because most teachers agree that the developmental levels of young children can vary a great deal. This factor makes it difficult to be certain that a specific rubric can claim reliability given the young child's differences in physical growth spurts and behaviors on any given day. Subsequently, *Moving With Words & Actions* offers three forms of evidence that ranges in complexity for teachers to consider when determining if specific content is age appropriate for their students and whether learning has taken place.

Evidence 1: The Child's Perspective

Effective teachers realize that preschool and elementary-age children can be creative when motivated to give their thoughts about the lesson (i.e., what they liked and didn't like and what they would do to improve the learning task). In the simplest sense, the teacher can ask the children to rate the lesson by raising their hands (e.g., raise your hand if you think it was excellent or good or you did not like it), or the teacher might ask the children to rate their individual performance by showing the appropriate number of fingers (e.g., three as excellent, two as good, and one as needing more practice). In addition, the children can rate the lesson if they learned something new by displaying a smile, pout, frown, or no expression. The following identifies additional ways to obtain the child's viewpoint concerning the lesson:

- Displaying thumbs-up, thumbs to the side, or thumbs-down.
- Standing tall if they liked the lesson, placing their hands on their knees if the lesson was OK, or sitting if they did not enjoy the lesson.
- Jumping forward, standing in place, or jumping back.
- Taking a giant step forward, standing in place, or taking a giant step back.
- Standing with hands on hips while bending forward and upward shows yes, hands on hips twisting side to side symbolizes OK, and stretching to touch the floor indicates no.
- Standing in front of a green paper taped to the wall signifies good, a yellow paper represents OK, and a red paper means poor.
- Writing a check-plus, which is good, or a check-minus, which is poor, on a piece of paper.
- Drawing a favorite activity within the lesson or drawing an aspect of the lesson that they did not enjoy as much.
- Drawing or writing something they learned, something they thought was important to know, or something they recalled from the lesson.

Soliciting the child's viewpoint at the end of the lesson is a good first step in involving the child in the assessment process. However, more assessment is needed to guide your decision making regarding long-term planning and in making referrals for children needing more skill work. A second step involves using higher-order-questions to gain insight into the child's cognitive and social abilities.

Evidence 2: Responses to Higher-Order Questions

One way to assess a young child's learning is to ask questions that require the child to purposefully think before responding to a question. In the simplest sense, these questions are called, *higher-order-thinking questions* and are also referred to as *higher-order-thinking skills*. The concept is based on the understanding that some educational tasks require more thought beyond a simple "yes" or "no" reply to the teacher's question. Over the years, higher-order thinking has been discussed by numerous educational theorists who believed learning is best achieved when the process involves active inquiry. This requires the teacher to plan lessons that evoke a young child's thinking and reasoning process.

Benjamin Bloom is probably the best known for his work reflecting higher-order thinking when he and four other scholars created a framework known as Bloom's *Taxonomy of Educational Objectives* (Bloom, Englehart, Furst, Hill, & Krathwohl, 1956). This taxonomy became a means for distinguishing basic questions within the kindergarten through grade 12 school systems in the United States as well as other countries. It has been used since that time by teachers and college professors to plan and assess lessons that coincide with how humans learn. Subsequently, these objectives are not only critical to lesson planning as discussed in chapter 2, but they also are the primary focus when assessing whether learning has taken place.

In this book's lesson plans, the questions at the end are identified as assessment questions. These questions are written to help you determine whether the lesson was age appropriate for the child's cognition, if the child's interactions with his or her peers assisted in the learning process, and whether the child demonstrated the correct elements of the selected movement or motor skill. New teachers will most likely identify the higher-order-assessment question as the specific question that challenges the child to do any of the following advanced forms of thinking:

- Use new words to describe an event
- Explain or describe a concept
- Use prior knowledge to answer a question at length
- Distinguish between objects
- Compare and contrast two objects or characters
- Recall facts about an event or setting
- Summarize happenings in their own words
- Explore and make simple discoveries
- Interpret how the child feels about an event or concept
- Discuss new ideas and their relationships
- Relate new understanding to other concepts
- Reflect on one's participation
- Apply new information to discussions
- Take part in basic problem-solving activities

- Recall or remember information presented in the lesson
- Apply the information in a new way
- Relate new information to prior experience
- Describe a visual representation of what they learned
- Apply ideas to new situations
- Predict what might happen next in a situation
- Connect new information with things already learned

When using the assessment questions to determine whether learning took place, the teacher must keep in mind that some learning tasks require more cognition, social engagement, and physical skills than others. This is especially true when exposing a young child to new concepts, and while the new content should challenge each child, it should not frustrate the young mind. Therefore, only one higher-order-thinking question is included in each lesson plan as part of the lesson's assessment. This question can awaken the child's interest in words, concepts, people, and things.

Evidence 3: Written Summaries and Progress Reports

Because it is critical that decisions not be made about young children on the basis of a single assessment tool, many teachers are asked to complete a written summary that they later share with the school's administrators and parents. The most common form of written summary is an assortment of materials collected over time and presented in a printed or in an electronic portfolio. In some cases, the physical education teacher works with the classroom teacher and gathers videotaped segments of the child participating in the class. This assessment evidence is gathered from a realistic setting and situations that reflect the child's actual performance.

Other physical education and classroom teachers prefer to use shorter forms of written summaries as an indication of the child's "strengths, progress, and needs." Some of these smaller forms of evidence include information retrieved from the teacher's ongoing observations that can be used to explain the active nature of the child's learning (The National Association for the Education of Young Children, 2003). The active nature of the young child's learning reflects the learning by doing philosophy made popular in this country by educational psychologist John Dewey (1859-1952). Dewey advocated for hands-on and dynamic learning experiences tied to -life situations to satisfy the child's curiosity (1916).

The lesson plans in *Moving With Words & Actions* include partner and group problem-solving activities, hands-on experiences, and moderate to vigorous games and movement narratives. In physical education, progress reports could include information concerning how the child used the teacher's feedback to improve his or her locomotor skill performance. This form of assessment tool is often favored over a rubric because it addresses the child's *progress* rather than claiming to be a precise measurement. Many school administrators prefer this method of assessment in the preschool years because it is very difficult to identify precisely a young child's level of functioning and learning because the child's physical performance can vary from day to day. These changes can occur for a variety of reasons. Perhaps the young child did not feel well on the assessment day or the child simply declined to fully participate because he or she was troubled by another event that had happened in the school.

Therefore, teachers of young children should be prepared to summarize in a printed or electronic format the child's advancements and identify areas needing additional work. The following are sample phrases to help teachers write progress reports for one lesson or a series of lessons. They are grouped according to the three domains of learning, but they can overlap.

Cognitive Abilities

The extent to which the child...

- Identifies the name of the body parts
- Visualizes items that cannot be seen
- Imagines the body is manipulating an object
- Recalls past experiences to yield new movement patterns (with a partner)
- Discovers how to link movements together (with a partner)
- Discusses facts related to objects or things (with a partner)
- Differentiates between what is fantasy and real (within a whole-group task)
- Responds verbally to suggestions (made by the teacher or group members)
- Critiques level of success and shows enthusiasm (for whole-group tasks)

Affective Abilities

The extent to which the child...

- Uses the body to express feelings and emotions
- Feels and shows confidence in trying novel ways of moving
- Appreciates the roles and actions of people or things that influence one's life
- Assists a partner in the demonstration of the activity
- Is willing to switch roles with a partner
- Shows respect for a partner's strengths, weaknesses, or disability

Psychomotor Abilities

The extent to which the child...

- Demonstrates static balance or dynamic balance while executing basic locomotor skills
- Imitates or duplicates the common movements of objects or things
- Uses combinations of body parts to produce one whole movement
- Successfully demonstrates locomotor skills within moderate to vigorous physical activity
- Stretches a group of body parts (with a partner)
- Manipulates a partner's body to move in a specific way
- Explores multiple movement responses (with a partner)
- Participates physically in all group tasks
- Finds ways to improve on the group movement response
- Responds successfully to whole-group challenges involving small- or large-muscle control
- Displays strength or coordination in the arms, legs, and shoulders

Summary

Overall, your ability to use more than one form of assessment, such as the child's viewpoint, questions that spark higher-order thinking, and written reports that are intended to be shared with parents and school administrators, increase the likelihood of obtaining a complete picture of the child's understanding and physical performance. These can complement existing formative and summative assessment tools.

PART II

Lesson Plans for Moving With Words & Actions

CHAPTER 5

Moving With Words & Actions to Create Healthy Bodies

In recent years, early childhood professionals, physical educators, classroom teachers, and health professionals have worked together to ensure that preschool and elementary school children gain knowledge of the essential elements required for healthy living. Throughout the United States, teacher education programs focus on content in areas such as understanding the systems of the human body and how they function, health and wellness, nutrition, the importance of healthy eating, and the need for daily physical activity. This knowledge is an important element of physical literacy.

When children in preschool through grade 2 are provided with moderate to vigorous physical activities and the opportunities to obtain an understanding of basic health-related concepts, they not only learn about their bodies and their physical capabilities, but they also develop an appreciation for physical activity. A love for physical activity is one of the most important gifts that teachers and parents can give their children. Therefore, the goal of this chapter is to provide you with content that will foster a child's joy for physical activity and the desire to be healthy.

To help accomplish that goal, we have included two distinguishing features within the learning tasks in this chapter. The first feature is aimed at expanding children's awareness of different body parts. That might be as simple as having children follow along in an action rhyme about body awareness or discovering healthy foods. Here are two sample action rhymes that you can recite to a class, having children demonstrate the actions in the rhymes.

Action Rhyme 1: Awareness of Body Parts

- *Shake* hands with yourself and say hello.
- How many parts of your body do you know?
- *Touch* your head. *Tap* your toes.
- *Rub* your stomach. *Wiggle* your nose.
- *Tap* your ears to hear, and *point to* your eyes to see.
- *Bend* your elbows and now *shake* your knees.
- So many body parts that are a part of you.
- We have named only a few!

Action Rhyme 2: Discovering Healthy Foods

- *Crouch* down low to the ground.
- Where juicy strawberries can be found.
- Now try to *move* while staying down low.
- *Reaching*, *stretching*, and *picking* fresh berries as you go.

The second feature is that all the movement tasks are moderate to vigorous physical activity in nature. Moderate physical activity is easily maintained and performed at an intensity that increases heart and breathing rates (NASPE, now known as SHAPE America, 2009). Vigorous physical activity is performed at an intensity that elevates the heart rate and breathing rate higher than that observed during moderate physical activity, and the child fatigues in a short amount of time (NASPE, now known as SHAPE America, 2009). Younger children might simply recognize these experiences as a fun way to strengthen their heart muscles while they play together. Learning tasks that incorporate moderate to vigorous physical activity provide opportunities for the children to discover their physical capabilities, practice a variety of locomotor and nonlocomotor skills, and test their physical prowess.

One example of a moderate physical activity action rhyme that you can use to warm children's muscles might follow this pattern:

We can *leap* over a tall building with a single bound,

Landing firmly on the ground.

Super Kids can *leap* again this way.

Because they practice every day.

A more vigorous form of physical activity might follow a pattern like this:

You *chase*. I will *flee*.

Running and *running*. Can you *catch* me?

All around our playing area we *sprint* and *run*.

Exercising this way is so much fun!

To help you plan your curriculum, the learning tasks in this chapter and throughout *Moving With Words & Actions* coincide with the **precontrol** and **control** levels found in **skill theme** developmental sequences (Graham, Holt/Hale, & Parker, 2012). Skill themes are fundamental movements that are later refined into more complex patterns in which learning tasks of greater complexity are built. The precontrol level is the stage at which a child is unable to control or repeat a movement consciously. At the control level, the child achieves the desired action through additional effort and concentration.

Unlike games containing competitive elements that declare a winner and discourage the loser, many of these learning tasks encourage children to use their imagination and assume the role of a character or object to perform a group task. For example, to create a fruit basket, challenge half of the children to stand in a large circle to form the rim of the basket. The remaining children make fruit shapes: round orange, apple, and plum shapes; long, thin banana shapes; and tiny, round grape shapes.

Other activities ask children to link their movements together to meet a group challenge, while others use a variety of expressive movements, creative pathways, fitness stretches, and creative images to stimulate group participation.

The five suggestions that follow should help you use the lesson plans in this book to expand children's understanding of healthful living:

1. Heighten group participation by stating the goal of the learning task beforehand and reinforcing it during the activity. Whenever possible, include content concerning the body (see Building Content Knowledge to Enhance Physical Literacy later in this chapter).

2. Emphasize that we can use our bodies to perform a group function (e.g., "In this task, we will use our bodies to build a creative structure.").

3. Substitute different types of locomotor skills children are to use in the learning task, and address the outcomes of those changes in the lesson's assessment questions.

4. Use age-appropriate picture books and posters, whenever possible, that identify body systems, human anatomy, bone structure, and food to reinforce the academic concepts presented in the learning task.

5. Use encouraging words and praise phrases to motivate children, and incorporate a sense of humor and a smile to inspire their love of physical activity (e.g., "I can see that you have been practicing"; "Super jumps! You bent your knees, and your landing was perfect."). You can find a list of additional words and phrases in chapter 3's section on Motivating Physically Literate Learners.

Building Content Knowledge to Enhance Physical Literacy

National Standard 3 states that individuals should be able to demonstrate the knowledge and skills needed to achieve and maintain a health-enhancing level of physical activity and fitness. When applying Standard 3 to lessons for young children, then, you should select content that focuses on the body and its functions. The lessons in this chapter contain facts related to the following topics: human cells, muscles, the heart, bones, good nutrition, lungs, and the brain. Physically literate learning takes place as you introduce a variety of "body facts" in each lesson that pique young children's curiosity about the capabilities of their bodies. See the lists of body facts on the next several pages for ideas. You can introduce body facts during the lesson's introduction or immediately following Learning Task 1. Also, you could use the body facts while children are working on Learning Task 3. Regardless, physically literate learning encompasses key words and understandings to enrich children's understanding of the body.

Our Body Is Made of Cells

Preschool and Kindergarten

- Our bodies are made up of many tiny pieces called human cells. Human cells come in all shapes and sizes because of the variety of jobs that they must to do.
- Some cells are round, others are flat like discs, and some look like rods. Cells are too small to be seen by the human eye.
- Our body has many types of cells, including skin cells, bone cells, brain cells, and blood cells.

Grades 1 and 2

- Every second, millions of cells die. The only cells in the body that are not replaced are brain cells. We are born with a surplus of brain cells to make up for this continual loss.
- Each cell is like a city in its structure and function. It produces the energy for the body.
- The center of the cell (i.e., the nucleus) is where the cell's information is stored.
- The outer membrane of a cell is like a city wall, protecting the cell from harmful substances.

Muscles Are Needed for Movement

Preschool and Kindergarten

- Muscles move our body like strings move a puppet.
- Muscles are made out of many stretchy, elastic materials called fibers.
- We have more than 600 muscles in our body.
- For a muscle to work, it must have a partner muscle. One muscle pulls a bone forward, and another muscle pulls a bone back. When one muscle is working (i.e., contracting), the other muscle is relaxing. Muscle pairs work well together.
- Muscles also help hold organs in place.

- We have a large muscle in our chest (i.e., the diaphragm) that helps our lungs breathe.
- Our heart is also a muscle, and it makes blood move through the body.
- Muscles help us to chew our food and even close our eyelids and help us to smile. It takes more muscles to frown than it does to smile.
- Caterpillars can have as many as 4,000 muscles.

Help children learn about the importance of their muscles by having them participate in the following action rhyme:

My Muscles Move Me

- Muscles help your body move.
- When you *stretch* them, they improve.
- Your muscles are always busy at work.
- They can *move quickly, slowly*, or with a *jerk*.
- Use your muscles to *move your eyes*,
- Then your *arms, knees, shoulders, fingers, feet*, and *thighs*.
- Muscles help you do everything.
- They help you to *jump forward*, and let your *arms swing*.
- *Move forward, backward*, and to the *side*.
- *Move* them so you are *tall and thin*, then *round, now wide*.
- *Make* yourself as *small* as a mouse,
- Then *stretch* your body as *large* as a house.

Grades 1 and 2

- Muscles are made of fibrous tissues bound together, and they act like bunches of rubber bands.
- Muscles can work in only one way, by pulling. They never work by pushing.
- The muscle system in our body is arranged so that even if we are pushing against something with all our strength, our muscles are really pulling.
- The ends of our muscles are attached to bones. One end is attached to a bone that the muscle is intended to move. The other end is anchored to a bone that the muscles will not move.
- Our muscles are usually attached to the bone by a short, tough cord called a tendon.
- Muscles are heavy. Our muscles make up half the weight of our body.
- There are more than three times as many muscles in the adult body as there are bones.
- We use 17 muscles to smile and 43 muscles when we frown.
- We use 72 muscles every time we speak one word.
- Muscles become stronger when they are used.

The Heart Is a Special Muscle

Preschool and Kindergarten

- Our heart is a strong pump that moves blood through the body.
- Our heart is located slightly left in the center of our chest, and it is about the size of a person's fist.
- The heart muscle works all the time, even when we sleep.
- It pumps blood, which is full of a gas called oxygen, and food through tubes called arteries. The blood travels throughout our body and feeds our tiny cells.
- Our heart pumps our blood to our lungs.
- It takes about one minute for our heart to circle the blood around the body and back again (i.e., circulation).
- We can hear our heart beating all the time. The beating sound is caused by the opening and closing of the doors (i.e., valves) inside the heart. They let the blood in and out of the heart.
- When we feel our heart beating, we know that blood is circling all around the body.

Grades 1 and 2

- Our heart is a pump that moves blood through the body. The blood is carried away from the heart in elastic tubes called arteries, and it returns to the heart in elastic tubes called veins.
- Together the heart, blood, arteries, and veins form what is known as the circulatory system.
- Blood carries oxygen and other important materials to every part of the body through tiny tubes called capillary arteries.
- The heart is really two pumps. One pump gets blood from the body and sends it out to the lungs. The other pump gets blood from the lungs and sends it around the body.
- Our heart is divided into four compartments (i.e., chambers).
- Every contraction and relaxation of the heart produces one heartbeat.
- A rabbit's heart is about the size of a ping-pong or golf ball.
- Large dogs have hearts the size of tennis balls, and a giraffe has a heart the size of a basketball.
- The heart's job is to pump blood. When blood enters the heart, the heart stretches. Then it squeezes together to push the blood out.

Our Bones Are Alive

Preschool and Kindergarten

- Our bones give our bodies shape and support and protect our organs.
- Bones help us to move from place to place.
- Our bones grow longer, and we get taller.
- Bones are strong, but they can break and mend.
- Half of the 206 bones in our body are in our hands and feet.

Grades 1 and 2

- The frame of the bones in our body is called the skeleton.
- The skeleton serves several purposes: The bones give the body its general support, they support and protect the softer parts of the body, and they provide leverage for the muscles that are attached to them.
- Inside the hard, outer material of our bones is a soft yellowish substance called marrow.
- The marrow in our bones contains many of the important materials that we need in order to live.
- The point at which bones meet is called a joint.
- The biggest, longest, and strongest bone in our body is the thigh bone (i.e., femur).
- The part of the skull that encloses the brain is made up of bones with immovable joints (i.e., cranium).
- At the joints where there is movement, the bones are bound together by strong bands called ligaments.
- Most people have 24 ribs that form a cage that protects their heart and lungs.
- Bones are made of living cells.

Good Nutrition and Tasty Foods

Preschool and Kindergarten

- The tongue is our most sensitive body part. The heel is the least sensitive part of our body.
- When we eat healthy foods, the food tastes sweet, bitter, sour, or salty.
- The way food tastes is determined when food touches our taste buds on the upper surface of the tongue.
- Not all of our taste buds are on the tongue. Some are on the palate and some at the top of the throat on the pharynx and tonsils.
- The taste buds at the tip of our tongue detect sweetness.
- The taste buds at the sides of our tongue detect sourness and saltiness.
- The taste buds near the base of our tongue detect bitterness.
- Healthy foods come in a variety of tastes.
- The stomach is like a stretchy storage bag that can hold up to two quarts (2 L) of food. When you are hungry, your stomach muscles contract. If there is air in your stomach, this contraction will make a growling or rumbling sound.

Grades 1 and 2

- The process of breaking down food is called digestion. Our food travels throughout the body, and on its way it is broken into smaller pieces.
- We use our teeth to bite, chew, and chop the food into tiny pieces. The tongue also helps to make the food smaller and softer.
- When we swallow food, it travels down our throat and through a long tube into our stomach.
- Our stomach stretches with the food, and acids help to break it down further.
- When food leaves the stomach, it travels down into the intestines, where the nutrients of the food go into our bloodstream.

- The food we eat must enter the bloodstream and go to the cells in our body.
- If we think of our body as a city, then the circulatory system would be the train that travels through it. The heart sends the blood with the good nutrients on hundreds of round-trips every day, each trip taking less than a minute. Every time the heart beats, it sends another wave of blood through the body.
- Our food consists of elements called protein, fat, carbohydrate, vitamins, minerals, and water. We need all of these to live. A balanced diet contains grains (e.g., bread, cereal, rice, pasta); fruit that is fresh, dried, or unsweetened; vegetables that are raw or lightly cooked; foods high in protein (e.g., red meat, poultry, fish, dried beans, eggs, nuts); and dairy (e.g., milk, yogurt, cheese).
- During our lifetime we eat about 60,000 pounds (27,215 kg) of food, about the combined weight of six elephants.
- Food is measured according to the amount of energy it produces. The unit to measure this energy is the calorie.

Healthy Lungs for a Long Life

Preschool and Kindergarten

- Our lungs help the body breathe.
- The upper part of our chest is almost totally filled with lungs.
- Our lungs are made up of millions of little sacs that fill up and let out air.
- Our lungs can hold about as much air as a basketball!

Grades 1 and 2

- Air comes into our body through the nose and mouth. It travels down the windpipe (i.e., trachea) through tubes (i.e., bronchial tubes), and then to both lungs.
- Our lungs trade air with the blood. The heart pumps used blood to the lungs. The lungs take the carbon dioxide and other things we can't use out of the blood.
- Our lungs give back fresh oxygen to the blood. In a short while, the blood goes back to the heart to work again.
- The strong muscle that helps make our lungs work is called the diaphragm.
- The diaphragm is under the lungs. It helps push out the lungs when they are filling up with air.
- The diaphragm also helps let our lungs back in to squeeze out the used air.
- When we take a large breath (i.e., inhaling) or when we breathe air out (i.e., exhaling), we know the lungs are working.
- We breathe faster while running or being physically active. This is caused by the need for additional oxygen for the body.
- Our lungs are like balloons filling up with air and letting air out.
- People can keep their lungs healthy by moving quickly, exercising, and not smoking.

The Brain Is Our Perfect Machine

Preschool and Kindergarten

- Your brain is located inside your skull, which acts like a turtle shell to protect it.
- Your brain has two sides.
- When we feel sad, happy, frightened, or excited, the feelings come from our brain.

Grades 1 and 2

- The right side of the brain receives messages and controls the left side of the body.
- Our brain does not move, but it uses more oxygen than any other part of our body.
- Our brain does not grow after we become 6 years old.
- The brain is our body's special computer. It constantly receives information from inside and outside the body and either uses it or saves the information for future use.
- Our brain looks like a mushroom of gray and white tissue, and it feels like jelly!
- Our brain is about 80 percent water.
- Our brain works best when we have had a long night's sleep and our body is in good health.
- People say that we do not use all of our brain's capacity, but learning helps us to exercise our brain.
- Playing outside is one way to get fresh oxygen to the brain.

BODY SHAPES AND CREATIONS

National Standards Addressed

- **Standard 1.** The physically literate individual demonstrates competency in a variety of motor skills and movement patterns.
- **Standard 4.** The physically literate individual exhibits responsible personal and social behavior that respects self and others.

Instructional Materials/Props

Lively music; a can of Play-Doh or modeling clay (optional); posters showing different shapes (optional); photographs of statues in the community, state, and nation (optional); device to play music; a whistle for safety

Central Focus

To reinforce that the body can form different shapes and poses.

Objectives

- **Cognitive:** The child will identify and describe a variety of shapes that his or her body can make.
- **Affective:** The child will interact in a friendly and respectful manner while molding and shaping their partner's body into familiar objects or things.
- **Psychomotor:** The child will manipulate and mold four or five classmates' bodies into one large connected shape and then describe the group pose to other classmates who have done the same. Then all groups come together to create a whole-group imaginary art gallery called Creative Body Gallery.

Component of Health-Related Fitness

Flexibility

Learning Task 1: Preparing Our Bodies to Move

Class organization: Children are scattered throughout general space.

Challenge the children to perform the following actions:

- Can you *curl* your body and create an egg or oval shaped statue?
- When I clap my hands, discover a way to make a box- or square-shaped statue.
- Who can show me what a silly statue might look like?
- Is it possible to change your body to create a very tall statue shape?
- How many body parts can you *wiggle* or *shake* to *relax* our muscles? Can you show me?

Learning Task 2: Partner Challenge

Class organization: Partners are scattered in self-spaces.

Present the following: *A sculptor is a person who uses materials to mold and shape in order to create an object or thing.*
Ask the children to explain how they can use Play-Doh to make different shapes and objects (e.g., by *bending, stretching, rolling,* and *twisting*).

- Encourage them to move quickly and select a partner (e.g., Who can find a partner that has the same color shirt or pants that you are wearing?).
- Suggest that one child pretend to be a large can of Play-Doh. The other partner pretends to be a sculptor and "molds" the Play-Doh into familiar shapes such as round, triangle, box, wide, long, and narrow. A child can also mold his or her partner's body into an object such as a tree, table, chair, or rocket. At the end of the learning task, the sculptor identifies and describes the partner's Play-Doh body shape and they exchange roles after three to four minutes.

Learning Task 3: Gallery

Class organization: Children are scattered in identified groups

Present the following: *A gallery is a place that displays art for people to view.*

- **Creative Body Gallery:** Divide the children into groups of five or six. One child from each group assumes the role of sculptor, while the remainder of the children in each group imagine they are molding clay or Play-Doh. The children acting as sculptors mold their group member's bodies into a large shape. Following this, one group at a time displays its creation for the remaining classmates and discusses the shapes they formed. For a greater challenge, ask two children to connect the group shapes to create an imaginary whole-group body gallery.
- **Fun Frozen Statue Shapes:** Children are encouraged to vigorously move about the playing area when the music begins. When the music stops, you call out, "Frozen Statue." All children freeze holding their pose until the music begins again. The next time the music stops, you call out, "rounded or circle statue" and the children respond. The action is followed by the words, "tall statue," "tiny statue," and "giant statue." With each trial, you may choose to vary the type of locomotor skills that the children perform (e.g., jump, gallop, or skip).

Assessment Questions

1. What kinds of shapes did we make today (e.g., narrow, tall, short, wide, box, circle)?
2. Which body parts were the easiest to bend into different poses?
3. Who can tell me how your body shape will change as you grow older?

Academic Language Demands

- **Language function:** Uses language to identify and describe shapes and objects that the body can make and offers opportunities for both partners to critique each other's imaginative pose each child created while in the role of sculptor.
- **Vocabulary:** Specific shapes the body can make (e.g., box, circle, square, oval, rectangle) while posing or while stretching (to become a greater width or length), and the word *sculptor* is defined as a person who uses materials to mold and shape in order to create an object or thing. The word *gallery* is defined as a place that displays pieces of art for people to view, and a *museum* is identified as a building that contains exhibits for people to study or learn about.
- **Syntax or discourse:** A verbal interchange focusing on the understanding that our body can change into many shapes in order to complete different physical tasks over time as we grow and become stronger and better movers.

STRONG BONES

National Standards Addressed

- **Standard 1.** The physically literate individual demonstrates competency in a variety of motor skills and movement patterns.
- **Standard 2.** The physically literate individual applies knowledge of concepts, principles, strategies and tactics related to movement and performance.

Instructional Materials/Props

Picture or plastic skeleton of the body (optional)

Central Focus

To isolate and name different body parts that can serve as specified targets in a vigorous movement activity.

Objectives

- **Cognitive:** The child will point to bones in different parts of the body and indicate how they move.
- **Affective:** The child will show signs of developing a positive self-concept after moving.
- **Psychomotor:** The child will demonstrate that he or she can collapse safely to the ground after moving vigorously.

Component of Health-Related Fitness

Cardiorespiratory endurance

Learning Task 1: Preparing Our Bodies to Move

Class organization: Children are scattered in self-spaces.

Challenge the children to perform the following actions while saying this rhyme:

My muscles and bones are inside of me. (*Point to chest.*)
My goal is to make them as strong as can be. (*Flex biceps.*)
So I happily *gallop, slide, skip,* and *jump*. (*Perform movements.*)
When finished, I use my bones to *pound* and *thump*! (*Pound arms on chest.*)

Learning Task 2: Partner Challenge

Class organization: Partners are scattered in self-spaces.

Present the following:

- Let's divide our bodies into different areas or zones.
- Show your partner how you can make three upper-body parts move one after the other as you both count the moves. Your partner imitates you, and then you exchange roles.
- Move two body parts on the right side of your body. Make one of those body parts the highest part of your body.
- One partner *points* to two lower-body parts. See if you can make those two lower-body parts move at the same time. Exchange roles.
- Both *wiggle* one body part that is on the left side of the body.

Learning Task 3: Bones, Bones, Everywhere

Class organization: Children are scattered in identified groups.

- Ask the children to designate a specific body part or body area to serve as a target (e.g., elbow, shoulder, below the knees, hip, or between the shoulder blades).
- Select two or more chasers, depending on the size of the group.
- Challenge the remainder of the children to scatter and flee from the chasers.
- When a child is tagged, he or she collapses into a "pile of bones." After everyone is tagged, select new chasers, or call out, "Strong bodies!" Children who are tagged continue in the game.

Assessment Questions

1. Which body part was the most difficult to tag?
2. Show me the movements you used to keep your body from being tagged (e.g., dodging and darting).
3. Who can remember a time when your bones needed to rest? How did you feel? Do you remember what you had been doing?

Academic Language Demands

- **Language function:** Uses language to explore the various body areas that are appropriate to serve as a space for tagging.
- **Vocabulary:** Collapse, elbow, hip, shoulder blades, strong
- **Syntax or discourse:** A verbal exchange concerning how to collapse and fall to the ground safely.

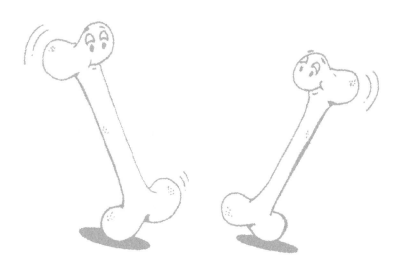

TWISTING BODY PARTS

National Standards Addressed

Standard 1. The physically literate individual demonstrates competency in a variety of motor skills and movement patterns.

Instructional Materials/Props

Picture or actual twisted pretzel (optional), photographs of twisted yoga poses (optional)

Central Focus

To explore a variety of twisted shapes by rotating specific body parts.

Objectives

- **Cognitive:** The child will make comparisons about how some body parts can naturally be twisted while others do not.
- **Affective:** The child will interact with a partner to respectfully and safely twist body parts to form the shape of a twisted pretzel.
- **Psychomotor:** The child will manipulate several classmates' bodies to create a large-group twisted pretzel shape and be able to hold the pose for a brief time.

Component of Health-Related Fitness

Flexibility

Learning Task 1: Preparing Our Bodies to Move

Class organization: Children are scattered throughout general space.

Challenge the children to perform the following actions:

Who can pretend to *open* a jar of peanut butter?

What body part were you *twisting* in this movement (wrist)? Show me.

Can you *twist* the upper part of your body without moving the lower part of your body?

Is it possible to *twist* one upper-body part around a lower-body part?

Learning Task 2: Partner Challenge

Class organization: Partners are scattered in self-spaces.

Ask children to quickly find a partner and use as many body parts as possible to form a *wide, narrow, curled*, and a *twisted* body shape.

Learning Task 3: Twisted Pretzels

Class organization: Children are scattered in identified groups.

- Divide the children into groups of five or six.
- Encourage children to make a giant pretzel shape by connecting with their classmates' shapes.
- Each group should maintain the pretzel shape until you say, "Twisted pretzels."

Assessment Questions

1. Which body parts were the easiest to twist (e.g., shoulders, neck, hips, wrists)?
2. What other objects have twisted pretzel-like shapes (e.g., gift bows, shoelaces, balloon animals, bow ties, wires)? Can you make one of these shapes?
3. Can anyone tell me the difference between twisting and turning a body part (e.g., turning is moving many body parts, and twisting is moving one body part around another)? Show me the difference.

Academic Language Demands

- **Language function:** Uses language to sequence ideas about how a partner's body can be twisted into a pretzel shape.
- **Vocabulary:** twist, bend, flexible
- **Syntax or discourse:** A verbal interchange reflecting the need to bend and twist in many ways in order to create objects with our bodies and to remain flexible.

MY SPECIAL BODY PARTS

National Standards Addressed

Standard 1. The physically literate individual demonstrates competency in a variety of motor skills and movement patterns.

Instructional Materials/Props

Samples of handwear (e.g., gloves, mittens, sport gloves) and footwear (e.g., shoes, sneakers, boots, sandals) (optional)

Central Focus

To suggest movements and develop actions that can be performed using specific body parts.

Objectives

- **Cognitive:** The child will locate and detect actions that require the use of their fingers and toes.
- **Affective:** The child will attempt to involve peers in challenges focusing on movements our feet can make.
- **Psychomotor:** The child will display a variety of uses for lower-body parts which challenges the child to work within a group and create a sequence of movements.

Component of Health-Related Fitness

Cardiorespiratory endurance

Learning Task 1: Preparing Our Bodies to Move

Class organization: Children are scattered throughout general space.

Present the following: *Some objects consist of parts that have the same name as one of our body parts (e.g., hands of a clock).* Challenge the children to participate in the following stretching task:

- Is it possible to *move* your arms and hands in a circle like the hands of a giant clock?
- Who can keep their feet still and *move* their hands from side to side while saying, "Tick tock"?
- Let's *shake* your whole body like the loud ringing of an alarm clock.

Learning Task 2: **Partner Challenge**

Class organization: Partners are scattered in self-spaces.

Present the following:

- Please find a partner and stand beside that person so that we can explore movements that our bodies can perform. What body parts do we cover with mittens (hands, fingers, palms, wrists)? Let's explore several hand movements. Who can *wiggle* their fingers, or *flutter* their fingers?
- Follow me as I make a *clapping* motion. Now *cup* your hands and *clap*. Do you hear a different sound?
- Make two fists and *pound* one fist on top of the other.
- Show me how you can *drum* your fingers on the floor. *Snap* your fingers together. *Shake* your fingers at the side of the body.
- Can you and your partner discover two other ways to move your fingers and hands (e.g., point, push, pull, grip, dig, scoop, flick, cross, throw, catch)?

Learning Task 3: **Small-Muscle Actions**

Class Organization: Children are scattered in identified groups.

- Divide the children into groups of four or five. Ask the children to identify the part of the body that we cover with socks (e.g., feet, toes, heels, ankles).
- Give each group three to five minutes to explore movements or gestures that they can perform with their toes and feet (e.g., wiggling, stomping, kicking, marching, and other vigorous movements).
- Bring the children together and ask each group to demonstrate two or three actions while the remainder of the class mimics their movements.

Assessment Questions

1. Which actions today involved stretching the fingers and toes?
2. Which actions involved curling or bending these body parts?
3. Is it possible to create a dance with special steps and movements and give it a name?

Academic Language Demands

- **Language function:** Uses language to integrate ideas to form a whole-group learning task involving the feet.
- **Vocabulary:** shake, clap, pound, drum, flutter, hand (of clock), toe, foot movements
- **Syntax or discourse:** A verbal interchange regarding the use of the tiny muscles in our hands and feet and why they are important for movement.

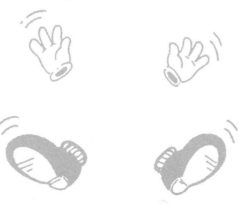

MUSCLE ACTIONS

National Standards Addressed

Standard 1. The physically literate individual demonstrates competency in a variety of motor skills and movement patterns.

Instructional Materials/Props

Pictures of or sample objects that show relaxed and tightened positions (e.g., piece of yarn, pictures of body parts, pictures of yoga poses) (optional)

Central Focus

To experience and explain the difference between a tightened muscle and a relaxed muscle.

Objectives

- **Cognitive:** The child will expound on the difference between a tightened and a relaxed muscle.
- **Affective:** The child will display cooperative behavior when asked to use a variety of muscle tensions with his or her partner.
- **Psychomotor:** The child will execute the ability to move, stretch, and bend in a variety of specific ways.

Component of Health-Related Fitness

Cardiorespiratory endurance

Learning Task 1: Preparing Our Bodies to Move

Class organization: Children are scattered throughout general space.

Challenge the children to perform the following actions:

- Muscles make it possible for the body to move. Our brain sends a message to a muscle or a group of muscles and tells them to tighten (i.e., contract) or to relax. To test this, we can tell our brain to make a tight fist or to grip. If you want to open your hand, tell your brain to relax your muscles.
- Show me how you can make a strong shape with your arms. Feel your muscle grow and tighten. Now *shake* your arms to *relax* the muscle like cooked spaghetti.
- Can you *stiffen* your legs and *tighten* the muscles? Now *bend* your legs to a low level.
- *Walk* around and *relax* your leg muscles.
- Who can show me an object or a person that *walks* with *stiff* legs (e.g., robot, soldier)?
- Is it possible to *tighten* your abdominal muscles? Show me.
- Let's lie down at a low level and *tighten* one arm's muscle. Now, *relax* that arm. *Tighten* the other arm's muscle. *Relax.* Try to *tighten* one leg's muscle, *relax*, and then *tighten* the other leg's muscle. *Relax.*

Learning Task 2: **Partner Challenge**

Class organization: Partners are scattered in self-spaces.

Present the following:

- Partners can exercise together and help one another tighten and relax muscles to make their muscles stronger.
- Select a partner, and *extend* one hand to each other in a *handshake* or *gripped* position, making your arms *tight* by *gripping* firmly. Switch hands. *Shake* your arms and hands to *relax* your muscles.
- *Place* the palms of your hands together. *Push* your hands and feel the muscles in your hands and arms *tighten*. Now try this with your partner. Facing one another, *touch* the palms of your hands to your partner's palms. Start by gently *pushing* against each other's hands.
- With your partner, can you *sit* down facing each other with toes touching? Who can make their legs *tight*? Now *relax*.

Learning Task 3: **Muscle Challenges**

Class organization: Children are scattered in self-spaces.

Read the following muscle challenges and ask the children to demonstrate these actions.

If becoming healthy is your aim,

Then *running* in place could be your game.

Our quadriceps help us to *jump*,

Back and forth our legs and arms *pump*.

There are so many healthy ways to have fun,

Sprinting forward while using our hamstrings is a special one.

Imagine you are *climbing* way up high,

On a giant, rocky mountain that rises to the sky.

Let's complete our muscle challenges, so *wiggle* and *shake* with all your might,

To keep your muscles from becoming tight.

Assessment Questions

1. How did you feel when you relaxed your muscles?
2. What happened to your body when you tightened your muscles?
3. See how many ways you can stretch your upper-body parts while naming a favorite muscle.

Academic Language Demands

- **Language function**: Uses language to determine a solution for the partner tasks involving muscular contraction and relaxation.
- **Vocabulary:** relax, tighten, contraction, quadriceps, hamstrings
- **Syntax or discourse:** A verbal interchange reiterating that our brain sends a message to a group of muscles and tells them to tighten (i.e., contract) or to relax.

BODY EXPRESSIONS

National Standards Addressed

Standard 1. The physically literate individual demonstrates competency in a variety of motor skills and movement patterns.

Instructional Materials/Props

Four to six large sheets of plain paper and one box of wide-tipped markers or crayons

Central Focus

To perform a variety of expressive movements and work in a group to collectively illustrate the key parts of a person's body.

Objectives

- **Cognitive:** The child will identify facial expressions and body gestures that reflect different emotions.
- **Affective:** The child will accept constructive criticism and find joy in contributing to a group drawing.
- **Psychomotor:** The child will perform a variety of locomotor skills at a vigorous pace while completing a group illustration of a human body on a large sheet of paper.

Component of Health-Related Fitness

Cardiorespiratory endurance

Learning Task 1: Preparing Our Bodies to Move

Class organization: Children are scattered throughout general space.

Challenge the children to perform the following actions:

- The look or expression on people's faces often shows us how they are feeling. How does your face tell me you are feeling *worried, daring, bashful,* and *angry*?
- Use your whole body to tell me you are feeling *mighty, beautiful, afraid,* and *sleepy*.
- How does your body move when you are feeling *droopy, fierce,* and *lazy*?
- Some people skip and dance when they feel playful. Can you *skip* and *dance* and *move* in a playful way?
- Show me how your favorite action heroes and heroines feel and move.

Learning Task 2: Partner Challenge

Class organization: Partners are scattered in self-spaces.

Present the following:

- While facing your partner, one partner uses his or her face and body to show a feeling. The other partner has three guesses to identify the correct emotion. Both partners discuss which clues helped them name the emotion (e.g., *angry*: stiff body, closed fists, staring, body squarely facing the other person).
- Exchange roles.

Learning Task 3: Creative Body Expressions

Class organization: Children are scattered in identified groups.

- Arrange the children into groups of no more than four children. Each group forms a behind-line with all group members facing the same direction.
- Place a large sheet of paper and a box of crayons at the opposite end of each group's playing area.
- Explain that the purpose of this learning task is to work with their group members to draw a person's body.
- To do so, the first child from each line runs to the group's designated sheet of paper and draws a large circle to represents a person's face. After completing the circle, the child returns to the rear of his or her line.
- The second child in line runs to the sheet of paper and draws one body part (e.g., eye, ear, or nose), followed by the third child who draws a body part. The fourth child adds another part, and so on until the face is complete with eyelashes, a chin, lips, teeth, cheeks, and hair, followed by larger body segments (neck, torso, arms, hands, fingers, legs, and feet). Vary the form of locomotor skill used to advance to the sheet of paper.

Assessment Questions

1. Who can tell me what the person they have drawn is feeling based on the completed drawing (e.g., surprised, silly, frightened)?
2. Can your body move in other ways to show how you are feeling?
3. If you could change one thing about your group drawing, what would it be?

Academic Language Demands

- **Language function:** Uses language to predict what a large drawing of a body might look like when composed by a group of classmates.
- **Vocabulary:** emotions (e.g., daring, bashful, angry, mighty), body parts (e.g., eyes, mouth, arms, torso)
- **Syntax or discourse**: A verbal interchange that identifies the emotion and expression that each group's illustration most closely represents.

JUMPING JILLS

National Standards Addressed

Standard 1. The physically literate individual demonstrates competency in a variety of motor skills and movement patterns.

Instructional Materials/Props

Large sheet of paper, marker, tape

Central Focus

To successfully perform the mechanics involved in a jumping jack and to work with a partner and group in the creation of an original exercise.

Objectives

- **Cognitive:** The child will recall the three separate actions that are required to perform a jumping jack.
- **Affective:** The child will contribute to the creation of an original exercise with a partner.
- **Psychomotor:** The child will use the time with a partner productively and demonstrate effort to create a unique exercise that classmates can perform and repeat.

Components of Health-Related Fitness

Cardiorespiratory endurance, muscular strength and endurance

Learning Task 1: Preparing Our Bodies to Move

Class organization: Children are scattered throughout general space.

Challenge the children to perform the following actions:

- Show me how you have learned to *jump* by using two feet and landing on your toes.
- Who can *jump* forward, backward, and side to side? What part of your foot touches the floor first (toes)? Can you *wiggle* these body parts?
- Today we will demonstrate a special exercise. It is called a jumping jack for boys and a jumping jill for girls. Many people like doing them to warm up their muscles. Let's begin by making our bodies very stiff and narrow with our arms at our sides. Is it possible to *jump* up and open your legs in a triangle shape?
- See if you can *clap* your hands over your head. Bring your arms back to your side. Now close the triangle.
- If you are having trouble coordinating your actions, simply *flap* your arms like a big bird.
- Try to perform five jumping jacks or jills.

Learning Task 2: Partner Challenge

Class organization: Partners are scattered in self-spaces.

Present the following: *The heart's job is to pump blood. When blood enters the heart, the heart stretches. Then it squeezes together to push the blood out.* Challenge the children to perform the following actions:

- Hold your partner's hands and *squeeze* close together.
- Imagine that your heart is filling with blood. As your heart fills up, slowly move apart, but continue holding hands.
- When you are completely *stretched*, quickly squeeze back together to *push*, or pump, the blood out. This represents one heartbeat.

Learning Task 3: Our Special Exercise

Class organization: Children are scattered in identified groups.

Organize the children into groups of four. Challenge the groups to create or invent a new exercise. Suggest that the exercise include bending, stretching, or curling the body into a shape. Groups should name their newly created exercise.

- After the groups have had time to create an exercise, bring all the children together.
- Encourage each group, one at a time, to demonstrate their group's original exercise to the class. Challenge the whole class to perform the exercise two or three times while the original group observes and provides positive reinforcement or suggestions for correction.
- List the names of the exercises on a large sheet of paper or on a bulletin board for all the children to view.

Assessment Questions

1. During the jumping jills and jacks, which body parts were the most difficult to control (hands or feet)?
2. How many of you found an exercise today that you would like to perform again at home? Can you show me?
3. See if you can think of another way we can make exercising fun.

Academic Language Demands

- **Language function:** Uses language to convince classmates that the original exercise is fun to perform and one that can make the body stronger or more flexible.
- **Vocabulary:** jump, stretch, bend, curl, heart pumping
- **Syntax or discourse:** A verbal interchange focusing on why the partners believe their original exercise was given a particular name.

TIME, FORCE, AND FLOW . . . ON THE GO

National Standards Addressed

Standard 1. The physically literate individual demonstrates competency in a variety of motor skills and movement patterns.

Instructional Materials/Props

Photos of a roadrunner and a coyote (optional)

Central Focus

To demonstrate the ability to move quickly, stop quickly, and perform a mature balance shape.

Objectives

- **Cognitive:** The child will recall facts about the bird called a roadrunner at the end of the lesson.
- **Affective:** The child will not hesitate to depend on his or her partner for stability when completing several balance tasks.
- **Psychomotor:** The child will perform a mature balance shape after moving vigorously.

Component of Health-Related Fitness

Cardiorespiratory endurance

Learning Task 1: Preparing Our Bodies to Move

Class organization: Children are scattered in self-spaces.

Challenge the children to perform the following actions:

- Who can *balance* on two different body parts at separate times without falling?
- Can you *balance* on the hand you use to drink a glass of water? What about the foot you use to kick a ball?
- See if you can *balance* on one foot while changing from a low to a high level.
- Make the letter O with your arms while *balancing* on one foot.
- Is it possible to *run* forward five steps, and then *stop* quickly and maintain your *balance*? Try this movement three times.

Learning Task 2: Partner Challenge

Class organization: Partners are scattered in self-spaces.

Ask the following:

- With a partner, see if you can *hold* hands, *stretch* into a wide shape, and maintain your *balance*.
- Is it possible to *hold* hands and only have three feet touching the ground while maintaining your *balance*?
- Which set of partners can *hold* hands and *balance* on just two feet instead of four?

Learning Task 3: **On the Go**

Class organization: Children are scattered in identified groups.

- Challenge the children to imagine themselves as being roadrunners. Explain that roadrunners are speedy birds found in California, Mexico, and Texas. They can obtain speeds up to 17 miles per hour (27 km/h) by running. These birds can grow up to 2 feet (61 cm) long.
- This activity is a variation of the popular game stork tag. Begin by selecting one or more children to be a coyote (i.e., the chaser). Designate a specific shoulder to be tagged.
- The remainder of the children pretend to be roadrunners and flee from the coyote.
- A roadrunner can avoid being tagged by balancing on one foot, folding the arms across the chest, and saying, "Meep, meep."
- When a roadrunner is tagged, he or she cooperates with the coyote to tag other roadrunners.

Assessment Questions

1. What body parts helped you to stop and hold your balance like a roadrunner?
2. Who can think of two sports that require an athlete to balance?
3. Can you use your body to move like athletes in those two sports (e.g., skaters, gymnasts)?

Academic Language Demands

- **Language function:** Uses language to describe the difficulty that one can experience when moving quickly and trying to stop and maintain one's balance.
- **Vocabulary:** balance
- **Syntax or discourse:** A verbal interchange concerning the strategy that one uses to balance and move the body at the same time (e.g., arms at the sides, lowering the center of gravity).

BODY OUTLINES

National Standards Addressed

Standard 1. The physically literate individual demonstrates competency in a variety of motor skills and movement patterns.

Instructional Materials/Props

A box of chalk or a roll of art paper with markers and tape to attach paper to the floor

Central Focus

To outline the shape of a partner's body and perform a variety of movement skills using one's own body outline.

Objectives

- **Cognitive:** The child will trace and illustrate a large recognizable body shape.
- **Affective:** The child will cooperate respectfully and take his or her turn while completing a variety of locomotor movements over and around the outline of a partner's body.
- **Psychomotor:** The child will correctly perform a specific locomotor skill around a collection of large illustrated body shapes.

Component of Health-Related Fitness

Cardiorespiratory endurance

Learning Task 1: Preparing Our Bodies to Move

Class organization: Children are scattered throughout general space.

Challenge the children to perform the following actions:

- Different people have different body shapes. Who can show me a very tall body shape, a short body shape, a strong body shape?
- Some people's bodies are long and narrow. Can you make this shape?
- Find a way to make a round body shape.
- Pretend your legs are rubber bands. *Stretch* your legs and make them the longest they can be.
- We can even make our bodies into silly shapes. Show me a silly shape and a strange, *twisted* shape.
- Tell the children that words like "fat" and "ugly" should not be used to describe a person's body. These words make people feel sad about their body's shape.

Learning Task 2: Partner Challenge

Class organization: Partners are scattered in self-spaces, and each set of partners receives a piece of chalk.

Present the following:

- One partner lies on the floor and makes a wide body shape. The other partner holds the chalk and traces around the head, arms, torso and trunk, and legs to form the outline of the body. When the body outline is completed, change places with your partner and draw his or her body shape.

- Partners can also trace each other's body using markers on art paper taped to the floor.
- Who can stand at the head of their body shape, on the arm, or at the feet?
- See if you can *walk, hop, gallop,* and *jump* around the outside of your body shape.
- Show me how you can *run, jump,* or *leap* over your body shape.
- Is it possible to *jump* from one hand to the other, from the feet to the head, and from one knee to an elbow?

Learning Task 3: **Follow Me Body Tour**

Class organization: Children are in a behind-line behind the teacher.

- All children form a behind-line, and you are the leader of the line. Remind the children to follow you by staying in line and to avoid stepping on the drawings as they begin their walking tour of all the body-outlines art.
- After they begin their follow-the-leader walk, challenge the children by changing locomotor skills (e.g., marching, tiptoeing, slide stepping).
- Change the speed of the locomotor skill (e.g., marching at a slower or faster pace) or vary the level (e.g., marching at a high, medium, or low level).
- For a greater challenge, divide the children into small groups and make the first child in each line the leader. He or she chooses a variety of physical actions to lead the group through the body illustrations (e.g., walk, run, slide step, or jump around the outside of the body shapes). After a certain amount of time, the leader goes to the back of the line and the children follow the new leader. Continue until all children have had a turn being the leader.

Assessment Questions

1. Who can tell me something special about their body shape?
2. How will your body shape change as you grow older? Show me.
3. Can you think of other movements or things you could do using the outline of your body's shape (e.g., standing on one hand and one leg, jumping in and out of the shape, standing on both knees, using the body shape as the "no tag" space while playing tag)?

Academic Language Demands

- **Language function:** Uses language to justify why a body illustration looks the way it does.
- **Vocabulary:** torso, trunk, body shape descriptors (e.g., tall, short, strong, long, narrow, round, twisted)
- **Syntax or discourse:** A verbal interchange to decide how difficult or easy it was to participate in the follow-the-leader learning task.

ACTIVE FRUITS AND VEGETABLES

National Standards Addressed

- **Standard 1.** The physically literate individual demonstrates competency in a variety of motor skills and movement patterns.
- **Standard 3.** The physically literate individual demonstrates the knowledge and skills to achieve and maintain a health-enhancing level of physical activity and fitness.

Instructional Materials/Props

Lively music (highly recommended), photographs of fruits and vegetables or plastic versions (optional)

Central Focus

To find enjoyment by participating in a variety of creative stretches and reflecting on the importance of eating fruits and vegetables.

Objectives

- **Cognitive:** The child will increase his or her understanding of fruits and vegetables by participating in a variety of creative stretches.
- **Affective:** The child will seek a partner to work with without disruption and will follow the teacher's suggestions regarding two active stretching and jumping tasks.
- **Psychomotor:** The child will collaborate with a small group of classmates and develop an innovative small-group dance using music and imagery to move in a creative way.

Components of Health-Related Fitness

Cardiorespiratory endurance, flexibility

Learning Task 1: Preparing Our Bodies to Move

Class organization: Children are scattered throughout general space.

Challenge the children to perform the following actions:

- A tomato is actually a fruit that we use as a vegetable. Show me how you can *stand* and *bend* forward to *touch* your toes to perform a "toma*toe*" (tomato) stretch.
- Pineapples are juicy fruits that look like large pine cones. Let's *stretch* our back and perform the "*spine*-apple" stretch by *bending* forward with both arms and letting them *dangle* near the floor and now *swinging* our arms up over our head behind our back.
- Green beans are high in fiber. Can you demonstrate the string bean stretch by *clasping* your hands over your head and *stretching* to one side and then to the other side?
- Peaches have fuzzy skin. Is it possible to *curl* your body into a round peach shape?
- Strawberries are very high in vitamin C and are the only fruit with their seeds on the outside of the skin. Find a way to *stretch* your body in three directions to perform a strawberry stretch.
- Spinach contains vitamin A. See if you can *stretch* at the waist to perform the spinning spinach. Use your elbows to start the spinning motion.

Learning Task 2: **Partner Challenge**

Class organization: Partners are scattered in self-spaces.

Present the following:

- Sweet potatoes are high in vitamin A, which is good for your eyes and skin. With your partner, perform the sweet potato stretch. Together create a wide and stretched shape.
- The Native Americans showed the pioneers how to pop corn. *Holding* hands with your partner, try to *jump* together like popping corn.

Learning Task 3: **Dancing Fruits and Vegetables**

Class organization: Children are scattered in identified groups.

- Organize the children into groups of four or five and encourage each group to use their imaginations and create an exercise or dance called the Watermelon Wiggle, Turnip Twist, Squishy Squash, Crazy Cucumber, or the Rocking Raspberries.
- Invite each group to demonstrate their original exercise or dance while the others imitate the movement.
- After all groups have had their turn, play lively music and let all the children perform their fruit and vegetable actions together.

Assessment Questions

1. Which body parts did we stretch today?
2. Stand and show me your favorite exercise. Raise your hand if you think you can perform this exercise three times every evening at home.
3. Explore a way to create a fun banana dance with a partner.

Academic Language Demands

- **Language function:** Uses language to compare the actual name of the vegetable with the fun changed name of a warm-up stretch in the initial activity.
- **Vocabulary:** bend, stretch, clasp, curl, twist, wiggle, rock, squishy
- **Syntax or discourse:** A verbal interchange meant to identify vegetables according to their color.

  Red: beet, radish, red leaf lettuce, red bell peppers, red-skin potato

  Orange: butternut squash, carrots, orange peppers, pumpkin, sweet potato

  Yellow: corn, yellow peppers, spaghetti squash, yellow wax beans

  Green: leafy greens (e.g., cabbage, lettuce, kale, spinach), asparagus, broccoli, Brussels sprouts, celery, cucumber, green beans, green peppers, peas, string beans

  Blue: blue potato

  Purple: eggplant, purple cauliflower

  White: cauliflower, onions, turnip, white potato

  Brown: mushrooms

  Rainbow colors: rainbow kale, rainbow Swiss chard

FRUIT SALAD TOSS-UP

National Standards Addressed

- **Standard 1.** The physically literate individual demonstrates competency in a variety of motor skills and movement patterns.
- **Standard 3.** The physically literate individual demonstrates the knowledge and skills to achieve and maintain a health-enhancing level of physical activity and fitness.

Instructional Materials/Props

Multicolored balloons (enough for one for each child) and lively music

Central Focus

To manipulate different body parts to keep a balloon afloat and depend on others to create an imaginary fruit salad.

Objectives

- **Cognitive:** The child will name and match fruits associated with a particular color.
- **Affective:** The child will contribute ideas and express an interest in finding ways to tap a balloon with a partner.
- **Psychomotor:** The child will demonstrate the ability to track a floating object and manipulate the object so that it lands on specific body parts and to move with peers in order to keep the object afloat.

Components of Health-Related Fitness

Cardiorespiratory endurance, flexibility

Learning Task 1: Preparing Our Bodies to Move

Class organization: Children are scattered throughout general space.

Challenge the children to perform the following actions:

- Who would like to select their favorite-color balloon? Can each of you think of a favorite fruit that is the color of your balloon? (e.g., **red:** apple, cherry, strawberry, cranberry, raspberry, watermelon; **orange:** orange, peach, nectarine, apricot, cantaloupe, tangerine, papaya; **yellow:** lemon, pineapple, pear; green: grapes, kiwi, pear, lime, honeydew; **blue:** blueberry; **purple:** grapes, plum, figs; **black:** blackberry, black currants, raisin; **white:** banana, coconut, white peach).

- *Toss* your fruit into the air. Let it fall and touch your arm. Try again, this time by *bouncing* it off your elbow. Now *bounce* your fruit off your knee.

- See if you can *toss* your fruit at different heights. *Catch* your fruit over your head, in the middle of your body, near the floor or ground.

- Can you think of a favorite game involving your fruit that you can play by yourself (e.g., keep it up)? Let's play keep it up using different body parts.

Learning Task 2: Partner Challenge

Class organization: Partners are scattered in self-spaces.

Present the following:

- Ask the children to select a partner and share one balloon.
- Is it possible to play keep it up while *holding* your partner's hand?
- At your signal, partners explore different methods of moving the balloons between themselves (e.g., tapping, kicking, or bouncing) and different ways to move the piece of fruit to the opposite end of the playing area (e.g., holding both hands and keeping the balloon in the air, using only lower-body parts to advance the balloon, using only one hand and one leg, using only the head).

Learning Task 3: Fruit Salad Creation

Class organization: Children are scattered in identified groups.

- Organize the children in groups of five. Four players form a circle and clasp hands. The fifth player asks the group what fruit they would like to have in their fruit salad and responds to their suggestion by tossing a balloon of that color into the circle. The circle players work cooperatively to keep the balloon afloat by sometimes using their elbows, heads, and other body parts since they are holding hands.
- Depending on the group's skill level, the tosser may add a second balloon, challenging the group to keep two fruits in the air, or he or she may wait for the group to lose control of the balloon so that it drops to the floor and then adds the group's second-favorite fruit. This continues until the children have tossed several fruits to create an imaginary fruit salad.

Assessment Questions

1. Which body parts were the easiest to use to move the balloon forward?
2. Who can tell me why it is important to eat fruits every day (e.g., Fresh fruits are high in vitamins.)?
3. Is it possible to use a classmate's body to create another healthy fruit shape? Show me.

Academic Language Demands

- **Language function:** Uses language to describe which colors reflect which fruits and why our diet should include fruits.
- **Vocabulary:** bounce, toss, catch, tap, fruit names and their colors
- **Syntax or discourse:** A verbal interchange identifying children's favorite fruits and how often they should eat fruits to maintain a healthy body.

SIZZLING VEGETABLES

National Standards Addressed

- **Standard 1.** The physically literate individual demonstrates competency in a variety of motor skills and movement patterns.
- **Standard 3.** The physically literate individual demonstrates the knowledge and skills to achieve and maintain a health-enhancing level of physical activity and fitness.

Instructional Materials/Props

Photographs of or an actual wok and frying pan (optional), photographs of vegetables or plastic versions (optional)

Central Focus

To increase the child's understanding of the textures, colors, and shapes common to different vegetables.

Objectives

- **Cognitive:** The child will identify shapes and colors of different vegetables.
- **Affective:** The child will be attentive to the suggestions of his or her partner while inventing a new heathy vegetable.
- **Psychomotor:** The child will imitate the actions described and demonstrate that he or she is aware of the change in speed when the imaginary heat increases.

Component of Health-Related Fitness

Cardiorespiratory endurance

Learning Task 1: Preparing Our Bodies to Move

Class organization: Children are scattered throughout general space.

Challenge the children to perform the following actions:

- *Raise* your hand if you have ever tasted stir-fried vegetables. We know that raw vegetables that snap and crunch are cut or chopped into tiny bite-size shapes that allow them to cook faster. Fewer vitamins escape when vegetables are cooked quickly. Can you use your arms and hands to show me a *chopping* movement?
- Pretend your body is a long, narrow stalk of celery. Make believe your body is a round, tearful onion.
- Who can use his or her body to *create* a thin, pointed carrot? A tiny green pea? A thin cabbage leaf?
- Show me how you can *create* a mushroom cap by *placing* your hands on your head and *stooping* to a low level.

Learning Task 2: Partner Challenge

Class organization: Partners are scattered in self-spaces.

Present the following:

- Who can select a partner and form as many different types of vegetables as possible using your bodies and imagination (e.g., peas and carrots)?
- See if you can invent a new vegetable and form its shape. Give it a name. Tell us what it might taste like.
- What color is your vegetable? As a class, decide how this new vegetable can help our body stay healthy (e.g., makes us stronger or quicker, improves our eyesight, fights diseases, keeps skin healthy, makes strong bones and teeth).

Learning Task 3: Frying Pan or Wok

Class organization: Children are scattered throughout general space.

- Ask the children to imagine that some space in the playing area is a large frying pan or wok. Ask them to imagine that their bodies are one of the vegetables that they made in their personal space. Encourage everyone to jump into the giant frying pan or wok as you begin to stir the vegetables. Tell the children that as the frying pan or wok begins to heat, they need to lift their feet off the floor and move vigorously to become stir-fried.
- Next, tell the children that the heat is being turned down. They can move more slowly. Finally, turn the heat off, and the children are ready to be "eaten"! On this cue, make a gesture with your arms (e.g., opening or closing), and the children all flee.

Assessment Questions

1. Who can tell me why it is important to eat fresh vegetables?
2. Can you think of any other vegetables that taste good uncooked (e.g., spinach, broccoli, cauliflower)? Use your body to create that shape.
3. What body parts did you use to create that shape?

Academic Language Demands

- **Language function:** Uses language to describe similarities and differences among vegetables.
- **Vocabulary:** wok, vegetable names and shapes
- **Syntax or discourse:** A verbal interchange about why it is better to eat vegetables that have not been overcooked.

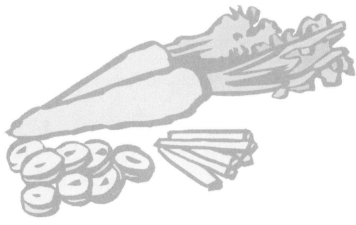

HEALTHY LUNCHTIME FOODS

National Standards Addressed

- **Standard 1.** The physically literate individual demonstrates competency in a variety of motor skills and movement patterns.
- **Standard 3.** The physically literate individual demonstrates the knowledge and skills to achieve and maintain a health-enhancing level of physical activity and fitness.

Instructional Materials/Props

Food chart for teacher to add names of foods from four of the five food groups that one would use to create a healthy sandwich (optional)

Central Focus

To exhibit the cooperation needed to partially support his or her group's weight and appreciate healthy foods.

Objectives

- **Cognitive:** The child will add to the teacher's list of foods that can be used to create a healthy sandwich.
- **Affective:** The child will have a say in selecting the types of foods that are used in creating a heathy sandwich.
- **Psychomotor:** The child will imitate the shape of a healthy food item.

Component of Health-Related Fitness

Muscular strength and endurance

Learning Task 1: Preparing Our Bodies to Move

Class organization: Children are scattered throughout general space.

Challenge the children to perform the following actions:

- Who can *stretch* their body so that it is an imaginary string bean *climbing* up a pole?
- Is it possible to *bend* and *hang* down low like a strawberry *dangling* from a vine?
- Let's *climb* an imaginary ladder and *reach* for an apple at the top of the tree.

Learning Task 2: Partner Challenge

Class organization: Partners are scattered in self-spaces.

Present the following:

- Explain that bread is an important food for good health because it provides vitamins, minerals, and nutrients. Bread is made from grains such as wheat, rye, and oats.
- Ask partners to imagine that they are being *rolled* and then are *formed* into round biscuit shapes and long loaf shapes. As they *slide* into the oven, they slowly become wider and larger as the yeast rises.

Learning Task 3: Hearty Healthy Sandwiches

Class organization: Children are scattered in identified groups.

- To create a friendly atmosphere, take one child's hand and place it horizontally between your two hands. Ask the children to guess the name of the object that you have created. After several attempts, tell the children that you have made a "hand sandwich."

- Introduce the idea that the children can use their bodies to create a healthy sandwich.

- Divide the class into groups of seven or eight children. Ask the groups to identify different foods and shapes that make up a sandwich (e.g., square slices of bread, round tomato slices, flat pieces of cheese, wide pieces of carved turkey).

- Begin by asking four children from each group to form the outside crust of a slice of bread while lying in a prone position (i.e., facing downward).

- Select two or three children to be food items that carefully lie inside the crust (e.g., first the lettuce, then the tomatoes, followed by the slice of cheese).

- Complete the top slice of bread by asking one child to stand and form an arch shape over his or her group members' bodies or lie in a wide shape at a low level over his or her group members' bodies.

- The task is complete when you circulate to the different sandwiches and pretend to take a large bite (i.e., by opening and closing your arms) of each sandwich.

Assessment Questions

1. Why was it necessary to work together to create the sandwich?
2. Who can name other healthy foods to use to create sandwiches?
3. Is it possible for you and a partner to create a sandwich in a different shape (e.g., submarine roll, round bun, hot dog roll) with your bodies? Show me.

Academic Language Demands

- **Language function:** Uses language to identify healthy foods that are commonly used in sandwiches.

- **Vocabulary:** a variety of healthy food items

- **Syntax or discourse:** A verbal interchange to identify how a sandwich can contain four of the five food groups (grains, protein, vegetable, and dairy).

CHAPTER 6

Moving With Words
& Actions in Our
Community

Increasing children's understanding of their local community is fundamental to the education process. This understanding helps children learn how their home environments differ from other home settings and, in the upper-elementary grades, serves as a foundation for learning about other cultures. The context for learning in a physical literacy lesson is for all children to physically repeat the actions and imitate the behaviors of common community workers and helpers. This new awareness that people's roles in the community dictate specific movements expands the child's appreciation for these jobs.

Simple classroom props can enhance the child's motivation for active participation. Preschool specialists can complement this chapter's content by providing the children with building block sets containing community workers, animals, and vehicles. For example, when implementing content regarding the role of construction workers and a construction site, you can discuss the purpose of bridges and tunnels and how they are constructed. Ask the children to create these structures with building set materials. In dramatic play, the child can use child-size uniforms and props or dress-up clothing to spark creative role-playing possibilities. Preschool children are especially delighted when construction workers are invited to the childcare center and bring their own tools for the children's viewing. Ask this visitor to describe the materials he or she uses to build houses. Show the differences between the types of nails, screws, bolts, and other fasteners used in building structures. Talk about the number of construction sites that exist near the school. Ask the children whether they live in a new house, an apartment building, or in a house that has been repaired, expanded, or changed.

In keeping with the construction example, teachers who work with kindergarten children can challenge them to draw objects that are seen at the construction site (e.g., trucks, cars, cranes, bulldozers). Kindergarten children have the cognitive capacity and are curious about the roles that different adults play, unlike the preschool child who tends to be more fascinated with the workings of objects. Storybooks serve as wonderful props for children in grades 1 and 2. Ask the children to role-play the actions of the main character (e.g., a construction worker, a foreman). Select a storybook containing vivid pictures of objects or things. Challenge the children to differentiate between objects that are man-made and objects that are found in nature. In short, physical literacy provides opportunities for children to think of their own home setting and local community and the special movements they see or experience each day.

COMMUNITY HELPERS

National Standards Addressed

- **Standard 1.** The physically literate individual demonstrates competency in a variety of motor skills and movement patterns.
- **Standard 4.** The physically literate individual exhibits responsible personal and social behavior that respects self and others.

Instructional Materials/Props

Plastic figurines (optional)

Central Focus

Discuss good versus evil character roles in a vigorous learning task.

Objectives

- **Cognitive:** The child will reflect on ways that we can help others in the community.
- **Affective:** The child will provide support willingly for his or her peers who need a safe haven during a learning task.
- **Psychomotor:** The child will perform dodging and numerous vigorous agility moves to evade a chaser and will exchange roles with classmates when tagged.

Component of Health-Related Fitness

Cardiorespiratory endurance

Learning Task 1: Preparing Our Bodies to Move

Class organization: Children are scattered throughout general space.

Challenge the children to perform the following actions:

- Can you combine *running* with any other kind of movement?
- Who can determine the best way to take as few *running* steps as possible to move to the other side of the playing area?

Learning Task 2: Partner Challenge

Class organization: Partners are scattered in self-spaces.

Present the following:

- Who can *skip* arm in arm with his or her partner?
- Can you help your partner *jump* over an imaginary mud puddle?
- Give your partner a light *pat* on the back to say, "Good job."
- Pretend that you are in a burning building. Show me how you would help a partner to safety (e.g., moving low to the ground on one's knees). Exchange roles.
- *Shake* your partner's hand to show your appreciation.

Learning Task 3: **Human Helpers**

Class organization: Children are scattered in identified groups.

Present the following:

- Divide children into two groups. In one group, partners are scattered throughout the playing area and join hands to form several caves. The other group pretends to be villains (e.g., well-known comic book, movie, or television characters).
- Designate two or more children to be the heroes and heroines.
- Select a body part to be tagged (e.g., the right leg, the left shoulder). The heroes and heroines chase the villains, who flee to avoid being tagged by standing under the raised hands forming caves.
- When a villain is tagged on the designated body part, he or she must switch roles with one of the children supporting the cave structure.
- Only one villain is allowed in a cave at a time, and no villain should stay in a cave for more than 10 seconds.

Assessment Questions

1. Who can give me examples of good behavior and bad behavior?
2. Demonstrate one movement that people use to show they are friends (e.g., shake hands, high-five). Can you show me other gestures of friendship?
3. Describe a time when people use their body to help a person in trouble.

Academic Language Demands

- **Language function:** Uses language to discuss the actions that are common to community heroes and heroines.
- **Vocabulary:** villains, heroes and heroines, flee, specific body parts that can be tagged
- **Syntax or discourse:** A verbal interchange stressing the need to tag classmates only on a designated body part.

FARM

National Standards Addressed

Standard 1. The physically literate individual demonstrates competency in a variety of motor skills and movement patterns.

Instructional Materials/Props

Plastic figures of farm animals and a picture of a farm (optional)

Central Focus

To name and imitate the sounds and movements common to farm work and barnyard animals.

Objectives

- **Cognitive:** The child will state several responsibilities that are common to the daily life of a farmer.
- **Affective:** The child will work eagerly with a partner to use their bodies to form the shape of food that is commonly grown on a farm.
- **Psychomotor:** The child will perform movements, and the actions display behaviors common to farm animals.

Components of Health-Related Fitness

Cardiorespiratory endurance, flexibility

Learning Task 1: Preparing Our Bodies to Move

Class organization: Children are scattered throughout general space.

- Explain that farms consist of large areas of land that can be used to grow food and raise animals. The first farmers raised just enough crops to feed their families. They used wooden plows pulled by horses to plant gardens.
- Challenge the children to perform the following actions:
  - Farmer Seekins awakens early in the morning to milk the cows. Help him by *squatting* and *sitting* on the milking stool. Show me the movement that farmers use to milk the cows.
  - Let's *throw* feed to the baby chicks.
  - Farmer Seekins enjoys plowing the garden. Pretend to *drive* the tractor through the field to gather vegetables.
  - *Grasp* the steering wheel tightly as you *move* over the bumpy land.
  - Can you use one arm to show me how a tractor *plows* the land?
  - Make believe you are using a shovel and *dig* a hole. Now *plant* a seed and *cover* it with dirt.
  - Demonstrate the action of a sprinkler watering the garden. *Stretch* your body upward like the vegetables when they grow.
  - Try to *lift* bales of hay from the fields. *Place* the bales on a large truck.
  - Who can *pump* water from a deep well?
  - Show how you can *skip* along a berry patch. *Stoop* low to the ground to *fill* a basket with strawberries.

Learning Task 2: **Partner Challenge**

Class organization: Partners are scattered in self-spaces.

Present the following:

- With a partner, choose a vegetable that grows on a farm and work together to form its shape with your bodies.
- Show me how you and a partner can use your bodies to form a fruit that might be found growing on a farm.

Learning Task 3: **Farmyard**

Class organization: Children are scattered in identified groups.

Present the following:

- Tell the children that they can use their bodies to form a farmyard fence.
- Divide the children in two groups. One group uses their bodies to form the fence by stretching upward and standing very still.
- The remaining children stand inside the fence and name and perform the movement, physical actions, and sounds of their favorite barnyard animals. Exchange roles.

Assessment Questions

1. Who can name their favorite farming action or animal movement that they performed today?
2. Copy me as I pretend to use a hammer to fix the barn door. Who can pretend that one of the walls in this room is the barn door?
3. What is the name of a building that farmers use to keep animals in (e.g., barn)? Would it be possible to use your classmate's bodies to form a large make-believe barn?

Academic Language Demands

- **Language function:** Uses language to recall common movements and actions that one might see on a farm.
- **Vocabulary:** plow, squat, lift, pump, responsibility, a variety of animal sounds (e.g., clucking chicken), bales of hay
- **Syntax or discourse:** A verbal interchange to identify a variety of tasks that farmers might have when growing food and raising animals.

FIRE STATION

National Standards Addressed

- **Standard 1.** The physically literate individual demonstrates competency in a variety of motor skills and movement patterns.
- **Standard 4.** The physically literate individual exhibits responsible personal and social behavior that respects self and others.

Instructional Materials/Props

Red or orange streamers, bubble wrap (optional), paper plate or floor spot, jump rope

Central Focus

To demonstrate activities common to a fire station.

Objectives

- **Cognitive:** The child will discuss several basic strategies for being safe if a fire should occur.
- **Affective:** The child will maintain a high level of alertness throughout the partner activities that ask the child to move in specific ways and show an appreciation for the role of the firefighter.
- **Psychomotor:** The child will perform lifesaving fire safety movements such as "stop, drop, and roll" and be able to work with classmates to create a make-believe firehouse ladder with their bodies.

Component of Health-Related Fitness

Cardiorespiratory endurance

Learning Task 1: Preparing Our Bodies to Move

Class organization: Children are scattered throughout general space.

Challenge the children to perform the following actions:

- *Grasp* the cord and *ring* the fire bell. This sound tells the firefighters that there is a fire.
- How quickly can you *pull on* your boots, *slip* into your fire coat, and *strap* on your helmet?
- Can you *slide* down the pole and *hurry* to the truck? Use your hands to *grasp* the pole.
- What color is the fire engine (e.g., red, lime green, yellow)? Show me how you can *move* quickly like a fire truck. *Honk* the horn. *Make* the sound of the siren.
- *Pretend* you are using the fire hose. Who can show me how the water *rushes* through the hose to put out the fire?
- Use your arms and legs to *climb* the ladder.
- Sometimes rooms are filled with smoke. To escape the smoke, the firefighters either use a mask and an air tank to get fresh air or they *cover* their faces and move quickly along the floor. This is called *stay low and go.* Can you *move* quickly on your hands and knees through a smoke-filled room? Remember to *stay low and go.*
- Let's practice what we should do if part of our clothes catch on fire. First we must *stop* very quickly, then *drop* to the ground, and *roll* to smother the flames. Let's try that again. *Stop, drop, and roll.*

Learning Task 2: **Partner Challenge**

Class organization: Partners are scattered in self-spaces.

Present the following:

- The fire station holds the fire trucks and provides a house where the firefighters eat and sleep. The men and women are always ready to *move* quickly when the alarm rings.
- Can you and a partner use your bodies to *make* a fire truck? One child *steers* the fire truck while the other child holds onto the driver's shoulders and *rings* the bell.

Learning Task 3: **Putting Out Fires**

Class organization: Children are scattered in identified groups.

- **Firehouse ladder:** Explain to the children that they can use their bodies to form a giant ladder along the floor. One child needs to lie facedown on the floor and stretch into a long shape. The next child should lie down and grab the first child's ankles. The next child in line connects until a long ladder shape is created.
- **Putting out the fire:** Divide the children into two groups. Group one vigorously waves red or orange streamers and (if available) stomps on a sheet of bubble wrap to make the crackling sound of fire. Group two represents a fire engine carrying firefighters by forming a behind-line and holding a rope (or jump rope) symbolizing the firehose. The first child in line holds a paper plate steering wheel. The second child in line holds a sheet of paper representing a map to the fire. The fire engine maneuvers throughout the playing area until it reaches the fire. The firefighters use the hose to extinguish the flames. The children pretending to be flames die down by collapsing to a low level.
- **Stop, drop, and roll:** Select two or three children to represent flames. The other children dodge and move away from the approaching fire. When a flame tags a child, the tagged child must stop, drop, and roll and then continue to move away from the flames.

Assessment Questions

1. Is it possible to create a giant water hose using our bodies?
2. Who can name other objects that firefighters might use when putting out a fire?
3. What kinds of things can we do to prevent fires in our homes?

Academic Language Demands

- **Language function:** Uses language to repeat the stop, drop, and roll sequence and the stay-low-and-go sequence when practicing.
- **Vocabulary:** strap; honk; smother; flames; stay low and go; stop, drop, and roll
- **Syntax or discourse:** A verbal interchange identifying the importance of fire safety and knowing how to prevent fires at home and at school.

TOY STORE

National Standards Addressed

Standard 1. The physically literate individual demonstrates competency in a variety of motor skills and movement patterns.

Instructional Materials/Props

Pictures of or actual play objects found in the toy store (optional)

Central Focus

To imagine their bodies have become their favorite playthings.

Objectives

- **Cognitive:** The child will acquire information regarding classic toys and playthings and participate in the actions associated with these objects.
- **Affective:** The child will express an interest in using his or her body and the body of a partner to imagine that he or she is a classic toy or plaything.
- **Psychomotor:** The child will enthusiastically participate with classmates and explore movements and actions common to toys.

Component of Health-Related Fitness

Cardiorespiratory endurance

Learning Task 1: Preparing Our Bodies to Move

Class organization: Children are scattered throughout general space.

Present the following: *Toys are objects created for the enjoyment of children. Let's begin by moving like several favorite toys.* Challenge the children to perform these actions:

- Who can show me how to *spin* like a top?
- Can you pretend to *wiggle* a Hula-Hoop around your waist?
- How high can you *bounce* your body into the air like a rubber ball?
- Jumping rope helps the heart grow stronger. Make believe you are *jumping* rope.
- The wooden toy rowboat has two oars. *Raise* your arms and pretend to *row* the boat down the river.
- The wooden rocking horse has been a favorite toy for many children. *Place* one foot in front of your body. Try to *rock* back and forth.
- The ballet dancer doll *stretches* up and *walks* on his or her toes. Find a way to *walk* on your toes and *twirl* around like the dancer.
- Show me how you can *march* like the toy robot.
- Let's pretend to *strap* on a pair of ice skates. Can you *slide* and *move* as if you were *skating* on slippery ice?
- Superhero dolls wear costumes in their adventure roles. Pretend to *step* into your costume and show me how *strong* you can make your body.
- Toy rockets blast off on a count of 10. Ready, *lower* your body and then *spring* up like a rocket.

Learning Task 2: Partner Challenge

Class organization: Partners are scattered in self-spaces.

Present the following:

- Children quickly find partners. To form a make-believe scooter, one child stands very tall and places his or her fists on the chest. The other child stands behind this person and grasps the partner's elbows.
- Together, partners move forward by taking sliding steps without bumping other sets of partners. Exchange roles.
- Explain to the children that wagons carry children's toys. To begin, one partner clasps his or her hands together to form a circle in front of the body. This is the handle of the wagon.
- The other partner grasps the handle and pulls the wagon along. Exchange roles.

Learning Task 3: A Classic Toy

Class organization: Children are scattered in identified groups.

Present the following:

Divide the children into two groups. Explain to them that they can use their bodies to form a large jill- or jack-in-the-box. Some of the children form the box by standing side by side to make a square. Within the box is a group of children who stoop low to the floor like a folded Jack or Jill. These children grasp their knees while balancing on their toes as they stoop. One child must stand outside the box to crank the handle as the children forming the box recite this poem:

Jack-in-the-box,

Jill-in-the-box,

Tucked down in your box today,

We'll *crank* the handle so you'll

Come out and play!

The Jills and Jacks spring up on the word *play*. Exchange roles.

Assessment Questions

1. Build a large soft toy using a partner's body.
2. Is it possible to name a toy that uses technology and show your classmates how it might move?
3. Who can think of a toy we did not see today and show us how it moves?

Academic Language Demands

- **Language function:** Uses language to guide a partner in movements that imitate the physical actions associated with a classic toy or plaything.
- **Vocabulary:** oars, strap, spring, crank, the names of a variety of classic playthings
- **Syntax or discourse:** A verbal interchange to conclude that a classic toy or plaything moves in a particular manner or can be formed using the bodies of several classmates.

PARK

National Standards Addressed

- **Standard 1.** The physically literate individual demonstrates competency in a variety of motor skills and movement patterns.
- **Standard 3.** The physically literate individual demonstrates the knowledge and skills to achieve and maintain a health-enhancing level of physical activity and fitness.

Instructional Materials/Props

Pictures of objects and activities viewed at a park (optional)

Central Focus

To remember experiences and demonstrate a variety of ways of moving outdoors.

Objectives

- **Cognitive:** The child will recall objects, living creatures, and physical activities one can perform at a community park.
- **Affective:** The child will seek a partner and jog or run for a predetermined amount of time.
- **Psychomotor:** The child will create and move like objects, living things, and activities commonly seen in the park.

Components of Health-Related Fitness

Cardiorespiratory endurance, muscular strength

Learning Task 1: Preparing Our Bodies to Move

Class organization: Children are scattered throughout general space.

Challenge the children to perform the following actions:

- We can use our imaginations and make believe that we are at our community park.
- Let's *move* like the animals we see in the park. Can you *scamper* along the ground like a squirrel? Use your hands and feet to *move* quickly.
- *Point* to the robin's nest. The young birds have hatched. Pretend to be a baby robin and *stretch* your brand new legs. Sometimes your legs *wobble* back and forth. You can pretend to *spread* your wings by *bending* your arms at the elbows. Now bring your hands to your shoulders. Can you *move* your wings back and forth in this position? *Hop* on one foot onto a branch. Now leave the nest and *flutter* your wings.
- Is it possible to *move* like the animals that wiggle, crawl, slither, or creep along the ground? Can you *wiggle* along the ground like an earthworm? Show me another creature that *moves* along the ground (e.g., spider, snake, bug).
- Imagine that you are *flying* a kite that is tied to a long string. *Run* with one arm *held* over your head.

- Can you *run* forward and pretend to *kick* a ball on the ground?
- *See* the people *playing* with bats and balls. Pretend to *catch* a ball that is hit high into the sky. *Run* and *chase* a ball that is rolling along the ground. *Stoop* to the ground to *pick* it up with your hands. Can you pretend to *swing* a bat and *hit* the ball?
- Our park also has a path for people to ride their bicycles on. Pretend to *ride* a bicycle by *holding* onto the handlebars. *Lift* your knees high as you *ride* down the path.
- How quickly can you *pack* your picnic basket and *skip* home?

Learning Task 2: Partner Challenge

Class organization: Partners are scattered in self-spaces.

Present the following: *People exercise their muscles by running along a jogging path. Can you* run or jog *alongside a friend?*

Learning Task 3: Scanning the Park

Class organization: Children are scattered in identified groups.

Ask the children to close their eyes and imagine an object or thing that moves in a park.

- Call out the name of one child and ask, "What did you see?"
- The child responds by saying, "I see a squirrel scampering on the ground."
- With that response, all children use their bodies to scamper along the ground.
- Ask a second child what he or she sees and encourage the child to respond with a different answer (e.g., "I see worms wiggling.") Continue until all children have responded.

Assessment Questions

1. Can you tell me what your favorite outdoor activity is?
2. Find a way to move like your favorite outdoor activity.
3. Let's summarize all of the objects and things that we saw in our imaginary park today. Who can identify one thing? Would you like to repeat this lesson in our local park?

Academic Language Demands

- **Language function:** Uses language to name items and activities that are common to a community park.
- **Vocabulary:** scamper, pedal, wobble, jog, objects and activities viewed or performed in a community park
- **Syntax or discourse:** A verbal interchange regarding the need to keep our parks cleaner by tossing garbage into cans.

SCHOOLYARD

National Standards Addressed

- **Standard 3.** The physically literate individual demonstrates the knowledge and skills to achieve and maintain a health-enhancing level of physical activity and fitness.
- **Standard 5.** The physically literate individual recognizes the value of physical activity for health, enjoyment, challenge, self-expression and/or social interaction.

Instructional Materials/Props

Pictures of objects and activities viewed at a schoolyard (optional)

Central Focus

To imitate the movements and actions associated with several large structures found in a schoolyard.

Objectives

- **Cognitive:** The child will compare playground equipment and activities in the community schoolyard to those described in the learning tasks.
- **Affective:** The child will encourage his or her partner to move in opposition in order to create the actions of a seesaw.
- **Psychomotor:** The child will manipulate his or her peers' bodies in order to generate the movements of a make-believe merry-go-round and school bus.

Components of Health-Related Fitness

Flexibility, muscular strength and endurance

Learning Task 1: Preparing Our Bodies to Move

Class organization: Children are scattered throughout general space.

Challenge the children to perform the following actions:

- Can you *hop* on one foot through a hopscotch shape? Use your arms for balance as you *hop* through the make-believe boxes.
- Use your arms and legs to *climb* up the make-believe monkey bars. What do you see at the top?
- Who can use their arms and legs again to *crawl* through an imaginary barrel?
- *Place* one leg in front of the other and show me how you would *rock* your body back and forth like the movement of a swing. Pretend to give a friend a gentle *push*.
- Imagine you are *gripping* the rungs of a horizontal metal ladder that has 10 rungs. *Swing* from one rung to another while keeping a tight *grip*.

Learning Task 2: **Partner Challenge**

Class organization: Partners are scattered in self-spaces.

Present the following:

- Let's use our bodies to *make* the movement of the seesaw.
- First, find a friend who is wearing a big smile. *Stand* so you can see your partner's smile.
- *Stretch* your arms in front of your body and *grasp* your partner's hands. *Hold* hands tightly.
- Take turns *standing* up and *stooping* down to make the movement of the seesaw. To create a three-person seesaw, one child makes a wide, stretched shape between the two outside players. Both outside children *hold* a hand of the middle person and take turns *moving* up and down.

Use the following rhyme:

> *Moving* like a seesaw at a low level with a friend,
> Becoming more fit as your muscles *stretch* and *bend.*

Learning Task 3: **Schoolyard Objects**

Class organization: Children are scattered in identified groups.

Present the following:

Merry-go-round: Tell the children they can use their bodies to make the movement of a merry-go-round. This is possible by having three friends stand back to back in a circle shape. Each child's arms are straight out in front of the body. The children move slowly around and around and up and down. Stop the merry-go-round so that other riders can join the children. Additional children can stand between the arms that make the sections of the merry-go-round. Encourage the children to move together safely. (To make a large merry-go-round, half of the class grasps hands to form a large circle. Everyone faces toward the center of the circle. The remaining children place one hand onto the shoulder of a person forming the circle. The children all move in the same direction as the merry-go-round slowly moves in a circle shape.)

School bus: School buses drop children off at the schoolyard. Ask the children to quickly stand beside a partner and hook elbows. Ask the partners to form a behind-line and invite the children to place their outside hand on the shoulder in front of them. Slowly move forward. The partners at the front of the line are the bus drivers and steer an imaginary wheel.

Assessment Questions

1. Who can identify their favorite piece of playground equipment?
2. Who can name three movement skills that we performed on our imaginary schoolyard?
3. Is it possible to design a totally new piece of playground equipment with a group of classmates?

Academic Language Demands

- **Language function:** Uses language to identify which body parts are needed to mimic the movements and actions of an object or thing found in a playground.
- **Vocabulary:** climb, swing, push, rock, objects and activities found on a playground (e.g., hopscotch, monkey bars, rung, horizontal, seesaw, merry-go-round)
- **Syntax or discourse:** A verbal interchange to organize classmates' bodies so that a make-believe merry-go-round is formed and all classmates are contributing to making the object move in a circular pathway.

FOOD MARKET

National Standards Addressed

- **Standard 1.** The physically literate individual demonstrates competency in a variety of motor skills and movement patterns.
- **Standard 3.** The physically literate individual demonstrates the knowledge and skills to achieve and maintain a health-enhancing level of physical activity and fitness.

Instructional Materials/Props

Chart or poster of the five food groups and a sample list or pictures of foods from each group (all optional)

Central Focus

To increase an awareness of healthy choices within food groups found in the food market.

Objectives

- **Cognitive:** The child will match foods to those found within the five basic food groups
- **Affective:** The child will attend to the task of forming a make-believe shopping cart and coordinating movements with a partner.
- **Psychomotor:** The child will develop an understanding of the five food groups as he or she collaborates within a small group to create the shape of food found in those categories.

Components of Health-Related Fitness

Flexibility, muscular strength and endurance

Learning Task 1: Preparing Our Bodies to Move

Class organization: Children are scattered throughout general space.

Challenge the children to perform the following actions:

- Show me how your face *smiles* when you see a favorite food at a grocery store.
- What does your body look like if you are *shivering* in the frozen-food section?
- Can you use your body to show me the shape of different foods? Pretend to be a *tiny* green pea, a *long* ear of yellow corn, a *bumpy* potato, a *round* green head of lettuce, a *thin* orange carrot, a *curved* banana, a *large* loaf of bread, an *oval*-shaped egg, and a *flat* slice of cheese.

Learning Task 2: **Partner Challenge**

Class organization: Partners are scattered in self-spaces.

Explain to the children that they can use their bodies to form the shape of a shopping cart by placing their arms in front of the body to make the basket. After selecting a partner, one child is the shopper and the other is the shopping cart. The shopper stands behind the shopping cart and guides it through the aisles of the food market without touching other carts. The shopper places imaginary foods into the basket as shopping continues. Exchange roles. Remind the children that healthy eating starts at the food market and to select foods from the five food groups:

- **Fruits** give your body nutrients to stay healthy.
- **Vegetables** supply your body with vitamins and minerals. Dark-green, yellow, and orange vegetables are the healthiest.
- **Grains** like pasta, rice, cereal, and bread should be eaten every day and give your body fiber.
- **Protein** such as meat, poultry, fish, eggs, nuts, and beans helps the body grow and repair itself.
- **Dairy** foods like milk, cheese, and yogurt contain calcium for strong bones and teeth.

Learning Task 3: **Food Groups at the Food Market**

Class organization: Children are scattered in identified groups.

Divide the class into groups of four or five children. Explain to the class that each group will use their bodies to form the shape of foods they find at the food market. Ask the groups to first form a fruit and show their creation to the other groups, followed by vegetables, grains, proteins, and dairy food.

Assessment Questions

1. Can you name five healthy foods found in the grocery store?
2. Who can draw their favorite food in the air?
3. Let's remember that healthy eating means knowing what to eat. Can you each use your body and create one food that you should eat more often?

Academic Language Demands

- **Language function:** Uses language to identify a variety of foods found in each of the five food groups.
- **Vocabulary:** market, nutrients, fiber, fruits, vegetables, grains, proteins, dairy food, a balanced diet
- **Syntax or discourse:** A verbal interchange that focuses on the body's need for a balanced diet to grow strong and healthy. Healthy eating means knowing what to eat.

PET SHOP

National Standards Addressed

Standard 1. The physically literate individual demonstrates competency in a variety of motor skills and movement patterns.

Instructional Materials/Props

Finger or hand puppets of pets found in a pet shop (optional), pictures or stuffed animals of pets (optional)

Central Focus

To exhibit the movements of common pets.

Objectives

- **Cognitive:** The child will associate specific movements with certain pets found at a pet shop.
- **Affective:** The child will show a desire to move at a low level by coordinating all of his or her muscles to swiftly hide behind the bodies of classmates.
- **Psychomotor:** The child will imitate the movements of fish by moving at different levels with the hands behind the back.

Component of Health-Related Fitness

Muscular strength and endurance

Learning Task 1: Preparing Our Bodies to Move

Class organization: Children are scattered throughout general space.

Present the following: *We need pet stores to help us to take care of our family pets.* Challenge the children to perform the following actions:

- Can you pretend to *cradle* a kitten in your arms? *Rock* your arms back and forth.
- There is a turtle. Show me how you can *move* close to the ground like a turtle.
- Look at the puppies learning to walk. Who can *move* quickly on their hands and feet?
- Is it possible to *slither* on the floor like the snake in the tank?
- The parakeet loves to fly. See if you can *flap* your arms like wings. *Fly* carefully around our playing area.

Learning Task 2: Partner Challenge

Class organization: Partners are scattered in self-spaces.

Present the following: *The lizard moves quickly to hide behind a rock.*

- With your partner, *make* the movements of a lizard.
- One of you will *crawl* like the lizard and the other will *stand still* like a rock.
- Take turns being the lizard and the rock.

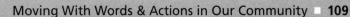

Learning Task 3: Fishbowl

Class organization: Children are scattered in identified groups.

Tell the children that they can use their bodies to make a giant fishbowl. Some children will be the bowl, and some will be the fish. Ask who would like to be part of the giant fishbowl. These children join hands to form a large circle. Everyone must hold hands or the water will escape. The other children can step into the circle and use their bodies to move like fish by placing both arms behind their backs, locking their fingers, and bending forward to swim like goldfish. Exchange roles.

Assessment Questions

1. If you could choose any pet, what would it be? Can you move like that pet?
2. Explore other ways to move like pets that live in glass cases.
3. Pets need people to help take care of them. What movements do people use to take care of pets?

Academic Language Demands

- **Language function:** Uses language to describe the movements of a variety of household pets.
- **Vocabulary:** cradle, escape, flap, slither, swim, fins
- **Syntax or discourse:** A verbal interchange focusing on how to move in a recognizable way to imitate the movements of common pets.

GAS STATION AND REPAIR SHOP

National Standards Addressed

- **Standard 2.** The physically literate individual applies knowledge of concepts, principles, strategies and tactics related to movement and performance.
- **Standard 3.** The physically literate individual demonstrates the knowledge and skills to achieve and maintain a health-enhancing level of physical activity and fitness.

Instructional Materials/Props

Pictures and actual objects found at a gas station and repair shop (e.g., gas pump, jack, piston, car engine, tow truck, hitch) (optional)

Central Focus

To use one's body to perform the actions associated with a gas station and repair shop.

Objectives

- **Cognitive:** The child will make a comparison between the fuel a vehicle needs (e.g., gasoline) and our body's need for healthy foods.
- **Affective:** The child will exhibit the willingness to make believe he or she has the ability to move a car that is in need of assistance by performing the role of an imaginary tow truck.
- **Psychomotor:** The child will imitate the actions of a driver whose imaginary car is moving at different speeds.

Components of Health-Related Fitness

Cardiorespiratory endurance

Learning Task 1: Preparing Our Bodies to Move

Class organization: Children are scattered throughout general space.

Challenge the children to perform the following actions:

- Can you use your body to *make* the shape of a car?
- Use your arms to show me the *movement* of the windshield wipers.
- Show me how you would use the steering wheel to *move* in different directions.
- Is it possible to *make* the shape of your car's tires?
- Your car's motor has pistons that move up and down. Show me this up-and-down *movement* as you pretend to *drive* along.
- The person at the repair shop is called a mechanic. He or she tunes your car's engine. Can you *move* like a car engine that needs repair?
- Use your arm like a jack that *lifts* your car up into the air.
- Can you *lie* on your back and use your legs to *move* under a car to make repairs?

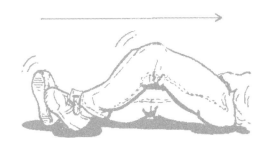

Learning Task 2: **Partner Challenge**

Class organization: Partners are scattered in self-spaces.

Present the following: *When a car runs out of gas, some drivers call a tow truck. Can you and a partner take turns* towing *each other's car? Your hand can be the hitch that* tows *the car throughout our playing area.*

Learning Task 3: **Refueling**

Class organization: Children are scattered in identified groups.

Divide the children into two groups. One group acts as gas pumps and stands still in a side-by-side line along one side of the room. They dangle their arms to form the gas pump hoses. The remainder of the children pretend to steer their cars throughout the playing area. When drivers need more gas, they move their cars to a pump and say, "Please fill it up." The gas pump touches the car's shoulder to fill the tank. The children can refuel their cars any time to keep moving. When a car is no longer able to move quickly throughout the playing area, the child can exchange places with a gas pump.

Assessment Questions

1. What foods make the best fuel for a healthy body?
2. Who can form a motorcycle with a friend and drive throughout our playing area?
3. What other things can we do for our body so that we can keep moving for a longer time (e.g., exercise)? Show me.

Academic Language Demands

- **Language function:** Uses language to discuss the role of a car mechanic and why a car and our body both need fuel to keep moving for an extended period of time.

- **Vocabulary:** dangle, tune, jack, hitch, pistons, names of healthy foods

- **Syntax or discourse:** A verbal interchange identifying the many foods that keep our body healthy and make it possible for our body to vigorously move for an extended period of time.

TRAIN STATION

National Standards Addressed

- **Standard 1.** The physically literate individual demonstrates competency in a variety of motor skills and movement patterns.
- **Standard 4.** The physically literate individual exhibits responsible personal and social behavior that respects self and others.

Instructional Materials/Props

Pictures of different types of trains, train cars, and engineer hats (optional)

Central Focus

To interact cooperatively while exploring three ways to move like a make-believe train.

Objectives

- **Cognitive:** The child will remember aspects of a typical community train station and describe ways in which trains travel along tracks.
- **Affective:** The child will contribute to the small-group discussion concerning which type of train to create in order to move through imaginary tunnels.
- **Psychomotor:** The child will move in unison within a small group in order to coordinate the movements of three imaginary trains.

Component of Health-Related Fitness

Cardiorespiratory endurance

Learning Task 1: Preparing Our Bodies to Move

Class organization: Children are scattered throughout general space.

Challenge the children to perform the following actions:

- Show me how the big clock outside the ticket station *moves* its hands.
- Is it possible to *move* your arms like the wheels of a train?
- *Use your arms* to show me how the railroad crossing gates *block* cars.
- Let's pretend we are repairing the railroad tracks. Can you *swing* a heavy hammer and *drive* spikes into the ground?
- Who can use his or her body to *make* the shape of a boxcar? You can use your legs, arms, and back to make this shape.
- *Stand* and *make* the movement of the train. *Blow* the whistle as you chug along.
- Can you say, "Chug-chug, clickity-clack, here we go around the railroad track," as you *move* along?
- *Wave* good-bye to your friends as you *chug* along our playing area.

Learning Task 2: Partner Challenge

Class organization: Partners are scattered in self-spaces.

With a partner, one child is the train engine and the second child is the train's caboose. The children pretend to travel on railroad tracks as the engine leads the train, discovering ways to chug up hills, changing directions and speed. After a specific amount of time, call out to pull into the train station. Partners then exchange roles.

Learning Task 3: Railroad Tracks and Tunnels

Class organization: Children are scattered in identified groups.

- Explain that we can use our bodies three different ways to show the movements of a community train. Divide the children into two groups. Ask the first group to select partners and use their bodies to form make-believe tunnels by joining hands to form a high arch shape for trains to move through. The tunnels should be scattered throughout the playing area. The second group now forms several trains by combining three or four bodies. The trains move through the tunnels. Exchange roles. For a greater challenge, the trains can move through the tunnels by performing any or all of the following actions:
  - **Chug-along:** Children create the train by putting their hands on the next child's shoulders and chugging along imaginary tracks in the playing area.
  - **Chug-a-chug:** Children create the train by placing their hands on the next child's waist and chugging along the imaginary tracks.
  - **Tug-and-chug (more advanced):** Children create the train by holding onto the next child's elbows. The elbows move forward and back in a pumping motion as the train moves along the tracks.

Assessment Questions

1. Who can explain why trains are important (e.g., transportation, carrying products)?
2. Is it possible to make a large-group tunnel for a small train to move through?
3. What body parts did we need to coordinate in order to make our three types of trains?

Academic Language Demands

- **Language function:** Uses language to discuss the three ways to create an imaginary train that can move through a tunnel.
- **Vocabulary:** engine, boxcar, caboose, tunnel, railroad crossing gates, chug
- **Syntax or discourse:** A verbal interchange to reinforce that all peers must coordinate their movements in order to move smoothly along imaginary tracks.

CAR WASH

National Standards Addressed

- **Standard 2.** The physically literate individual applies knowledge of concepts, principles, strategies and tactics related to movement and performance.
- **Standard 4.** The physically literate individual exhibits responsible personal and social behavior that respects self and others.

Instructional Materials/Props

Pom-poms, bubbles, jump ropes or short pieces of clothesline, sponges or towels, red and green construction paper (all optional)

Central Focus

To explore and identify various movements and actions related to a car wash.

Objectives

- **Cognitive:** The child will repeat steps necessary for washing and cleaning an imaginary car.
- **Affective:** The child will participate actively with a partner and assume the roles of people who work at the community car wash.
- **Psychomotor:** The child will use his or her arms to vigorously create the ongoing rolling movement of the giant brushes that clean a car as it passes through a car wash as well as using props (if available) to simulate additional movements and actions commonly observed at a car wash.

Component of Health-Related Fitness

Cardiorespiratory endurance

Learning Task 1: Preparing Our Bodies to Move

Class organization: Children are scattered throughout general space.

Challenge the children to perform the following actions after explaining that car washes are places where people get their cars and trucks cleaned:

- Before we have our car washed, we should vacuum the inside to remove dirt. Can you pretend to *push* a vacuum cleaner along the floor? *Push* and *pull* the vacuum cleaner along the floor.
- Pretend to use a sponge and *wash* the tires of the car. Your body should be at a low level near the ground.
- Can you *spin* around like the brushes you see in a car wash?
- Large rollers move the car through the car wash. Can you use your arms in front of your body to *make a rolling* movement? Try making small circles with your arms *stretched* out at your sides.
- Is it possible to *hold* your arms in a circular shape and *move* like the soap bubbles that clean the car?
- Show me how the water *sprays* all over the car.

Learning Task 2: Partner Challenge

Class organization: Partners are scattered in self-spaces.

Present the following:

- With a partner, imagine you both have large towels for drying the car. Together, *stretch* and *reach* to dry the roof. Use your hands to *make* a *circular* movement with your towel.
- One child *sprays* the inside of the car windows and the other child *wipes* the windows dry.
- Now exchange roles and one partner *sprays* the hub caps and the other partner *shines* them.

Learning Task 3: Car Wash

Class organization: Children are scattered in identified groups.

- Divide the children in two groups. Explain to them that they can use their bodies to form a long car wash. One group forms the two walls of the car wash by standing side by side. They use their arms to make rollers in front of their bodies. The remaining children drive their cars through the car wash. Exchange roles.
- Try using pom-poms as brushes, bubbles as soap, jump ropes or short pieces of clothesline to represent water hoses, and sponges or towels to dry off the newly washed cars. Hold red and green circular pieces of construction paper to signal when the cars are to advance or stop at stations while traveling through the car wash.

Assessment Questions

1. Let's see your bright and shiny car. Can you start the engine and grasp the steering wheel to drive home? Drive carefully and don't bump other cars.
2. Name another place that helps to keep things clean in your home or community (e.g., laundromat).
3. What movement do we use to make our hands clean before we eat (e.g., scrub)? Show me.

Academic Language Demands

- **Language function:** Uses language to discuss the role of a car wash in a local community and why adults like to keep their car and other possessions clean (e.g., so that they will look new or good).
- **Vocabulary:** vacuum, hub caps, rollers, brushes, push and pull, spray, scrub
- **Syntax or discourse:** A verbal interchange about parts of the car wash and how all classmates can play a role in imitating the actions that are commonly seen.

PIZZA PARLOR

National Standards Addressed

- **Standard 1.** The physically literate individual demonstrates competency in a variety of motor skills and movement patterns.
- **Standard 3.** The physically literate individual demonstrates the knowledge and skills to achieve and maintain a health-enhancing level of physical activity and fitness.

Instructional Materials/Props

Pictures of pizza toppings (optional)

Central Focus

To discover ways to form a popular family food with their bodies.

Objectives

- **Cognitive:** The child will identify several healthy pizza toppings.
- **Affective:** The child will cooperate with a partner to form with their bodies the shapes of healthy foods commonly used to create a pizza.
- **Psychomotor:** The child will use his or her body to help create a large imaginary pizza containing healthy foods and prepare the pizza for eating by performing several locomotor skills to cook and then cool the pizza.

Components of Health-Related Fitness

Cardiorespiratory endurance, flexibility

Learning Task 1: Preparing Our Bodies to Move

Class organization: Children are scattered throughout general space.

Challenge the children to perform the following actions:

- Who can tell me what pizza dough is made from (e.g., flour)?
- Let's pretend to make a pizza. To begin, everyone must imagine a large lump of pizza dough. Can you *roll* your pizza dough with a rolling pin? *Move* the pizza dough from hand to hand. Can you *flatten* the dough? Show me how you would *make* the dough smooth. Try to *toss* the dough above your head and *catch* it.
- We need tomato sauce. Is it possible to *make* our bodies very flat like the pizza sauce on the dough?
- What toppings can we add to the dough? Who can *make* a round pepperoni circle with their body?
- Discover a way to *shape* your body like narrow slivers of cheese. Mushrooms look like little stools when they are picked. Show me how you can *stoop* low to the ground like a mushroom.

Learning Task 2: **Partner Challenge**

Class organization: Partners are scattered in self-spaces.

Present the following:

- To make a large mushroom, one partner kneels on the floor to form the stem and the other partner stretches his or her arms over the stem to form a mushroom cap.
- Together try to form a green pepper ring. Now form a round tomato slice.

Learning Task 3: **Large Pizza Pie**

Class organization: Children are scattered in identified groups.

After dividing the class into three groups, challenge the children to use their bodies to form a large pizza pie.

- Ask one group to lie down in a large circle shape to form the outside crust.
- The second group of children becomes slivers of cheese, round pepperoni shapes, tiny mushrooms, and pizza sauce.

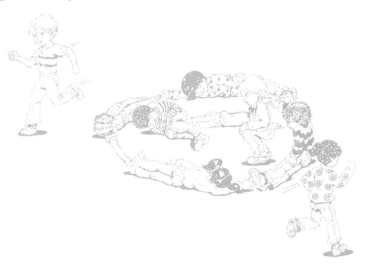

- To cook the pizza in a large oven, the third group of children begins by walking, and then jogging, and finally running around the outside to cook the pizza until the cheese is very hot and melts.
- To complete the activity, all the children run and skip around the pizza shop while the pizza cools.

Assessment Questions

1. Who can use their body to create another pizza topping (e.g., black olives, spinach, onion, pineapple)?
2. Now work with a partner to try to make a pizza shape (e.g., round, triangle) with your bodies.
3. Can you tell me other ways we can move quickly to cook our imaginary pizza? Show me one of those movements.

Academic Language Demands

- **Language function:** Uses language to discuss the food elements that go into the creation of a large pizza and why it is fun to eat pizza.
- **Vocabulary:** skip, kneel, stem, stool, sliver, oven, healthy pizza toppings
- **Syntax or discourse:** A verbal interchange focusing on popular healthy choices for pizza toppings.

CONSTRUCTION SITE

National Standards Addressed

- **Standard 1.** The physically literate individual demonstrates competency in a variety of motor skills and movement patterns.
- **Standard 4.** The physically literate individual exhibits responsible personal and social behavior that respects self and others.

Instructional Materials/Props

Pictures of objects found at a construction site (optional), tools or toy tools (optional)

Central Focus

To manipulate classmates' bodies to perform movements similar to those found in a construction site.

Objectives

- **Cognitive:** The child will recognize a variety of movements and actions specific to various materials and tools found at a construction site.
- **Affective:** The child will display cooperative behavior with a partner while imitating the actions or shape of three construction tools.
- **Psychomotor:** The child will participate actively alongside other classmates in the creation of imaginary large structures.

Component of Health-Related Fitness

Muscular strength and endurance

Learning Task 1: Preparing Our Bodies to Move

Class organization: Children are scattered throughout general space.

Challenge the children to perform the following actions:

- Can you pretend you are a very tall building by *stretching* upward?
- *Put on* a hard hat to protect your head. Use your arms and legs to *climb* the steel ladder.
- Is it possible to *walk* along a narrow steel beam without falling off? *Place* your arms out at the side of your body to help you *balance*.
- Show me how you can *walk* with giant steps to *move* from beam to beam.
- Let's *move* our body like an elevator down to the ground level.
- Pretend to *unload* tools from a large truck.
- Can you *lift* a heavy tool by using your leg muscles? Slowly *lower* your body and *place* your arms around the bottom of the large tool. Now *lift* the tool by *raising* your leg muscles. This movement prevents you from injuring your back.
- Find a way to *make* a noise like a drill and *spin* around in a circle.
- The concrete mixer has a large container. It churns cement, gravel, sand, and water to make concrete. Can you use both arms to *imitate* the turning movement of the mixer? See if you can *turn* your whole body like the concrete mixer.

Learning Task 2: **Partner Challenge**

Class organization: Partners are scattered in self-spaces.

Present the following:

- Show me how one partner can make believe he or she is a jack hammer breaking the concrete by *pumping* their arms up and down very quickly. The other partner controls how fast or slow the jack hammer moves by *turning* an imaginary button on the shoulder. Exchange roles.
- People use wheelbarrows to carry tools, dirt, and small pieces of concrete. Let's work with a friend to make the shape of a wheelbarrow. One child should *lie* on his or her back. The partner *holds* the ankles upward to make the handles of the wheelbarrow.
- Pretend you and your partner are a giant bulldozer *pushing* dirt. Find space along a wall and *push* the dirt together while making the sound of the bulldozer.

Learning Task 3: **New House on the Block**

Class organization: Children are scattered in identified groups.

Explain to the children that the word construction means "building."

Challenge the children to use their bodies to form a house. Ask them to stand tall and become the walls of the house. Add more children and make the door or archway into the house. Decorate the outdoors with children pretending to be a driveway, a mailbox, trees, hedges, or flowers in a flower bed.

Assessment Questions

1. Who can recall three movements common to a construction site?
2. Who would like to help build a neighbor's house? With your friends, show me how you could do this.
3. Can you use your bodies and create a larger house that could hold many people?

Academic Language Demands

- **Language function:** Uses language to identify the basic actions of several common tools found in a construction site.
- **Vocabulary:** jack hammer, hard hat, drill, construction, churn, building, archway, decorate
- **Syntax or discourse:** A verbal interchange focusing on common elements that encompass a large house with a yard.

LAUNDROMAT

National Standards Addressed

- **Standard 1.** The physically literate individual demonstrates competency in a variety of motor skills and movement patterns.
- **Standard 4.** The physically literate individual exhibits responsible personal and social behavior that respects self and others.

Instructional Materials/Props

Picture of a clothespin or actual clothespin, picture of a washing machine and clothes dryer, and a picture of a clothesline (all optional)

Central Focus

To show appreciation for and exhibit movements linked to a laundromat.

Objectives

- **Cognitive:** The child will remember vocabulary words associated with washing and drying clothes.
- **Affective:** The child will display cooperative behavior while working with a partner to create the shape of a bubble and move safely throughout the playing area.
- **Psychomotor:** The child will eagerly take part in the creation of a large imaginary laundromat.

Component of Health-Related Fitness

Cardiorespiratory endurance

Learning Task 1: Preparing Our Bodies to Move

Class organization: Children are scattered throughout general space.

Challenge the children to perform the following actions:

- Can someone tell me what we do in a laundromat?
- Who can *make* the sound of the washing machines?
- Let's use our arms to *make* the shape of the soap bubbles.
- See if you can *twist* your hips like the movement of a washing machine.
- Show me how you can use your feet to *stomp* out the dirt.
- *Move* your body back and forth as if you were the clothing being washed.
- Determine the best way to *spin* your body like the washing machine when it rinses the clothes.
- Use your hands and pretend to *squeeze* the extra water out of the clothing.
- Is it possible to *spin* your body quickly like the clothes dryer?

Learning Task 2: **Partner Challenge**

Class organization: Partners are scattered in self-spaces.

Partners join hands to form a giant soap bubble shape while moving cooperatively throughout the playing area without bumping into other bubbles. On your signal, partners join another set of partners to make a larger floating soap bubble.

Learning Task 3: **Washing Machine**

Class organization: Children are scattered in identified groups.

Explain that the children can use their bodies to make the movements of the washing machine.

- Divide the children into three groups.
- The first group forms a large circle and makes the vigorous churning movement of the washing machine. The second group stands in the middle of the washing machine and moves like the clothing being washed. The third group makes large, round soap bubbles with their arms.
- Challenge the children to coordinate their movements in order to wash a load of laundry.
- Instruct the children to exchange roles.
- At the end of the activity, ask the whole group to run in a large circle to make believe they are the parts of a giant dryer heating and drying the clothes so they can be worn.

Assessment Questions

1. Why is it important to care for your clothes? Some people hang their washed clothes on a clothesline to dry in the sun. Pretend your hands are clothespins. Show me how your fingers would move.
2. Can you hang your shirt or blouse from the clothesline?
3. Who can fold their body in half like a bedsheet that is placed in the closet?

Academic Language Demands

- **Language function:** Uses language to identify how clean clothes help keep our bodies healthy.
- **Vocabulary:** laundry, squeeze, clothespins, clothesline, bubbles, detergent
- **Syntax or discourse:** A verbal interchange concerning the elements that one commonly sees when going to a laundromat and when using a washing machine.

LIBRARY

National Standards Addressed

- **Standard 1.** The physically literate individual demonstrates competency in a variety of motor skills and movement patterns.
- **Standard 4.** The physically literate individual exhibits responsible personal and social behavior that respects self and others.

Instructional Materials/Props

Different types of books on display (optional)

Central Focus

To explore a progression of movements and expressive feelings related to characters, objects, and things similar to those found in categories of books in a library.

Objectives

- **Cognitive:** The child will recall and discuss characters, objects, and things associated with different types of books.
- **Affective:** The child will observe a classmate's creation of his or her favorite plaything without ridiculing the performance.
- **Psychomotor:** The child will engage in group efforts to convey emotions and poses that are common to a particular type of book.

Component of Health-Related Fitness

Cardiorespiratory endurance

Learning Task 1: Preparing Our Bodies to Move

Class organization: Children are scattered throughout general space.

Challenge the children to perform the following actions:

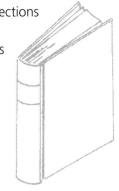

- Explain to the children that the books in a library are organized into sections to make it easier to find their favorite type of book.
- The adventure section might have books about stomping angry dragons and brave knights *galloping* on horses. Who can *stomp* both feet loudly?
- In the fairy tale section you can read and make believe you are flying on a magic carpet. Show me how you would *fly* with your arms in the air.
- Biographies are stories about famous people such as the ones who climb to the top of tall mountains. Is it possible to *walk* along as if you were on a narrow and rocky mountain ledge?
- The pet section has books that show playful puppies chasing each other. How quickly can you *run* without bumping into another classmate?
- Gardening books help people to grow fruits and vegetables. Imagine you are *stretching* and *plucking* an apple from a tall tree.
- Books that focus on music sometimes show people marching. Who can *lift* their knees while *playing* an instrument in a large marching band?

- Many people enjoy books about sports. Can you vigorously use your arms in a swimming race?
- Travel books help people to learn about new places and things. Who can make believe they are riding a wild bull as it *bucks, twists,* and *turns* in the western part of the United States?

Learning Task 2: Partner Challenge

Class organization: Partners are scattered in self-spaces.

Present the following: *A mystery is a special type of book that tells a story and usually has a surprise ending.* Ask one partner to think of a favorite plaything and then use his or her body to act out or form the shape of the plaything. The other partner tries to guess what the mystery object is. The children exchange roles.

Learning Task 3: Your Favorite Book

Class organization: Children are scattered in identified groups.

- Divide the class into groups of five or six.
- Assign each group a type of book (e.g., adventure: rowdy pirates digging for buried treasure; animals: creepy, slimy, slithering living creatures; biography: fearless race car drivers racing on the track; music: members of a music group enthusiastically playing their instruments).
- Ask each group to pose to create a picture for the cover of their book.
- Walk among the groups making believe you are taking photos that will be used on the covers of books for the classroom.

Assessment Questions

1. Who can name the title of his or her book and tell the class what action takes place in the book?
2. Can you use your body to show me what type of book is your favorite?
3. Is it possible to act out the movements in a book that your mother or father might like to read?

Academic Language Demands

- **Language function:** Uses language to compare or contrast different types of books and a few of the movements that are common to those books.
- **Vocabulary:** stomp, pluck, fearless, adventure, mystery, ledge, buck
- **Syntax or discourse:** A verbal interchange focusing on how every child must use his or her body in a similar way to identify a particular object or thing that is found in a particular type of book.

AIRPORT

National Standards Addressed

- **Standard 2.** The physically literate individual applies knowledge of concepts, principles, strategies and tactics related to movement and performance.
- **Standard 4.** The physically literate individual exhibits responsible personal and social behavior that respects self and others.

Instructional Materials/Props

Pictures and models of toy aircraft on display (optional), photos of an airport (optional)

Central Focus

To imagine the body has transformed into several objects that can move quickly and can also fly.

Objectives

- **Cognitive:** The child will describe differences in types of aircraft found at the community airport and their movements.
- **Affective:** The child will combine his or her body with a partner's body in a cooperative manner in order to imitate the movement of a single-engine airplane.
- **Psychomotor:** The child will move in relation with a partner and in a small group in order to imitate the movements of a single-engine plane and a make-believe passenger airplane as they take off from a runway and soar through the air.

Component of Health-Related Fitness

Cardiorespiratory endurance

Learning Task 1: Preparing Our Bodies to Move

Class organization: Children are scattered throughout general space.

Challenge the children to perform the following actions:

- Can you *lie* on the floor and *make* an airplane shape with wings?
- *Stand* and *place* your arms out to your sides to make a small airplane. Who can *imitate* the sound of the airplane's engine?
- Show me how you can *run* and take off from a long runway.
- Find a way to *land* your small plane safely on the ground.
- The helicopter is another type of small aircraft. Helicopters have a large propeller on top of them. When the propeller blades *whirl* around, they create a strong wind to *lift* the helicopter. Can you *spin* your arms like helicopter blades? Slowly *rise* into the air. Can you *travel* around our playing area without touching other helicopters while *spinning* slowly?
- The jet aircraft is built to move quickly. Can you *make* the pointed nose of the airplane with your arms and *zoom* through our playing area?

Learning Task 2: Partner Challenge

Class organization: Partners are scattered in self-spaces.

Present the following: *There are two basic types of airplanes. The first airplane can carry only one or two passengers because it has a small engine. This is called a single-engine airplane.* Challenge the children to perform the following actions:

- First, *stand* beside a partner. *Move* close together so that you are shoulder to shoulder.
- Can you *put* your arm around your partner's shoulders as good friends do?
- See if you can *move* together by using your two outside arms as wings.
- Let's practice air safety by making a long line of partner planes. Each plane should find a space to *stand* along the runway. On my signal, one plane *leaves* the runway and begins to *fly* through the skies. After the first plane has left the runway, the second plane may leave.

Learning Task 3: A Passenger Plane

Class organization: Children are scattered in identified groups.

Present the following: *A second type of airplane is large and typically has four powerful engines. It can carry many people to places around the world. This is called a passenger plane.*

Divide the children into groups of four.

To build the passenger plane, two children stand behind two other children, who are using their arms as wings. The front children are the pilots. The two children in the back place their hands on the shoulders of the pilots.

Slowly, the four children move together pretending to fly to a faraway place or across the ocean.

Assessment Questions

1. Raise your hand if you have been in a real passenger plane. Can you tell your classmates where you went?
2. Sometimes, airplanes fly in bad weather and strong winds. This is called bumpy air. Who can create an airplane and pretend to fly in bumpy air?
3. Let's see if we can name different parts of an airplane and a helicopter.

Academic Language Demands

- **Language function:** Uses language to describe two types of planes and how they are different and alike.
- **Vocabulary:** whirl, propeller, blades, aircraft, bumpy, runway, single-engine, take-off
- **Syntax or discourse:** A verbal interchange about how to move swiftly and at different levels throughout the playing area with a partner and a small group of peers.

<u>BEACH</u>

National Standards Addressed

- **Standard 1.** The physically literate individual demonstrates competency in a variety of motor skills and movement patterns.
- **Standard 4.** The physically literate individual exhibits responsible personal and social behavior that respects self and others.

Instructional Materials/Props

Pictures of objects found at or used at the beach or the actual items on display (e.g., sunscreen, hat, sunglasses, beach ball, shovel, sand, sand crab, seagull, sailboats, and sandcastles) (optional)

Central Focus

To identify and explore beach-related activities while recognizing ways to stay safe.

Objectives

- **Cognitive:** The child will point to actions one can take to protect the body against natural elements found at the beach.
- **Affective:** The child will show a willingness to follow the pathway of his or her partner while imitating the action of a sailboat and while moving in a fleet formation.
- **Psychomotor:** The child will participate in the creation of a human sandcastle and use his or her body to produce a tower or walls of the structure or other items from the child's imagination or books.

Component of Health-Related Fitness

Cardiorespiratory endurance

Learning Task 1: Preparing Our Bodies to Move

Class organization: Children are scattered throughout general space.

Challenge the children to perform the following actions:

- Here we are at our favorite beach. Let's begin by putting on sunscreen. *Rub* it on your arms, legs, face, neck, and ears. Now wear your sunglasses and hat. This will protect you from the sun's harmful rays.
- Show me how you can use your arms to make a beach umbrella. It should stand in the sun to block the sun's hot rays.
- Who can use a hand shovel and *dig* in the sand?
- Use your body to *make* the round shape of a beach ball. *Roll* it carefully along the sand.
- Is it possible to *walk* in the deep sand while *lifting* your legs high?
- Let's *run* along the beach and *jump* over a small wave.
- Make believe you are using a long fishing pole and *reeling* in a large fish.
- Pretend to *inflate* a large rubber sea horse. Take a deep breath, get ready, and *exhale*. Again, *inhale* deeply and *exhale*.

- If you look closely in the sand, you can see small sand crabs. Crabs walk backward. Try to move like the crab by *squatting* down. Now *reach* back and put both hands on the floor. Try to keep your rear end from touching the sand. *Move* throughout the playing area like a crab.

- Let's make the *flapping* wing actions of a seagull. Who can *swoop* down from the sky and low to the water?

Learning Task 2: **Partner Challenge**

Class organization: Partners are scattered in self-spaces.

Present the following: *Sailboats glide on the water by using the wind to push them along the water.*

- Ask children to make a sailboat by holding one arm straight up at the side of the head to form the mast. The other arm stretches out to the side of the body with the palm up. This shape makes the mast of the sailboat. Challenge partners to sail their boats near one another and throughout the playing area without touching other boats for increased spatial awareness.

- On your signal, partners can join another set of partners to create a fleet of sailboats. Challenge the children to create different fleet formations (e.g., one behind the other) to sail throughout the playing area.

Learning Task 3: **Human Sandcastle**

Class organization: Children are scattered in identified groups.

Present the following: *Who can name books or television programs that include a castle as part of the story? You can use your bodies to build a large human sandcastle.*

- Ask the children to make a tower by raising their arms and pointing to the sky.
- See if they can make a box shape on their hands and knees.
- Challenge the children to build a sand castle by having some classmates pretend to be blocks of sand while others make towers or flags or other related items with their bodies.

Assessment Questions

1. Can you name one activity you enjoy participating in at our imaginary seashore?
2. Who can name their favorite book or television show that includes a castle in the story?
3. Is there a sea creature you would like to see at the beach? Show me how it would move.

Academic Language Demands

- **Language function:** Uses language to identify items that commonly move or are seen in a beach environment and how adults and children can protect their skin from the sun's rays on hot summer days.
- **Vocabulary:** glide, reel, fleet, sandcastle, mast, tower, sunscreen, hat, beach, sea-shore
- **Syntax or discourse:** A verbal interchange identifying books or televisions programs known to the children that include a castle in the story.

BUILDING STRUCTURES

National Standards Addressed

- **Standard 2.** The physically literate individual applies knowledge of concepts, principles, strategies and tactics related to movement and performance.
- **Standard 4.** The physically literate individual exhibits responsible personal and social behavior that respects self and others.

Instructional Materials/Props

Pictures of arches and archways (optional)

Central Focus

To maintain a compact shape while moving through obstacles of different heights and widths.

Objectives

- **Cognitive:** The child will describe an archway and its purpose and apply this knowledge during the learning tasks.
- **Affective:** The child will happily interact with a peer to create an archway.
- **Psychomotor:** The child will perform a variety of locomotor skills in order to move through archway shapes of different heights and widths that have been created by peers.

Components of Health-Related Fitness

Cardiorespiratory endurance, flexibility

Learning Task 1: Preparing Our Bodies to Move

Class organization: Children are scattered throughout general space.

Challenge the children to perform the following actions:

- Is it possible to *walk* on only your toes, heels, inside of the foot, outside?
- See how many different ways you can *run*.

Learning Task 2: Partner Challenge

Class organization: Partners are scattered in self-spaces.

Present the following:

- Who can describe what an archway is and the purpose it serves (e.g., an opening, a place to walk through)?
- Can you demonstrate how to make a strong human archway by *standing* and facing a partner, *clasping* your hands together, and *extending* them over your heads? (The arch should allow enough space for a third child to move freely between the two bodies.)

Learning Task 3: **Human Architecture**

Class organization: Children are scattered in identified groups.

- Divide the children into groups of three. Two of the three children should form an arch, and the third child practices locomotor skills through the archway. Exchange roles.

- After each group member has completed the task, suggest that the two stationary partners lower the arch by kneeling. Encourage children to explore moving through the arch at this new height.
- For a greater challenge, divide the children into two groups. One group uses their bodies to form strong arches of different heights, while the other group moves through them. Exchange roles.

Assessment Questions

1. Which body parts were the most difficult to keep close to your body when you were in a tiny compact shape?
2. Who can identify why archways are important in our homes, school, and community?
3. What types of locomotor skills did you use when height of the archway was lowered? Show me.

Academic Language Demands

- **Language function:** Uses language to analyze the best way to move through an archway that has been lowered to a level that is challenging for the child to move through and continue onward.
- **Vocabulary:** arch, archway, pathway, opening, a variety of locomotor skills
- **Syntax or discourse:** A verbal interchange identifying the value of archways in our community.

WINTERTIME HOLIDAYS

National Standards Addressed

Standard 4. The physically literate individual exhibits responsible personal and social behavior that respects self and others.

Instructional Materials/Props

Photos of holiday items or the actual items on display (optional)

Central Focus

To be actively engaged in a variety of winter holiday movements.

Objectives

- **Cognitive:** The child will associate certain objects and activities with winter holidays.
- **Affective:** The child will happily combine his or her body with a partner to form three different objects seen commonly during the winter holidays.
- **Psychomotor:** The child will demonstrate the ability to work within a group and use his or her body to produce six holiday items that reflect winter holidays of different cultures.

Component of Health-Related Fitness

Flexibility

Learning Task 1: Preparing Our Bodies to Move

Class organization: Children are scattered throughout general space.

Challenge the children to perform the following actions:

- Can you *walk* like a gingerbread person with your arms *outstretched*?
- Show me how Rudolph the reindeer *gallops* and *flies* through the air.
- *Sway* back and forth like a Christmas bell.
- Show me a long and thin chimney shape. *Wiggle* your fingers like smoke rising from the chimney.
- *March* like a tin soldier throughout general space.
- Find the best way to *form* your body into a tiny, round bulb that we see on Christmas trees.
- Who can *create* a five-pointed star with his or her body? Which body parts make the points of the star?
- Use your body to *make* the shape of a large, round wreath.
- Show me how a dreidel *spins*.

Learning Task 2: Partner Challenge

Class organization: Partners are scattered in self-spaces. Challenge partners to combine their bodies to make the shape of a candy cane, a snowperson, and a sled and rider.

Learning Task 3: Wintertime Wonders

Class organization: Children are scattered in identified groups.

Present the following: *Many places have snow fall during the winter time. Snow provides many fun activities for children and their families.*

- **Igloos:** Ask the children to make an igloo by having some children stand to form the large dome and other children kneel on their knees to make the tunnel entrance.
- **Toboggan:** Ask the children to sit and position their bodies in a straddling formation as if they were riding a long imaginary toboggan with friends.
- **Snowflake:** Invite the children to place their bodies at a low level on the floor. Everyone then forms a wide shape and connects to other wide shapes to form one gigantic class snowflake.
- **Noel:** The word *noel* comes from the French word meaning Christmas. Challenge the children to use their bodies to spell the word *noel*.
- **Kwanzaa:** Kwanzaa honors the African heritage in African American culture, and it occurs from December 26 through January 1. Challenge the children to create the word Kwanzaa using their bodies.
- **Menorah:** A menorah holds nine candles. Eight candles represent the eight days of Chanukah and the ninth candle is called the shamos. The shamos candle is used to light the other candles and then stands taller to watch over them. Prompt the children to create a menorah by asking eight children to stand in a side-by-side line to represent candles. A ninth child represents the shamos and lights the other candles by tapping them on the shoulder. As the candles are lit, the flames flicker and flutter, causing the candles to melt to the floor.

Assessment Questions

1. Can you think of an object that is red or green? See if you can shape your body like the red or green object.
2. During winter holidays we sometimes see two types of angels. Show me how you can lie at a low level and move your arms and legs to create a snow angel.
3. Who can recall an activity they do during a holiday with their family that involves moving in a fun or special way?

Academic Language Demands

- **Language function:** Uses language to categorize items that are common to several winter holidays and those that are used during winter activities in cold climates.
- **Vocabulary:** sway, gallop, spin, wreath, igloo, toboggan, menorah, Kwanzaa, noel
- **Syntax or discourse:** A verbal interchange aimed at identifying objects that the child has experienced at home during the winter months and addressing questions regarding how fun holidays can be.

CHAPTER 7

Moving With Words
& Actions
Like Living Creatures

The young child's first experience with his or her surroundings begins within the home and later extends throughout the community (chapter 6). As children gain confidence of the home environment, they develop greater curiosity about their school surroundings and beyond. Children become fascinated with living creatures that are not common to their home. They soon learn that these creatures can be classified according to where they most often live. They also find enjoyment in imitating the movements, characteristics, and behaviors of specific animals while gaining an appreciation for the different patterns and physical skills needed to "become" the animal.

You can enhance this experience by making comparisons between the child's human body and that of the living creature while also recognizing physical differences among other groups such as animals, birds, fish, and insects. This chapter will enable you to increase the child's appreciation for living creatures and satisfy the child's natural curiosity of the unknown through their participation in moderate to vigorous learning tasks. You can use the following introductory information and activities in physical education classes or perhaps after story time in the classroom setting to spark children's interest in animal behaviors and movements.

Living Creatures Fun Facts

- Elephants cannot jump.
- The giraffe is the tallest animal in the world.
- Tigers have striped skin, not just striped fur.
- The hummingbird can fly straight up like a helicopter.
- The giant squid has the largest eyes in the world.
- Butterflies taste with their feet.
- An ant can lift 50 times its body weight.

Animal Actions

Jungle Animals

- **Antelope:** dashing
- **Baboon:** swinging
- **Cheetah:** running
- **Gazelle:** leaping
- **Hyena:** surrounding
- **Jackal:** exploring
- **Monkey:** climbing
- **Puma:** sneaking

Woodland Animals

- **Bat:** swooping
- **Bear:** charging
- **Fox:** sneaking
- **Hawk:** searching
- **Mountain lion:** stalking
- **Porcupine:** roaming
- **Possum:** swinging
- **Raccoon:** scattering

Lake and Pond Creatures

- **Beaver:** slapping
- **Otter:** flipping
- **Salamander:** crawling
- **Snake:** slithering
- **Swan:** swimming
- **Turtle:** walking

Sea Creatures

- **Barnacle:** clinging
- **Barracuda:** swimming
- **Clam:** opening and closing shell
- **Eel:** wiggling
- **Octopus:** squeezing
- **Shark:** gliding

Alphabet Animals

- **A:** alligator, anteater, antelope, armadillo
- **B:** baboon, bat, bear, beaver, bobcat, buffalo
- **C:** camel, cat, cheetah, chicken, chipmunk, cougar, coyote, crocodile
- **D:** deer, dog, donkey
- **E:** eagle, elephant, emu
- **F:** ferret, fox, frog
- **G:** gazelle, gecko, gerbil, giraffe, goat, gorilla, guinea pig
- **H:** hamster, hare, hedgehog, hippopotamus, horse, hyena
- **I:** iguana, impala
- **J:** jackal, jaguar
- **K:** kangaroo, kiwi, koala
- **L:** lemming, lemur, leopard, lion, lizard, llama, lynx
- **M:** mole, mongoose, monkey, moose, mouse, mule
- **N:** newt, numbat
- **O:** ocelot, opossum, orangutan, ostrich, otter
- **P:** panther, parrot, peacock, penguin, pig, polar bear, porcupine, possum
- **Q:** quail, quetzal, quokka, quoll
- **R:** rabbit, raccoon, reindeer, rhinoceros
- **S:** seal, sheep, skunk, sloth, snake, squirrel
- **T:** tapir, tarsier, tiger, tortoise, tree frog
- **U:** umbrellabird
- **V:** vampire bat, vulture
- **W:** walrus, warthog, wolf, wolverine, wombat
- **X:** xerus
- **Y:** yak
- **Z:** zebra, zebu

Alphabet Sea Creatures

- **A:** abalone, anchovy, angelfish
- **B:** barnacle, barracuda, blowfish
- **C:** catfish, clownfish, conch, crab
- **D:** dolphin, dragonet
- **E:** eel
- **F:** flounder, flying fish
- **G:** grouper
- **H:** halibut, hermit crab, herring
- **I:** isopod
- **J:** jellyfish
- **K:** kingfish
- **L:** lobster
- **M:** mackerel, mahi-mahi, manatee, manta ray
- **N:** needlefish
- **O:** octopus, orca whale, oyster
- **P:** plankton, porcupinefish, porpoise, pufferfish
- **Q:** quillfish
- **R:** ray
- **S:** scallop, sea horse, starfish, swordfish, shark, sponge
- **T:** tuna, turtle
- **U:** unicornfish, urchin
- **V:** velvetfish, viperfish
- **W:** whale
- **X:** X-ray tetra
- **Y:** yellow tang fish
- **Z:** zebra fish, zooplankton

LIVING CREATURES NEAR AND FAR

National Standards Addressed

- **Standard 1.** The physically literate individual demonstrates competency in a variety of motor skills and movement patterns.
- **Standard 2.** The physically literate individual applies knowledge of concepts, principles, strategies and tactics related to movement and performance.

Instructional Materials/Props

Photographs of animals (e.g., the African elephant, giraffe, gorilla, and monkey) (optional)

Central Focus

To learn how animals from different regions move and to demonstrate these actions.

Objectives

- **Cognitive:** The child will recall movements or behaviors of specific animals.
- **Affective:** The child will praise his or her partner and small-group members for being able to gallop in the same rhythm.
- **Psychomotor:** The child will successfully make a swinging motion while playfully manipulating the body of a classmate who is standing firm and treelike.

Component of Health-Related Fitness

Cardiorespiratory endurance

Learning Task 1: Preparing Our Bodies to Move

Class organization: Children are scattered throughout general space.

Present the following: *We can pretend to visit the zoo to learn about different animals and practice their movements.*

- African elephants can grow to be 10 feet (3 m) tall at the shoulders. They have big ears and a nose called a trunk. They use their trunks to tear off leaves and clumps of grass to eat and to smell and squirt water into their mouths. Show me how you can *bend* forward and use your arms to make a trunk that is low to the ground. Can you *swing* your trunk from side to side as you *move* like the heavy elephant?
- The giraffe can grow to be 19 feet (5.8 m) tall. They get most of their food and water from leaves high in the trees and can go a month without water. *Grasp* your hands together and *stretch* them upward like the long neck of the giraffe. *Gallop* forward.
- Is it possible to *swing* your arms low to the ground and to the side like a gorilla?
- The fastest land animal is the cheetah. It can run up to 65 miles an hour (105 km/h). Show me how you can *run* fast by *pumping* your arms at the side of your body and *sprinting* forward.
- Some African frogs can jump 10 feet (3 m). See if you can *stoop* low to the ground and *spring* forward using the muscles in your legs.
- Kangaroos live in Australia and use their powerful legs to jump as far as 40 feet (12 m) and as high as 10 feet (3 m). *Tuck* your hands to the side of your chest and see how far you can *jump* forward from a standing position.

- Alligators have short legs and a long body. You can move like an alligator by *lying* on the floor and *moving* your hand and foot on one side of your body and then the other hand and foot. *Bend* your knees and elbows as you move.
- The pink flamingo is a large, web-footed bird with long and slender legs and neck. This bird loves to wade in water. Try to *balance* on one foot like the pink flamingo.
- The bear is a heavy animal with thick fur and sharp claws. The bear shifts its body from side to side to move forward. Who can *bend* forward and *touch* the ground with both hands and feet? Now *move* a front and a back paw on the same side of your body. *Shift* to the other front and back paw while you *move* and growl.
- The seal is a flesh-eating sea animal and has large flippers. Its long body is covered with thick fur or bristle. The seal uses its front flippers and drags its tail to move along the ice. Is it possible to *move* forward by *using* only your hands and *dragging* your feet?

Learning Task 2: **Partner Challenge**

Class organization: Partners are scattered in self-spaces.

Present the following:

- Buffalo and horses gallop when moving at a fast speed.
- With a partner, pretend to be buffalo, moving at a fast *gallop* and then *stopping* for a drink of water.
- Can you *gallop* in the same rhythm as your partner?
- Now find another set of partners to create a small herd of buffalo. See if you can *gallop* in rhythm with the other buffalo in your herd.

Learning Task 3: **Monkeys on the Move**

Class organization: Children are scattered in identified groups.

- Explain to the children that monkeys are active animals that use their strong arms to move among vines and tree branches. Challenge the children to use their bodies to make believe they are a group of monkeys swinging playfully.
- Dividing the class into two groups. Half of the class use their arms to form vines or tree branches. The remaining children are monkeys and make believe they are swinging from branch to branch by moving under the branches (i.e., arms) of the trees. Ask the monkeys to demonstrate how they can swing on every branch. Exchange roles.

Assessment Questions

1. Who can demonstrate the movements and sounds of their favorite animal?
2. What kinds of things might animals talk about to other animals when they make different sounds?
3. If you could travel anywhere in the world, what animal would you like to see living in its natural habitat? Can you show me how this animal moves?

Academic Language Demands

- **Language function:** Uses language to explain unique characteristics that certain animals possess.
- **Vocabulary:** swing, pump, sprint, stoop, spring, shift, tuck, bristle, herd, trunk
- **Syntax or discourse:** A verbal interchange focusing on how to use the body so that it is a strong treelike structure for the children to manipulate in a playful way.

ANIMAL ACTIONS

National Standards Addressed

- **Standard 1.** The physically literate individual demonstrates competency in a variety of motor skills and movement patterns.
- **Standard 2.** The physically literate individual applies knowledge of concepts, principles, strategies and tactics related to movement and performance.

Instructional Materials/Props

Ribbon, scarves, or cloth 18 inches (46 cm) long; floor markers to identify the monkey tree, optional recording of animal sounds

Central Focus

To identify and perform the action words of a simple animal rhyme.

Objectives

- **Cognitive:** The child will recognize a variety of creatures that live in a tropical rain forest.
- **Affective:** The child will communicate effectively with a partner in order to create the sounds and movements of a specific animal.
- **Psychomotor:** The child will imitate the movements and sounds of monkeys and gorillas in a vigorous chase-and-flee game that requires the children to switch roles.

Component of Health-Related Fitness

Cardiorespiratory endurance

Learning Task 1: Preparing Our Bodies to Move

Class organization: Children are scattered throughout general space.

Challenge the children to perform the following actions:

In tropical rain forests,
With funny-looking trees,
There are *crawly* bugs, and *slithering* snakes,
Colorful *flying* birds and *swinging* chimpanzees.
Now, *bend* your legs a little,
And *place* your hands down on the floor.
Stretch your body forward,
And *make* the sound of a tiger's roar!

Learning Task 2: Partner Challenge

Class organization: Partners are scattered in self-spaces.

Present the following: *With a partner, imitate a jungle animal complete with sounds (e.g., gorilla, monkey, elephant, cheetah, rhinoceros) and the common way the animal moves. If it is possible, add features that make the animal different from another animal.*

Learning Task 3: Monkeys and Gorillas

Class organization: Children are scattered in identified groups.

Ask the children to identify how a monkey is different from a gorilla (e.g., monkeys have tails). Divide the class into two groups. Children in one group are the monkeys. Each monkey is given a strip of ribbon or cloth to place in their waistbands so that at least 6 inches (15 cm) is showing. Children in the second group are gorillas and scatter throughout the jungle. In the middle of the jungle is a clearly marked circular area designated as the monkey tree.

On your signal, the monkeys leave the tree to search for imaginary bananas while gorillas try to snatch a tail. Whenever a gorilla is successful, he or she retreats to the monkey tree where he or she tucks in the tail and becomes a monkey. The child whose tail was pulled is now a gorilla. However, gorillas cannot take away a monkey's tail while the monkey is in the tree.

All monkeys leaving the tree have five free seconds in which their tails cannot be taken. This keeps gorillas away from the tree. Children can perform a variety of movement patterns while adding monkey and gorilla sounds and actions. Remind the children that the monkey tree is used only to adjust tails and is not a resting area.

Assessment Questions

1. Who can name five other jungle animals?

2. Can someone show us how one of those animals moves? We will copy you.

3. Does anyone know what the word "species" means (e.g., animals having the same characteristics)? Can you tell me what the term "endangered species" might mean?

Academic Language Demands

- **Language function:** Uses language to determine the type of animal that the child and his or her partner can create and discusses distinguishing features that the animal possesses.

- **Vocabulary:** crawl, slither, swing, bend, stretch, tropical rain forest, chimpanzee, monkey, gorilla, species

- **Syntax or discourse:** A verbal interchange focusing on how different jungle animals move and sound and look different from other animals in the same animal category.

UNDER THE SEA

National Standards Addressed

Standard 5. The physically literate individual recognizes the value of physical activity for health, enjoyment, challenge, self-expression and/or social interaction.

Instructional Materials/Props

Photographs of sea creatures (optional), hand puppets to demonstrate specific sea creature movements (optional), paper crowns for the King or Queen of the Sea (optional)

Central Focus

To practice basic physical skills while identifying sea creatures and differentiating between their movement patterns.

Objectives

- **Cognitive:** The child will recall a variety of sea creatures with unique movements and physical characteristics.
- **Affective:** The child will maintain a high level of attentiveness while learning how to move like creatures found in sea and ocean water.
- **Psychomotor:** The child will select one specific sea creature and be able to move like that creature.

Component of Health-Related Fitness

Flexibility

Learning Task 1: Preparing Our Bodies to Move

Class organization: Children are scattered throughout general space.

Challenge the children to perform the following actions:

- Fish are sea creatures and they have backbones. Jellyfish do not have a backbone or a skeleton. Let's *jump* into the water and use your arms to *float* like jellyfish.
- The flying fish swims to the surface and leaps out of the water. Its fins are spread out to help it glide through the air. Can you *spread* your fins and *move* like a *flying* fish?
- The sea horse has a horselike head, a hard shell like an insect, and a pouch like a kangaroo. The sea horse swims by wiggling its back fin and moves up and down almost like a horse on a merry-go-round. Who can *swim* like a sea horse?
- Pufferfish and porcupinefish make themselves swell up like a balloon so that larger fish have problems swallowing them. Try to make your body *expand* to a large round shape.
- The octopus has eight arms with suckers along the bottoms of each arm for gripping. Demonstrate how an octopus might *move* along the ocean floor.

Learning Task 2: Partner Challenge

Class organization: Partners are scattered in self-spaces.

Present the following: *Whales with large teeth such as the orca, or killer whale, are considered large dolphins. They have one blowhole at the top of their head that they use to breathe air. They move their tails up and down for speed. Fish move their bodies and tails side to side when they swim.* Challenge each partner to place his or her arms together to make a fin. One partner shows how the dolphin moves up and down and the other partner shows how fish swim side to side as they move through the playing area.

Learning Task 3: Big Swim

Class organization: Children are scattered in identified groups.

Organize the children in a side-by-side line on one end line facing the opposite end of the playing area. The two end lines are clearly marked. Designate one child to be the King or Queen of the Sea and ask that child to stand in the center of the playing area. Individual children choose a specific sea creature to imitate. When the King or Queen of the Sea says, "Swim, swim, swim," the children move like their selected sea creature to the other end of the playing area while the King or Queen tries to tag the fleeing children.

If a child is tagged in the center of the playing area, that child joins the King or Queen of the Sea. The King or Queen of the Sea can try to trick the children by using phrases like "Swim flipper, swim" instead of simply saying, "Swim, swim, swim." The last three or four remaining sea creatures are declared "starfish" and become the next Kings or Queens of the Sea. Remind the children to avoid stepping on the hands of children choosing to be slithering sea creatures.

Assessment Questions

1. Let's use all our bodies to create a giant whale or starfish shape.
2. As a human, what sea creature and its movements are easiest to imitate? Why?
3. Who can tell me about the major role that the King or Queen had in our activity Big Swim?

Academic Language Demands

- **Language function:** Uses language to describe how specific sea creatures move throughout the water.
- **Vocabulary:** float, spread, fly, expand, search, tropical, backbone, suckers, blowhole
- **Syntax or discourse:** A verbal interchange used to differentiate the responsibilities of the King or Queen of the Sea in the whole-group learning task.

CRUSTACEANS

National Standards Addressed

Standard 1. The physically literate individual demonstrates competency in a variety of motor skills and movement patterns.

Instructional Materials/Props

Photographs of crustaceans (optional), a sheet of paper to designate each of the following areas: rocky beach, dune area, lagoon, sandy beach, and sandbar (optional)

Central Focus

To show an appreciation for the unique movements of a crustacean while coordinating stepping actions with other children.

Objectives

- **Cognitive:** The child will identify pairs of a human's body parts, mentally noting that humans have one pair of legs, while crustaceans possess five pairs.
- **Affective:** The child will interact with a partner in order to slide together in specific directions.
- **Psychomotor:** The child will interact with a group of classmates to use their bodies to imitate the movements of a crustacean.

Component of Health-Related Fitness

Cardiorespiratory endurance

Learning Task 1: Preparing Our Bodies to Move

Class organization: Children are scattered throughout general space.

Challenge the children to perform the following actions:

- Lobsters, crabs, and shrimp are sea creatures that have five pairs of jointed legs. A pair of something means two. How many pairs of body parts do we have (e.g., two legs, eyes, ears, hands, arms, knees, elbows, and ankles)?
- Can you *squeeze* your two elbows together? *Twirl* your wrists? *Dangle* your arms down by your toes?
- Who can *blink* both eyes at the same time? *Tap* your ears?
- Is it possible to *shake* your knees? Now *shake* your hands.
- Find a way to *move* both ankles at the same time.

Learning Task 2: Partner Challenge

Class organization: Partners are scattered in self-spaces.

Present the following:

- Our activity today requires everyone to be able to move together at the same time.
- While standing beside a partner, follow me as we take three *sliding* steps in this direction.
- Can you and your partner take *sliding* steps in three different directions? Move together.
- Is it possible for you and your partner to make long *sliding* movements in the same direction?

Learning Task 3: Lobsters on the Move

Class organization: Children are scattered in identified groups.

- Remind the children that lobsters have five pairs of jointed legs. Therefore, they need five pairs of legs, or five children, to form one lobster. Ask the children to form groups of five. Each group of five quickly forms a behind-line, each child placing their hands on the shoulders of the child directly in front. The child at the front of each group uses his or her arms to form the lobster's claws.

- Introduce the fact that lobsters can move backward. Standing in one spot, the children stomp three times on one side of the body and then stomp three times on the other side. The group as a whole then shuffles backward three steps.

- For a greater challenge, designate specific locations within the playing area for each group to move through (e.g., a make-believe rocky beach, dune area, lagoon, sandy beach, or sandbar).

Assessment Questions

1. Who can tell me what part of a lobster helps the sea creature swim backward (i.e., the tail)?
2. How difficult was it to coordinate your bodies in order to move like the lobster?
3. Can you think of other sea life that we can create with our bodies? Show me.

Academic Language Demands

- **Language function:** Uses language to communicate the direction and the movements used in the partner activity involving sliding.
- **Vocabulary:** slide, shuffle, stomp, pairs, jointed, lagoon, sandbar, crustaceans
- **Syntax or discourse:** A verbal interchange to facilitate the coordination needed for groups of five to form a lobster's body and imitate its movements.

FEATHERED FRIENDS

National Standards Addressed

- **Standard 2.** The physically literate individual applies knowledge of concepts, principles, strategies and tactics related to movement and performance.
- **Standard 4.** The physically literate individual exhibits responsible personal and social behavior that respects self and others.

Instructional Materials/Props

Photographs of different types of birds (optional)

Central Focus

To explore unique ways birds move.

Objectives

- **Cognitive:** The child will differentiate between the ways that specific birds can move.
- **Affective:** The child will extend his or her interest in birds and imitate several behaviors.
- **Psychomotor:** The child, while working in a small group, will explore several movement patterns that birds take while in flight and on the ground.

Components of Health-Related Fitness

Cardiorespiratory endurance, muscular strength and endurance

Learning Task 1: **Preparing Our Bodies to Move**

Class organization: Children are scattered throughout general space.

Challenge the children to perform the following actions:

- All birds have wings but some birds cannot fly. Penguins have wings and waddle when they walk. See if you can *waddle* like a penguin.
- The ostrich cannot fly but is the fastest running bird in the world. When it runs 40 miles per hour (64 km/h), it holds its wings straight out to the sides for balance. Try to *move* like an ostrich. Can you demonstrate how an ostrich *squats* and *stretches* its long neck along the ground to *hide* from enemies?
- Some birds have webbed feet. Webs are flaps of skin between the toes that act as small paddles to help the birds move quickly through the water. While *lying* on your back with your legs *raised* in the air, show how a duck's feet would *move* under water.
- The male peacock spreads its large tail to attract the attention of female birds. The male turkey also spreads his tail and puffs his body to look much bigger and more colorful. Show me how you can *strut* around like a peacock or turkey, showing off your colorful feathers.

Learning Task 2: **Partner Challenge**

Class organization: Partners are scattered in self-spaces.

Ask partners to pretend to be birds, flying about the playing area gathering imaginary objects to build their nests. Sample objects include twigs, sticks, cloth, leaves, weeds, string, ribbon, and yarn.

Learning Task 3: Ducks in a Row

Class organization: Children are scattered in identified groups.

Present the following: *When the mother duck leads her ducklings to the pond for a swim, all the ducklings waddle in a behind-line following her.* Divide the children into four groups. One child in each group is the mother duck, and the other children are the ducklings. The children imitate bird movements while waddling throughout the playing area following the mother duck to the water.

For an additional challenge, tell the children that in the fall, many birds fly in groups called flocks to relocate to a warmer climate. Many birds fly in a V formation. Ask the children to make a fist and extend the index and middle fingers to form a V shape. When the lead bird is tired, that bird drops back to the end of a line and another bird takes the lead. Divide the children into four groups. Designate one child in each group as the lead bird. When you announce "Change," the leader will fall back while another bird takes the lead.

Assessment Questions

1. Do all birds move in the same way?
2. Can you think of a bird we did not talk about today and how it moves? Show me.
3. We discussed how ducks like to fly in a V shape. Who can name another letter pattern that would allow a flock to keep flying forward?

Academic Language Demands

- **Language function:** Uses language to analyze and distinguish behaviors common to different birds.
- **Vocabulary:** waddle, run, balance, flock, migration, webbed feet, V formation
- **Syntax or discourse:** A verbal interchange to discuss the pattern that some birds use to fly to different locations for food and warmer climates in various seasons.

PENGUINS

National Standards Addressed

- **Standard 1.** The physically literate individual demonstrates competency in a variety of motor skills and movement patterns.
- **Standard 2.** The physically literate individual applies knowledge of concepts, principles, strategies and tactics related to movement and performance.

Instructional Materials/Props

Floor markers to symbolize icebergs, photographs of penguins and their habitat (optional), stuffed animal or toy penguin (optional)

Central Focus

To exhibit responsible and personal behavior while participating in an action rhyme.

Objectives

- **Cognitive:** The child will point to parts of his or her body that are similar to those belonging to a penguin.
- **Affective:** The child will modify his or her behavior to maintain waddling steps in order to follow or lead a partner through the playing area.
- **Psychomotor:** The child will demonstrate how best to imitate the actions of a penguin and then move to the teacher's directions and the words of an action rhyme.

Component of Health-Related Fitness

Cardiorespiratory endurance

Learning Task 1: Preparing Our Bodies to Move

Class organization: Children are scattered throughout general space.

Challenge the children to perform the following actions:

- The penguin has a long, pointed beak. What body part do you have that is like the penguin's beak? Can you *point* to it?
- The penguin's wings are at the sides of the body. Try to *flap* the two body parts you have at the sides of your body.
- Let's pretend you are a community of penguins *waddling* across the ice. See if you can *stand* tall like the king penguins that live in Antarctica, where it is very cold.
- Who can keep their legs *stiff* and take a tiny *step* forward with one leg? Now take a tiny *step* forward with the other leg.
- Penguins waddle along the ice by shifting one side of the body at a time. Show me how you can keep your arms at the sides of your body while you *waddle*.

Learning Task 2: Partner Challenge

Class organization: Partners are scattered in self-spaces.

One child stands behind his or her partner. The first child is the lead penguin and waddles throughout the playing area along the pathway of his or her choice. The second child follows the first child. Exchange roles.

Learning Task 3: Giant Iceberg

Class organization: Children are scattered throughout general space.

Markers are situated on the floor or ground to represent a large, imaginary iceberg. The children are challenged to stay on the iceberg and practice their waddling skills. At your signal, the penguins freeze (i.e., stop moving) and you decrease the size of the iceberg by moving the markers closer together. Challenge the children to continue waddling without touching another child's body. The activity continues until the iceberg becomes too small for all of the penguins. When the "iceberg melts" and becomes too small to hold them all, they jump off the iceberg into imaginary water. They use their arms as fins to swim to the safety of another iceberg (i.e., another designated area).

As a special treat, ask the children to imagine they are penguins and to act out the movements in the following rhyme:

Penguins *waddling* on the ice,
They think the ice is nice.
But the hot sunshine in the day,
Starts to *melt* the ice away.
Then, the ice becomes much too small,
Much too small to hold them all.
So they *slide* and *slide* and *leap*,
They all *splash* into the deep.
And they *swim* away a little faster,
Until they meet and *swim* once more,
On a *shivering* cold and icy shore.

Assessment Questions

1. Who can tell me how we can walk on slippery ice and not fall?
2. What body parts did you use to move like the penguin?
3. Can you think of another animal that lives where there is ice and snow? Let's try to imitate that animal's movements.

Academic Language Demands

- **Language function:** Uses language to react to the teacher's comparison of a human body to that of a penguin.
- **Vocabulary:** shift, waddle, flap, stiff, leap, slide, splash, swim, shiver, iceberg
- **Syntax or discourse:** A verbal interchange focusing on the words of an action rhyme that asks the children to perform seven movements to complete the activity.

EAGLES AND CHICKENS

National Standards Addressed

- **Standard 1.** The physically literate individual demonstrates competency in a variety of motor skills and movement patterns.
- **Standard 4.** The physically literate individual exhibits responsible personal and social behavior that respects self and others.

Instructional Materials/Props

Photographs of eagles and chickens and their habitat (optional)

Central Focus

To differentiate between the behavior and movements of two birds and find enjoyment in being expressive.

Objectives

- **Cognitive:** The child will make comparisons between eagles and chickens.
- **Affective:** The child will display cooperative and safe behavior with classmates when performing three vigorous roles.
- **Psychomotor:** The child will perform vigorous movement skills to successfully evade the chasers.

Component of Health-Related Fitness

Cardiorespiratory endurance

Learning Task 1: Preparing Our Bodies to Move

Class organization: Children are scattered throughout general space.

Present the following: *Let's see if you can tell me the difference between an eagle and a chicken after we perform the movements in our action story.*

One day, a young eaglet became lost in the barnyard of a chicken farm.

Not knowing any better, the eaglet thought that it must be a chicken.

So, it did all the things it saw the chickens do.

They *scratch* (children *scratch* the ground with toes of one foot three times),

And *peck* (children *make* pecking motions with their heads three times),

And *cluck* (children click their tongues as they *tip* their heads from side to side three times),

And *squawk* (children *squawk* three times),

And occasionally *cock-a-doodle-doo*, too (children *crow* cock-a-doodle-doo three times)!

The eagle *grew* larger and stronger (children *puff* out their chests).

It *grew* bigger than the chickens (children *stretch* outward).

It *grew* taller than the rooster (children *reach* upward).

And it could *run* and *jump* higher than any other bird (children *jump* up).

The eagle became very *sad* because it needed more space to run and jump.

One day, the eagle *looked* up and saw an eagle soaring in the sky.

It said, "Now, that is a BIG bird. I wonder whether I could fly like that."

So it *ran* as fast as it could (children *run* in place).

And it *flapped* its wings as hard as it could (children *flap* their arms).

And it *jumped* as high as it could (children *jump* up).

And it *flew* up into the air to the top of a tall mountain, where it saw many *proud* eagles.

And it began to do all the things that eagles do.

They *fly* (children *run flapping* their arms),

And *glide* (children *stretch* their arms out straight as they *run*),

And *swoop* (children *bend* and *move* their knees and bodies as though *swooping* down),

And *soar* (children *rise* on their toes and *reach* their arms straight up).

And one particular eagle, when no one is looking,

Will occasionally *cock-a-doodle-doo* (children *crow* cock-a-doodle-doo three times).

Learning Task 2: Partner Challenge

Class organization: Partners are scattered in self-spaces.

Present the following:

- A young bird learning to fly is called a fledgling.
- Together with a partner, practice short, low *jumps* as you *flap* your arms like wings.
- Continue by taking longer and higher *jumps* until you both *fly* around the playing area together.

Learning Task 3: Eagle's Nest

Class organization: Children are scattered in identified groups.

- Organize the children into three groups. One group performs the actions and behaviors of an eagle. The second group creates an eagle's nest, or aerie, which can be as large as 9 feet (2.7 m) in diameter and form a circle with their bodies. The third group pretends to be fish, an eagle's favorite food.
- On your signal, the eagles soar throughout general space, tagging as many fish as possible. When a fish is tagged, the fish is escorted to the nest by the eagle that tagged it. After all the fish are caught, the groups exchange roles.

Assessment Questions

1. Does anyone have a favorite bird that we did not talk about today? How does that bird move?
2. The chicken is a bird that has wings but cannot fly well. Show me how a chicken walks.
3. The eagle is able to see both forward and to the side at the same time. Who can think of a special ability that humans have?

Academic Language Demands:

- **Language function:** Uses language to describe several differences between a basic farm bird and a wild forest bird.
- **Vocabulary:** scratch, peck, cluck, flap, run, fly, glide, soar, swoop, aerie
- **Syntax or discourse:** A verbal interchange to identify the benefits of being strong or fast when considering imaginary characters.

SPIDER WEB FORMATIONS

National Standards Addressed

- **Standard 1.** The physically literate individual demonstrates competency in a variety of motor skills and movement patterns.
- **Standard 2.** The physically literate individual applies knowledge of concepts, principles, strategies and tactics related to movement and performance.

Instructional Materials/Props

Photographs of different types of spiders and their webs (optional)

Central Focus

To differentiate between wide and narrow shapes in a vigorous chase-and-flee activity.

Objectives

- **Cognitive:** The child will make comparisons between wide and narrow shapes.
- **Affective:** The child will happily link his or her body with a classmate's body to create a variety of wide shapes.
- **Psychomotor:** The child will maintain a wide shape as part of a large-group structure so that one or two children can safely walk through the structure.

Component of Health-Related Fitness

Cardiorespiratory endurance

Learning Task 1: Preparing Our Bodies to Move

Class organization: Children are scattered throughout general space.

Challenge the children to perform the following actions:

- How would you *stretch* your body into a wide shape? The distance between one hand and the other hand is long, which creates a wide shape. When we talk about objects being wide, we are describing a great distance from one side of the object to the other.
- Show me a wide shape at a low level.
- Can you *make* a thin, narrow shape at a low level?

Learning Task 2: Partner Challenge

Class organization: Partners are scattered in self-spaces.

Present the following:

- Is it possible to work with a partner and *use* both your bodies to *make* a wide shape at a high level? Try this at a low level while *lying* on the floor.
- How many wide shapes can you and your partner *create* at a low level?

Learning Task 3: Creating a Giant Spider Web

Class organization: Children are scattered in identified groups.

- Assign two children to be the chasers, or spiders. The rest of the children are flies, and they flee from the two spiders. Explain that as each child is tagged, he or she moves to a designated space in the spider's web (i.e., the playing area) and makes a wide shape while lying flat on the floor.
- Other children who are tagged join the first child, and combine their wide body shapes to form one giant spider web.
- Encourage the children to connect their bodies in a variety of positions (e.g., head to head, foot to knee, elbow to hand).
- After all flies are tagged, permit the two spiders to carefully walk through the web by stepping into the spaces between the children's bodies. Select new spiders each time the children perform this activity.

Assessment Questions

1. Who can identify different places where spiders might like to create spider webs (e.g., small trees, doorways, bushes, under houses)?
2. Can you show me a wide shape using only your legs? Why was it important to form a wide body shape, and not a narrow shape, when you are forming the spider web?
3. How much floor space would be covered if the flies formed narrow shapes instead of wide shapes?

Academic Language Demands

- **Language function:** Uses language to differentiate between wide and narrow shapes.
- **Vocabulary:** wide, narrow, spider web
- **Syntax or discourse:** A verbal interchange to reinforce that it is safest when all children maintain a wide shape after being tagged in the whole-group learning task since the spiders will walk through the web at the end of the activity.

INSECTS AND BUGS

National Standards Addressed

Standard 5. The physically literate individual recognizes the value of physical activity for health, enjoyment, challenge, self-expression and/or social interaction.

Instructional Materials/Props

Photographs of large insects and bugs in their habitat (optional), mat or padded floor covering (optional)

Central Focus

To make comparisons and demonstrate relationships between the human body and insect body.

Objectives

- **Cognitive:** The child will name insects and bugs that creep, squirm, wiggle, or crawl and be introduced to additional bugs and insects having unique characteristics.
- **Affective:** The child will praise his or her partner for the ability to follow while marching throughout the playing area.
- **Psychomotor:** The child will work with classmates to use their bodies to create three large bugs or insects and coordinate their movements so that the bugs and insects are recognizable to other classmates and the teacher.

Component of Health-Related Fitness

Flexibility

Learning Task 1: Preparing Our Bodies to Move

Class organization: Children are scattered throughout general space.

Challenge the children to perform the following actions:

- Can you name things that move by creeping, squirming, wiggling, or crawling? There are millions of insects, and it would be impossible to name them all. We can participate in a physical activity to learn more about insects. For example, crickets hear with their legs. *Touch* the body part we use to hear sounds. *Show* me ways we use our legs.
- Insects have feelers called antennae. They can smell food with their antennae. *Tap* the body part we use to smell foods. How do you *move* when you smell bread baking in the oven?
- Insects breathe through holes in their sides. Take a deep breath and *point* to the body parts we use for breathing. Can you *run* in your personal space until you are breathing very quickly?
- Insects use the hair on their bodies to taste and feel things. *Wiggle* the body part we use to taste food and *shake* the body parts we use to feel objects.
- Termites make nests in the soil. These nests have many tunnels. Can you *make* your body into a tunnel shape?
- Pretend you are a firefly *hiding* in the daylight. Make believe it is dark and *use* your light to find other fireflies.
- Bugs have a stylet which is their mouth shaped like a straw to drink liquids from plants and flowers. Show me how you would *drink* a large glass of milk.

Learning Task 2: **Partner Challenge**

Class organization: Partners are scattered in self-spaces.

Present the following: *Army ants are always moving and searching for food. In lands where it is hot, they march in large groups.* Encourage each set of partners to march throughout the playing area, one partner in front of the other. On your signal, partners exchange roles and then join other sets of partners to march along.

Learning Task 3: **Big Bugs and Insects**

Class organization: Children are scattered in identified groups.

Present the following: *You can work together in groups to form large bugs and insects with your bodies.*

Dragonfly: The dragonfly is a swift-flying, graceful insect that patrols the edges of streams and ponds. You can recognize it by its jeweled eyes that cover more than half of its head. The dragonfly has two pairs of transparent wings, six legs, and a long slender body. It also has two sets of jaws, with piercing teeth to eat mosquitoes and blackflies. Divide the children into groups of three and ask each group to create a dragonfly by forming a behind-line. The first two children in line extend their arms at the side of the body to represent the dragonfly's wings. The third child reaches over the second child and grasps the shoulders of the first child. The three children coordinate leg movements to move and fly forward.

Tarantula: The tarantula is a spider that lives on the ground, where it digs deep burrows. It is known for its hairy body, painful bite, a body 3 inches (7.6 cm) long, and legs 5 inches (13 cm) long. Like other spiders, the tarantula has four pairs of legs. To create a make-believe tarantula, groups of four children huddle close together, with their arms on each other's shoulders. Each group moves throughout the playing area by coordinating leg movements and keeping their heads close together to represent the tarantula's body.

Centipede: The centipede is a wormlike bug that has one head, three mouths, one pair of antennae, two front claws, and a segmented body that can grow to 12 inches (30.5 cm) long. By day, they live under rocks or in the bark of trees. Most types of centipedes have 10 pairs of legs, although some families may have as many as 177 legs. To form a centipede, groups of five children form a behind-line. Each child curls his or her body slightly forward to grasp the thighs of the child standing in front. The group slowly moves forward. If a mat or floor covering is available, the children can form a behind-line, kneel down, and grasp the ankles of the child in front. In this position, the groups move forward in a slow shuffling motion.

Assessment Questions

1. Is it possible to form groups of three and create an imaginary insect?
2. Can you find a way for your imaginary insect to move from one space to another space?
3. Today you learned about many types of insect, bugs, and spiders, and how they move. Who can recall three facts we learned today?

Academic Language Demands

- **Language function:** Uses language to identify characteristics of four large bugs or insects familiar to this age level.
- **Vocabulary:** creep, squirm, wiggle, crawl, curl, grasp, huddle, march, antennae, transparent, burrow, segmented, insect, bug
- **Syntax or discourse:** A verbal interchange comparing parts of an insect's body with the corresponding part of a human's body.

BUMBLEBEES

National Standards Addressed

- **Standard 1.** The physically literate individual demonstrates competency in a variety of motor skills and movement patterns.
- **Standard 2.** The physically literate individual applies knowledge of concepts, principles, strategies and tactics related to movement and performance.

Instructional Materials/Props

Six or seven bean bags or similar small objects that can be gripped, lively background music

Central Focus

To make comparisons between the child's own body parts and a bee's anatomy while participating in a variety of physical learning tasks.

Objectives

- **Cognitive:** The child will discover similarities and differences between his or her body and that of a bumblebee.
- **Affective:** The child will show an appreciation for his or her partner's creative dance and freely imitate those movements before exchanging roles.
- **Psychomotor:** The child will vigorously move from classmate to classmate by using rapid arm movements for an extended period of time before exchanging roles and assuming a stance that focuses on moderate movements.

Component of Health-Related Fitness

Cardiorespiratory endurance

Learning Task 1: Preparing Our Bodies to Move

Class organization: Children are scattered throughout general space.

Challenge the children to perform the following actions:

- We can learn how the bumblebee's body is like or unlike our own body. Bumblebees have two sets of eyes on each side of their head. *Point* to your own eyes. How many sets of eyes do you have (one set)?
- Bees hear through antennae. *Touch* the body parts we use to hear sounds. The bee's stinger projects from its abdomen. Can you *rub* your abdomen?
- The bee's skeleton is on the outside of its body. Our skeleton is on the inside of our body. Find a way to *stretch* your fingers to make your hand very wide, and *point* to a bone inside your hand.
- We use our legs to walk. Bees use their wings to fly. The buzzing sound is made from the rapid movement of the wings. Can you *place* two closed fists in front of your chest to form the wings of the bee? Who can *make* the movement and the buzzing sound of the bee?

Learning Task 2: Partner Challenge

Class organization: Partners are scattered in self-spaces.

Present the following:

- People talk or communicate through their mouths or with their hands. Bees communicate by dancing. The tail-wagging dance, which looks like a wiggle, tells other bees where to find food.
- While working in sets of partners, one partner performs what he or she thinks the tail-wagging dance might look like and the other bee imitates the first partner's movements. Exchange roles.

Learning Task 3: Bee Activities

Class organization: Children are scattered in identified groups.

Present the following:

Collecting pollen: Divide the children into two groups. Children in the first group join hands and form a large round circle, representing the opening to a beehive. The remaining children display the actions and sounds of the bees as they fly around collecting pollen (i.e., beanbags or other small objects). The bees take the pollen to the beehive. The children exchange roles after the pollen is collected.

Bee's sonnet: Organize the children into two groups. One half of the children pretend to be flowers scattered throughout the playing area. The remainder of the children assumes the role of bees and fly to each flower as lively music plays. Exchange roles.

Balancing bee: Encourage the children to move at different levels throughout general space. On your signal, the children hover (i.e., freeze) and balance on one foot.

Flight of the bumblebee: Encourage the children to move to lively music as you signal fun actions that are characteristic of bees, such as bee quick, bee fast, bee round (e.g., tiny, fast, light, and at a high, medium, or low level) while moving throughout the general space.

Assessment Questions

1. The bee needs to move its wings very quickly to keep its body in the air. Show me how quickly you are able to move your arms.
2. What body parts can we exercise in order to move more quickly (e.g., legs)? Can you exercise your legs?
3. Which activities were the most challenging? Why?

Academic Language Demands

- **Language function:** Uses language to identify parts of the bee and how these parts contribute to the bee's survival.
- **Vocabulary:** wiggle, wag, scatter, collect, tiny, fast, light, levels, hover, skeleton, pollen, beehive, abdomen
- **Syntax or discourse:** A verbal interchange to determine when to switch roles and to use this knowledge to assume another activity related to bees.

LIFE CYCLE OF THE BUTTERFLY

National Standards Addressed

Standard 1. The physically literate individual demonstrates competency in a variety of motor skills and movement patterns.

Instructional Materials/Props

Two crepe paper streamers per child, photographs of flowers displayed throughout the playing area

Central Focus

To discover the four phases of the life cycle of the butterfly and to engage in activities experienced during their life span.

Objectives

- **Cognitive:** The child will remember the four stages of the life cycle of the butterfly.
- **Affective:** The child will show an appreciation for reenacting the life cycle of the butterfly when using his or her own body to demonstrate the major steps in the process.
- **Psychomotor:** The child will use props to assist in making vigorous arm movements imitating the wings of a butterfly and will demonstrate the ability to dart, dash, and use different pathways in his or her attempt to evade a chaser.

Components of Health-Related Fitness

Cardiorespiratory endurance, flexibility

Learning Task 1: Preparing Our Bodies to Move

Class organization: Children are scattered throughout general space.

Present the following: *The word butterfly comes from the Old English word "buter-fleoge," which means butter and flying creature. The butterfly goes through four stages of development.* Challenge the children to perform the following actions:

- The first stage is the egg. Eggs are tiny and can be round, oval, cylindrical, or other shapes. Can you *curl* your body into the shape of a butterfly egg?
- Inside each egg is a caterpillar. The caterpillar has 16 legs, a hairy back, and small eyes and mouth. Show me how you *wiggle* your body like a soft caterpillar.
- The caterpillar pushes out of the egg and immediately begins to eat, growing rapidly. This is the larval stage. The caterpillar's main activity is eating, and as it grows, it becomes too large for its skin. The caterpillar sheds its outer skin, called the exoskeleton, and develops new skin. Can you show me how the caterpillar *pushes* out of its egg, eats, and then *sheds* its skin?
- The third stage of the development of the butterfly is the pupa stage. When the caterpillar becomes an adult, usually after two weeks, it finds a high twig or leaf, hangs on, usually upside down, and covers its body with a sticky liquid. This shiny liquid hardens to become a gold-colored shell. Demonstrate the caterpillar in this pupa stage by *shaping* your body into the letter J. This is the shape of the chrysalis when suspended from the twig or leaf.
- The butterfly is now ready to emerge from the pupa. Its wings are damp and crinkled. Try to free yourself from your chrysalis and show how you practice *flapping* your wings until they unfold and are ready for flight.

Learning Task 2: Partner Challenge

Class organization: Partners are scattered in self-spaces.

Present the following: With a partner, one child skips in the yard (i.e., playing area) trying to catch his or her partner, who is a butterfly flying from one flower to another. When the child touches the butterfly on the shoulder or back, partners exchange roles.

Learning Task 3: Butterfly Activities

Class organization: Children are scattered in identified groups.

Flight of the butterfly: Explain to the children that butterflies flutter and fly to flowers, using their proboscis, a long sucking tube, to suck nectar and other liquids. Provide each child with two streamers to flutter as they fly throughout the playing area. Ask the children to fly to flowers displayed on walls.

Butterfly chase and flee: Tell the children that butterflies have enemies called predators, which include birds and other insects. Many butterflies protect themselves by blending into the colors of their surroundings. Give each child two crepe paper streamers to serve as wings. Select two children to be birds that will fly throughout the playing area. The other children are butterflies who flutter and fly. When the butterfly feels that it will be captured (i.e., touched) by a bird, the butterfly freezes (i.e., blends into its surroundings). If the butterfly is caught, it exchanges its wings with the bird and flies away.

Assessment Questions

1. Why do you think people enjoy watching butterflies?
2. What happens to the wings of the butterfly when it first emerges from the chrysalis? Show me.
3. Who can identify different stages of our life cycle we will go through, beginning with being a baby (e.g., baby, child, teenager, and adult)?

Academic Language Demands

- **Language function:** Uses language to identify the life cycle of the butterfly.
- **Vocabulary:** curl, wiggle, push, shed, flap, flutter, larval stage, exoskeleton, chrysalis, pupa stage, proboscis, predator
- **Syntax or discourse:** A verbal interchange focusing on the word *predators* in the whole--group learning task.

HORSES

National Standards Addressed

- **Standard 1.** The physically literate individual demonstrates competency in a variety of motor skills and movement patterns.
- **Standard 2.** The physically literate individual applies knowledge of concepts, principles, strategies and tactics related to movement and performance.

Instructional Materials/Props

Photographs of various types of horses (optional)

Central Focus

To identify and exercise a variety of actions associated with specific types of horses.

Objectives

- **Cognitive:** The child will draw upon prior knowledge of horses and build on that awareness with new information regarding how different horses move.
- **Affective:** The child will actively attempt to tag his or her partner, who is in an imagery role and needs to be rescued.
- **Psychomotor:** The child will eagerly take part in an action rhyme that encourages the child to use a variety of locomotor skills in order to learn about how different horses move.

Component of Health-Related Fitness

Cardiorespiratory endurance

Learning Task 1: Preparing Our Bodies to Move

Class organization: Children are scattered throughout general space.

Challenge the children to perform the following actions:

- Pretend you are a pony *galloping* around in a large circle. This is the way many horses are trained.
- Who can *prance* like a show horse that *lifts* its legs with a lively step?
- Can you act as if you are a tired work horse *plodding* along with a slow and heavy step back to the stable?

Learning Task 2: Partner Challenge

Class organization: Partners are scattered in self-spaces.

Present the following: *On a ranch, cowboys and cowgirls round up, or gather, cattle that wander away from the others.* One partner pretends to ride a horse, chasing after the partner who is a runaway cow. When the rider tags the runaway cow, both exchange roles.

Learning Task 3: Horse Actions

Class organization: Children are scattered throughout general space.

Present the following: *We can use our bodies and learn how different kinds of horses move. Can you begin by making the sound of horses' hooves by slapping your legs with your hands? Now, let's see who can move like different horses.*

Wild mustangs *run* free,

Galloping across the open prairie.

Can you *gallop* and keep one foot in front of your body?

>Bucking broncos *jump* and *kick,*

>As if *jumping* on a pogo stick.

>Show me how you can *jump* up and down like a *bucking* bronco.

Beautiful show horses stand tall as they *prance.*

It sometimes looks like a fancy *dance.*

How would you *prance* around our playing area like a proud show horse?

>Tiny, *prancing* Shetland ponies are small.

>Giant, *plodding* work horses are tall.

>If you can, *prance* while being small. Now, to be tall, *stretch* upward like the work horse.

Cowboys and cowgirls *ride* horses to *chase* cows.

Work horses are used on farms to *pull* heavy plows.

Is it possible to *move* like a cowboy or cowgirl *riding* on a horse?

>Thoroughbred horses love to gallop in a horse race.

>They *gallop* around an oval track at a fast pace.

>How quickly can you *gallop* on an oval-shaped track like a race horse?

Merry-go-round horses *move* up and down,

As the carousel goes round and round.

Who can raise and lower their body while *moving* in a circle like the merry-go-round horse?

>Rocking horses can move fast or slow.

>You are its rider calling out "Giddyup" or "Whoa."

>Try *rocking* back and forth by *shifting* your weight from one foot to the other.

Real horses *stomp* their feet and *paw* the ground,

Then *leap* and *jump*, *bucking* all around.

Who can *leap* forward? Now *jump* and *buck* by *stretching* your body.

>Horses also *walk, run, trot,* and *jump.*

>Then *shake* all over, from their head to their rump.

>Determine the best way to *walk*, then *run*, and finally *trot* like a horse.

Assessment Questions

1. Can you name another animal that also can gallop (e.g., dog, zebra, rhinoceros, buffalo, cow)?
2. Who can tell me why many people think horses are special animals?
3. Of all the horses that you pretended to be to, which would you like to have at your home? Why?

Academic Language Demands

- **Language function:** Uses language to describe the similarities and differences in the way specific horses move and behave.
- **Vocabulary:** slap, gallop, jump, buck, prance, kick, plod, rock, cattle, bronco, rump, trot
- **Syntax or discourse:** A verbal interchange emphasizing why and how horses are distinctive animals and can serve various purposes.

LEARNING ABOUT NATURE

National Standards Addressed

Standard 1. The physically literate individual demonstrates competency in a variety of motor skills and movement patterns.

Instructional Materials/Props

Photographs of animals in their natural environment (optional)

Central Focus

To use the body to form animal homes and the objects naturalists use.

Objectives

- **Cognitive:** The child will describe the role of the naturalist and the outdoor environment.
- **Affective:** The child willingly uses his or her body to create the shape of an animal's home and exchange roles when asked.
- **Psychomotor:** The child will demonstrate how classmates' bodies can be linked and intertwined to form the shape of common insect and animal homes found in nature.

Component of Health-Related Fitness

Flexibility

Learning Task 1: Preparing Our Bodies to Move

Class organization: Children are scattered throughout general space.

Challenge the children to perform the following actions:

- A naturalist is a person who knows all about outdoor life and can identify insects, animals, birds, and other living creatures. Make believe you are putting on a backpack. Let's *carry* a camera to take photos of nature and *tuck* a map into our pocket.
- Can you *rub* on sunscreen and *put* on a hat and sunglasses?
- *Hop* inside the jeep, *buckle* your seatbelt, and off we go for our adventure.
- Our first stop is the duck pond. Can you *quack* and *waddle* like a duck? Use your body to *form* the shape of a duck's pond.
- Insects live in the grass. *Stand* tall and pretend to be blades of grass.

Learning Task 2: Partner Challenge

Class organization: Partners are scattered in self-spaces.

Present the following: *Squirrels find holes in tall trees to build their homes in. Select a partner. With your bodies,* create *a tree and find a way to* make *a home for the squirrel.*

Learning Task 3: **Homes Found in Nature**

Class organization: Children are scattered in general space.

Present the following: *You can use your bodies and imaginations to create the homes of several creatures.*

   Wasp's nest: Point to an imaginary gray nest hanging just below a tree branch. Tell the children that some wasps make their nests out of a papery substance, which is dry wood moistened into a paste. Explain that they can make a paper wasp's nest by forming a large circle and stretching their arms either up or down. Ask three or four wasps to fly around inside the nest.

   Bird's nest: Ask the children to use make-believe binoculars and look up to the bird's nest. Challenge them to discover a way to make a round bird's nest with their bodies. One or two children can form tiny egg shapes in the middle of the nest.

   Lily pads: Explain that certain plants floating on top of the pond are called lily pads. Frogs jump and land on lily pads. Half of the children make several lily pads by sitting face to face in pairs with their legs stretched in a wide shape and their toes touching. The rest of the children pretend to be frogs and jump throughout the playing area. Every frog should land on at least two lily pads.

   Here are names for the homes of other animals:

- **Rabbit:** burrow
- **Spider:** web
- **Snake:** nest
- **Bear:** cave
- **Bee:** hive

Assessment Questions

1. Is it possible to work with a partner and create a home for your pet?
2. Who can think of something else we might need to bring when exploring in the woods?
3. Can you name three more living creatures we might find on a walk in the woods? What do you think their home would look like? Show me with your bodies.

Academic Language Demands

- **Language function:** Uses language and their bodies to explore an imaginary environment and several creatures that live in the forest.
- **Vocabulary:** pack, hop, rub, waddle, jump, land, lily pad, wasp
- **Syntax or discourse:** A verbal interchange giving suggestions about how to best create the home of the imaginary animal or insect.

CHAPTER 8

Moving With Words & Actions in Science and Math

Science education for young children aims to increase their understanding of their communities, local environments, and living creatures common to their region. In this chapter, the lesson plans help children apply their curiosity to learning how objects and living things move. This includes participating in learning tasks that focus on areas such as energy, water, forestry, weather, and rock formations. In addition, the lessons offer science learning tasks relating to colorful natural objects, machines, our solar system, and dinosaurs. These science-related challenges are followed by a series of tasks designed to increase children's interest in learning about numbers, shapes, measurement, size, relationship, and time. In a physically literate sense, the children will combine movement and locomotor skills with mathematical concepts for a meaningful and fun experience.

Science

SUBSTANCES, SURFACES, AND TEXTURES

National Standards Addressed

Standard 1. The physically literate individual demonstrates competency in a variety of motor skills and movement patterns.

Instructional Materials/Props

Sample objects to represent different types of substances, surfaces, and textures listed throughout the lesson plan (e.g., fuzzy, sticky, sharp, smooth, rough, slick) (optional)

Central Focus

To differentiate between unique surfaces and substances while imitating movements associated with specific surfaces and substances.

Objectives

- **Cognitive:** The child will associate surfaces and substances with specific objects having those unique characteristics.
- **Affective:** The child will express an interest in participating actively when it is his or her turn to respond.
- **Psychomotor:** The child will imitate the action or movements that coincide with the texture that he or she has been given.

Component of Health-Related Fitness

Cardiorespiratory endurance

Learning Task 1: Preparing Our Bodies to Move

Class organization: Children are scattered throughout general space.

Present the following: *One way to learn about our environment is by exploring as many surfaces and substances as possible. The word "surface" refers to the outside covering of an object. The word "substance" refers to what something is made from, and "texture" describes how something feels when you touch it.* Offer the children the following questions and challenges:

- Who can describe their favorite plaything? Can you describe its shape and color and how to use it for play?
- Is your favorite object fuzzy and soft, or hard and smooth?
- I will say a word that describes how something feels when it is touched or used. For example: I am thinking of **fuzzy** objects or things. Show me how you *hug* a teddy bear. (The children should respond by pretending to *squeeze* a stuffed fuzzy bear.)
  - Who can use a make-believe fuzzy **cotton ball** to *powder* their face like a clown?
  - Put on your fuzzy **mittens** and make believe you are *building* a snowperson.
  - *Pull* on your fuzzy winter **cap** or **hat** and *roll* in the snow.
  - Make believe you are *shaking* a round, fuzzy **rug**.
- Now I am thinking of **sticky** objects or things.
  - Pretend your body is **bubble gum** being *chewed*.
  - *Show* me sticky **fingers**.

- What would happen if both hands were covered in sticky **glue** and you *touched* your ankles?
- How would you *move* if it were a hot, muggy, sticky day?

- Now I am thinking of **sharp** objects or things.
  - Use a make-believe **knife** to *cut* a banana into slices.
  - *Shoot* an **arrow** from a bow into a target.
  - *Thread* a **needle** and pretend to *sew* a pair of pants.
  - Walk as if you have a sharp **pain** in one leg.

Learning Task 2: Partner Challenge

Class organization: Partners are scattered in self-spaces.

Present the following: *Now, we will play a partner challenge activity, and you will take turns acting out the responses to my instructions.* With a partner, one child acts out the first response followed by the second partner performing the second response, and so on. When you ask the children to think of an additional object at the end of a set of responses, partners help each other identify an additional object. For example: Now I am thinking of **smooth** objects and things. Partners might respond as follows:

- Partner 1: *Swing* a baseball **bat** and *hit* a home run.
- Partner 2: *Feel* the **skin** on your face and arms.
- Partner 1: Pretend to *pat* a cat's **fur**.
- Partner 2: Make believe that you are ice *skating* on a smooth **pond**.
- Both partners: Can you and your partner think of other **smooth** objects?

Following are sample textures and cues.

- I am thinking of **rough** objects and things.
  - Use **sandpaper** to *polish* a wooden chair.
  - Show me how a bulldozer *pushes* **gravel** into large piles.
  - Can you use a shovel to *fill* a pail with **dirt**?
  - Make believe you are *shaving* a **beard** from your face.
  - Can you and your partner think of other **rough** objects?

- I am thinking of **slick** objects and things.
  - Make believe you are *swimming* in a brook filled with slick **rocks**.
  - How would you *walk* on a slippery **sidewalk**?
  - *Drive* a sled over the slick **ice**.
  - Show me how you *position* your body when you are moving down a **slide**.
  - Can you and your partner think of other **slick** objects?

- I am thinking of some special **substances** found in or near our home.
  - Show me how **Jell-O** *moves* when you eat it.
  - *Spread* **peanut butter** on two slices of bread.
  - Is it possible to *make* your body light and fluffy like **whipped cream**?
  - Make believe you are *stirring* a large pot of **vegetable soup**.
  - Show me how **sand** *runs* through your fingers at the beach.
  - Can you *shape* and *pat* a **mud pie**?
  - Can you and your partner think of other special **substances**?

Learning Task 3: **Surface Creations**

Class organization: Children are scattered in identified groups.

Divide the class into four groups. When you call out a word to describe a surface, the children in each group combine their bodies to form a favorite plaything that has that type of surface (e.g., fuzzy, rough, smooth, sharp). Groups show off their creations and others see whether they can identify the play object.

Assessment Questions:

1. Move like your favorite object that we discussed today.
2. Can you think of an object that has a wooden surface that you can move on?
3. See whether you can identify one more object that you find at home that has a special surface. Work together with your classmates to create that object with your bodies.

Academic Language Demands

- **Language function:** Uses language to generate ideas about how best to move to reflect a specified texture or substance.
- **Vocabulary:** squeeze, pull, push, shake, roll, swing, and names of substances, surfaces, and texture types
- **Syntax or discourse:** A verbal interchange focused on creating the best possible plaything with the type of surface that you've assigned.

POWER SOURCES

National Standards Addressed

- **Standard 1.** The physically literate individual demonstrates competency in a variety of motor skills and movement patterns.
- **Standard 3.** The physically literate individual demonstrates the knowledge and skills to achieve and maintain a health-enhancing level of physical activity and fitness.

Instructional Materials/Props

Poster that reads "Race Car, Airplane, Train" (optional)

Central Focus

To imitate the movements associated with small objects that use batteries and to participate in a vigorous learning task.

Objectives

- **Cognitive:** The child will name objects that use batteries and restate why we use batteries.
- **Affective:** The child will accept constructive criticism from a partner after he or she has moved vigorously for one minute and asks for feedback based on the observations of his or her partner.
- **Psychomotor:** The child will reproduce the movements of three objects that move vigorously until becoming fatigued and will imagine that he or she is being energized in order to proceed onward.

Component of Health-Related Fitness

Cardiorespiratory endurance

Learning Task 1: Preparing Our Bodies to Move

Class organization: Children are scattered throughout general space.

Challenge the children to perform the following actions:

- Who can tell me why we use batteries (e.g., to make things go)?
- Show me what a battery looks like.
- Can you use your body to *create* types of toys that use batteries (e.g., airplanes, trains, robots, trucks, remote control cars)?
- Who can name an object in their home that uses batteries? Find a way to *move* your body like that object (e.g., clock's hands, flashlight).
- Let me see how your body *moves* when it is feeling strong and energized.
- How does your body *move* when it is tired and needs to rest?

Learning Task 2: **Partner Challenge**

Class organization: Partners are scattered in self-spaces.

After children have selected partners, one partner runs in place as quickly as possible. The other child observes what happens when the child running starts to get tired (e.g., speed slows, breathing rate increases). Signal the children to exchange roles after one minute. Children discuss their observations with their partners.

Learning Task 3: **Energizers**

Class organization: Children are scattered in identified groups.

- Select several children to be "rechargers." All other children scatter throughout the playing area and assume the role of a nonworking battery that must be "energized" by a recharger.
- The rechargers run or gallop to each stationary battery. The recharger crosses his or her hands and gently lays them on top of the battery or the battery's shoulders. The recharger counts to three and loudly says, "Energized." At that moment, the energized battery moves throughout the playing area by pretending to be a race car. At some point, the child fatigues and finally stops. He or she remains stationary until a recharger approaches and reenergizes his or her battery.
- After being recharged a second time, the child is free to move by pretending to be an airplane flying throughout the playing area. Upon fatiguing and stopping for the third time, the child is energized and moves like a train chugging throughout the playing area.
- A recharger should have a turn at being a battery before the learning task is completed.

Assessment Questions

1. Our body needs healthy foods to stay energized. Who can name some of these healthy foods?
2. Is it possible to use another word to describe being energized (e.g., charged, boosted, motivated, powered-up)?
3. Can you show me three movements that tell me your body is strong and healthy?

Academic Language Demands

- **Language function:** Uses language to discuss ways that we can reserve our energy so we don't become tired too quickly.
- **Vocabulary:** fly, chug, energize, recharge
- **Syntax or discourse:** A verbal interchange focusing on the actions and movements of how three objects move in vigorous ways.

WAVE ACTIONS

National Standards Addressed

Standard 4. The physically literate individual exhibits responsible personal and social behavior that respects self and others.

Instructional Materials/Props

Photos of oceanic waves (optional)

Central Focus

To gain an understanding of water movement by depicting the action of a wave individually and while working in a group.

Objectives

- **Cognitive:** The child will explain the basic action and transfer of energy made by ocean waves.
- **Affective:** The child will be considerate of his or her partner's ability to jump while imagining that the two of them are jumping into a variety of ocean waves.
- **Psychomotor:** The child will participate and assist classmates when the group uses their bodies to create three types of wave motions. This will require timing and, in some cases, basic strength.

Component of Health-Related Fitness

Flexibility

Learning Task 1: Preparing Our Bodies to Move

Class organization: Children are scattered throughout general space.

Present the following: *Today we will use our bodies to learn about waves. Waves are made from water. They begin far at sea when the wind blows. As the waves are pushed to the land, the ocean's floor stops the water from moving. The wave topples onto the land.* Challenge the children to perform the following actions:

- Let's make the movement of a wave by *swinging* both of our arms back and forth. Try not to move your feet.
- Can you make your whole body *sway* back and forth without moving your arms and feet?
- Use your arms to make a *tumbling* action in front of your body. Your hands should move in circles to make this movement.
- Show me how you can *lie* at a low level and *roll* your body like a wave coming to shore.
- Is it possible to *roll* at a low level again and *open* your body into a wide shape when you stop? *Lie* very still.

Learning Task 2: Partner Challenge

Class organization: Partners are scattered in self-spaces.

Present the following: *At the beach we should always enter the water with a buddy.* Challenge the children to perform the following actions.

- With a partner, *hold* hands as you *jump* together into the waves.
- Discover new ways to *jump* with your partner into the waves.

Learning Task 3: Special Waves

Class organization: Children are scattered in identified groups.

Present the following:

Wave: Explain that the children can work together to create one large wave. To form the first wave, the children form a side-by-side line and all grasp hands. On the count of three, the first child in line raises his or her hand followed by the next person in line raising his or her hand high. The next child immediately raises his or her hand until everyone's hand is raised.

Big Wave: Ask the children to stoop in a side-by-side line. Hands remain clasped. On the count of three, the first child stands up, slowly pulling on the hand of the next child, who rises, followed by the next child rising until all of the children are standing.

Breaker Wave: The children form this wave by kneeling in a side-by-side line without holding hands. The first child in line falls forward and breaks the fall by moving his or her hands forward to lower the body slowly. Encourage the children to bend their elbows as they lower their bodies. After the first child begins to fall forward, the second child begins the action, and so forth until all the children have all fallen forward.

Assessment Questions

1. Who can think of places where we play in the waves (e.g., sea, ocean, lake, beach, pond, pool)?
2. Can you show me how you use your body to swim in the waves?
3. Why is it important to play in large waves only when an adult is close by?

Academic Language Demands

- **Language function:** Uses language to explain the action and movements made by ocean waves.
- **Vocabulary:** topple, swing, sway, tumble, jump, grasp, high and low levels, tide, breaker wave, break
- **Syntax or discourse:** A verbal interchange aimed at convincing classmates of the importance of good timing when performing movement tasks.

UNDERSEA TRAVEL

National Standards Addressed

Standard 2. The physically literate individual applies knowledge of concepts, principles, strategies and tactics related to movement and performance.

Instructional Materials/Props

Photographs of submarines (optional)

Central Focus

To adjust one's level while moving throughout the playing area.

Objectives

- **Cognitive:** The child will develop an awareness of the body's ability to move at different horizontal planes or levels.
- **Affective:** The child will actively take part in the creation of a large structure and happily participate with group members when moving efficiently at different levels throughout the playing area.
- **Psychomotor:** The child will assemble an imaginary submarine by combining his or her body with a small group of friends' bodies and be able to move at different levels through obstacles.

Component of Health-Related Fitness

Muscular strength and endurance

Learning Task 1: Preparing Our Bodies to Move

Class organization: Children are scattered throughout general space.

Challenge the children to perform the following actions:

- A submarine is a type of ship that can travel underwater. The prefix "sub" means under or below. Submarines have propellers that force the hull or body of the submarine forward. Can you *rotate* your arms like propellers and *move* slowly throughout the playing area?
- See if you can change the depth of your submarine and *move* at a low level near the bottom of the ocean.
- Now try to *surface* at a high level.
- A periscope is a tool that helps people see objects above the water. It is a long tube that can be raised, lowered, or moved in any direction. *Raise* your arm like a periscope at a high level. *Turn* from side to side so you can see the surface of the water. Lower the periscope down to a medium level.

Learning Task 2: **Partner Challenge**

Class organization: Partners are scattered in self-spaces.

Present the following: *A recreational submarine is a small submarine used for fun or studying underwater life.* Each child finds a partner. Some partners form submarines by holding onto the shoulders of their partner and traveling underwater. Other partners place their arms behind their backs and become a school of fish traveling together for those in the sub to view. Encourage submarines to travel close to the fish without making contact. Exchange roles.

Learning Task 3: **Submarines**

Class organization: Children are scattered in identified groups.

Divide the children into two groups. One group scatters throughout the playing area and pretends to be waves by rocking their bodies back and forth. The remainder of the children use their arms as propellers to move around the waves. Encourage the submarines to move at different levels. Exchange roles.

Challenge groups of children to create two or three submarines by using one hand to hold onto the shoulder of the person in front. The other hand acts like a propeller. Each submarine should try to remain in a long narrow shape as it moves at different levels throughout the playing area.

Assessment Questions

1. Who can name activities we do at a low level?
2. Show me two ways to stretch the body to a high level.
3. What objects and things might you see if you were traveling in a real submarine? Can you move like one of those objects or things?

Academic Language Demands

- **Language function:** Uses language to identify and describe movements that a submarine makes, as well as the parts of a submarine.
- **Vocabulary:** high, medium, low levels; submarine, propellers, periscope, hull, surface
- **Syntax or discourse:** A verbal interchange focusing on the understanding that a person's body can change levels (low, medium, and high) and that numerous activities can be performed at each level.

LIFE CYCLE OF A TREE

National Standards Addressed

Standard 1. The physically literate individual demonstrates competency in a variety of motor skills and movement patterns.

Instructional Materials/Props

Photographs of a forest (optional)

Central Focus

To use the body to imitate the life cycle of a tree.

Objectives

- **Cognitive:** The child will recall the growth process of a tree and individuals who benefit from products made from trees.
- **Affective:** The child will interact with a partner and grasp hands to pretend they are cutting down an imaginary tree.
- **Psychomotor:** The child will roll and manipulate classmates' bodies in order to move them from one place to another place in general space.

Component of Health-Related Fitness

Muscular strength and endurance

Learning Task 1: Preparing Our Bodies to Move

Class organization: Children are scattered throughout general space.

Challenge the children to perform the following actions:

- *Make* yourself into a small seedling planted deep into the ground. Show me how you begin to *grow* until you are a large tree and can provide shade.
- What happens as the season changes? Can you show me how the wind blows your leaves and *moves* your branches?
- The snow is falling. Who can show how their branches freeze by *making* their muscles very tight?
- The lumberjack is here and is cutting us down. Try *stretching* your arms over your head to make yourself into a long log. Is it possible to *roll* to the river and *float* to the sawmill?
- Can you *use* your body to show me the type of product you have become (e.g., firewood, a wooden table, wood blocks, a wooden toy train, a folded newspaper)?

Learning Task 2: **Partner Challenge**

Class organization: Partners are scattered in self-spaces.

Present the following: *Lumberjacks work together to cut down trees. A two-person crosscut saw has wood handles on either end so that lumberjacks can push and pull the saw back and forth between them as the sharp teeth of the saw cut down a tree or saw a downed tree into pieces. With your partner,* grasp *hands and pretend you are lumberjacks* sawing *together back and forth to cut down a tree.*

Learning Task 3: **Timb-er-r**

Class organization: Children are scattered in identified groups.

- Designate one-third of the children to be lumberjacks. These children act as chasers and move through the forest looking for trees.

- The remaining children are trees and flee from the lumberjacks. When a tree is tagged, the lumberjack yells, "Timb-er-r!" and the tagged tree collapses to the ground in a long, narrow log shape.

- After all of the trees are tagged and lying in a log position, the lumberjacks stoop to the floor and roll each log to the specified river area. When all the trees have been rolled to the river, the children make believe they are planting more trees so that the activity can begin again.

Assessment Questions

1. Who can tell my why it is important to plant trees after cutting them down in the forest? Which body parts were used to demonstrate the actions of cutting trees?

2. Why was it important to collapse safely to the floor when you were tagged?

3. What other objects have long and thin shapes? Show me.

Academic Language Demands

- **Language function:** Uses language to describe the role of the lumberjack and the strength needed to fulfill those responsibilities.

- **Vocabulary:** stretch, roll, float, push, pull, collapse, lumberjack, timber, seedling, log, sawmill, crosscut

- **Syntax or discourse:** A verbal interchange to give reasons why it is important to plant trees after cutting down forest dwellings.

CAVE STRUCTURES

National Standards Addressed

- **Standard 1.** The physically literate individual demonstrates competency in a variety of motor skills and movement patterns.
- **Standard 2.** The physically literate individual applies knowledge of concepts, principles, strategies and tactics related to movement and performance.

Instructional Materials/Props

Photographs of caves (optional)

Central Focus

To pose the body in two positions to form cave structures.

Objectives

- **Cognitive:** The child will match the shape of a cave opening by manipulating and bending his or her own body.
- **Affective:** The child will brainstorm with a partner three or four shapes that the body can make in order to create a cave for the partner to move through.
- **Psychomotor:** The child will rely on his or her strength and use of the arms and legs to move through two large cave structures formed by classmates' bodies.

Component of Health-Related Fitness

Muscular strength and endurance

Learning Task 1: Preparing Our Bodies to Move

Class organization: Children are scattered throughout general space.

Challenge the children to perform the following actions:

- Who can use his or her body to *show* me a round shape?
- Is it possible to *enlarge* the round shape to *make* a hole?
- Show how you can *make* a round shape with your hands and feet while *touching* the floor?

Learning Task 2: Partner Challenge

Class organization: Partners are scattered in self-spaces.

Present the following:

- Now that you have made a round shape with your hands and feet while touching the floor, select a partner and take turns *crawling* through the hole.
- Can one partner *stand* upright as the second partner *crawls* between his or her legs? Use your arms and legs to *crawl* through quickly. Exchange roles and *explore* three other ways that your body can form a cave shape.

Learning Task 3: Caves

Class organization: Children are scattered in identified groups.

Present the following: *A cave forms in the side of a mountain when water wears away rock and makes a hole.*

Mountain caves: Divide the class into two groups. One group creates a long cave by forming a behind-line and opening their legs to make the cave. The other group crawls through the long cave structure. Exchange roles.

Sea caves: A more complex cave is formed by children in one group making a side-by-side line. On your signal, children bend forward so that they support their weight on their hands and feet. The remaining children crawl under this long cave structure. The structure can be a twisted shape. Exchange roles.

Assessment Questions

1. Which body parts helped us the most to move through our imaginary caves?
2. Which cave that we created today was the most difficult to crawl through?
3. Who can name animals and creatures that live in caves (e.g., bears, bats, salamanders, spiders, snakes)? Show me how these cave creatures move.

Academic Language Demands

- **Language function:** Uses language to assess how difficult it would be to move through caves using only arms and legs.
- **Vocabulary:** creep, crawl, bend, round shape, twisted shape, cave
- **Syntax or discourse:** A verbal interchange identifying several creatures that move and live in caves.

WIND PATTERNS

National Standards Addressed

- **Standard 1.** The physically literate individual demonstrates competency in a variety of motor skills and movement patterns.
- **Standard 4.** The physically literate individual exhibits responsible personal and social behavior that respects self and others.

Instructional Materials/Props

None required

Central Focus

To comprehend changing wind patterns by performing a variety of moderate to vigorous movements associated with the Beaufort scale.

Objectives

- **Cognitive:** The child will make comparisons to how wind strength and the changing severity of weather influence our environment and the way our bodies move.
- **Affective:** The child will depend on his or her partner to demonstrate how to move safely when strong winds are pushing the body.
- **Psychomotor:** The child will reenact the actions and elements common to a dangerous storm.

Component of Health-Related Fitness

Muscular strength and endurance

Learning Task 1: Preparing Our Bodies to Move

Class organization: Children are scattered throughout general space.
Challenge the children to perform the following actions:

- Discover how many ways you can *walk*.
- How would strong winds affect the way a person walks? Show me.

Learning Task 2: Partner Challenge

Class organization: Partners are scattered in self-spaces.
Present the following:

- Can you and your partner *hold* hands while a very strong wind blows in your face and tries to push you backward?
- While still *holding* hands with your partner, show me how you would *move* if the strong wind were hitting your back and pushing your forward.

Learning Task 3: **Wind Strength**

Class organization: Children are scattered in identified groups.
Present the following:

Activity A: Wind on the Move. *The weather forecaster shares weather information with people. The weather forecaster also warns people if a large storm is approaching. The greatest cause of weather is wind. Large masses of air, some of which are hot and some cool, constantly move over the earth's surface. The Beaufort (pronounced Bo-fert) scale classifies wind strength. As a class moving together, use your bodies to move like the following actions associated with the Beaufort scale.*

Rating: 0
The effects on land: Calm, smoke rises straight up.
Learning task: Can you slowly *raise* your body upward?

Rating: 1
Effects on land: Weather vanes are inactive. Smoke drifts gently.
Learning task: Is it possible to *move* smoothly throughout the playing area?

Rating: 2
Effects on land: Wind is felt on face. Leaves rustle.
Learning task: See if you can *run* and *feel* the wind on your face.

Rating: 3
Effects on land: Leaves and twigs start to move. Light flags begin to unfurl.
Learning task: *Make a fluttering motion* with your fingers and arms.

Rating: 4
Effects on land: Small branches sway. Dust and papers blow around.
Learning task: Try to *hold* your hands close and in front of your body. *Make a swishing motion* back and forth.

Rating: 5
Effects on land: Small trees sway.
Learning task: Find a way to s*way* your upper body back and forth smoothly.

Rating: 6
Effects on land: Large branches move.
Learning task: Determine the best way to *shake* your arms and legs vigorously.

Rating: 7
Effects on land: Whole trees move. Walking is difficult.
Learning task: Pretend to *walk* while *leaning* forward in heavy wind.

Rating: 8
Effects on land: Twigs break off.
Learning task: Who can *make a bending motion* with their arms?

Rating: 9
Effects on land: Chimneys blow off roofs.
Learning task: Show me you can *jump* into the air and pretend to *crash* to the ground.

Rating: 10
Effects on land: Trees are uprooted.
Learning task: Can you *fall* forward from a standing position? Use your hands to safely cushion your fall.

Rating: 11-12
Effects on land: Widespread damage and destruction occurs.
Learning task: Pretend to be in a tropical storm, *moving* vigorously throughout the playing area.

Activity B: The Imaginary Thunderstorm. To create an imaginary thunderstorm, organize the class into seven groups scattered along the perimeter of the playing area. Explain that you will assign each group a weather element that they must imitate as you tell a story. When a group hears its element mentioned in the story, the children must move to the center of the playing area and demonstrate the action. Begin by whispering the element to each group, and then share the following story:

Once upon a time, two children lived in a large castle. They loved to be active and play outside. One morning, the sun was shining in their large backyard and the children were running about to become more physically fit. (The children pretending to be the sun *walk* to the center and *create* a circle over their heads with their arms.)

However, by the afternoon it began to sprinkle rain. (The children pretending to be rain enter into the circle and *flutter* their fingers from high to low.)

To the children's surprise, the clouds began to roll in and the sun went away. (The children pretending to be clouds enter and *roll* their arms and the sun exits.)

Soon the children heard crashing thunder. (The children pretending to be the thunder enter while *stamping* their feet.)

Then, hail stones bounced down from the sky. (The children pretending to be hail enter and *pound* their fist into the air as if throwing stones.)

The children became very afraid, and ran inside because a lightning bolt raced across the sky. (The children pretending to be lightning *run* in a jagged pathway.)

And, to make things worse, a giant twister twirled through the children's backyard. (The children pretending to be a twister *hold* hands and *twirl* in a circular motion.)

Just as the two children peered out the window, they saw a happy sight. The sun entered their yard and *whisked* all the rain, clouds, hail, thunder, lightning, and the twister far away. (The children pretending to be the sun reenter and the other elements exit.)

And the children entered their yard with all of their classmates and skipped merrily along. (The entire class *skips* happily throughout the playing area.)

Assessment Questions

1. How important was it that each weather element waited for his or her turn to move in our castle story?
2. Winds rated 12 on the Beaufort scale are called a hurricane. Can you spin your bodies like the winds of a hurricane?
3. Animals and sea creatures can sense changes in approaching weather conditions. Who can demonstrate what birds might do when strong winds with a rating of 7 are approaching (e.g., fly away)?

Academic Language Demands

- **Language function:** Uses language to identify consequences that can occur in dangerous weather.
- **Vocabulary:** flutter, swish, jump, sway, jagged pathway, whitecaps, rustle, uprooted, twigs, chimney
- **Syntax or discourse:** A verbal interchange regarding how best to move like different forms of weather events, from mild to severe.

VINES FOUND IN THE JUNGLE

National Standards Addressed

- **Standard 1.** The physically literate individual demonstrates competency in a variety of motor skills and movement patterns.
- **Standard 5.** The physically literate individual recognizes the value of physical activity for health, enjoyment, challenge, self-expression and/or social interaction.

Instructional Materials/Props

Chalk or tape, two 10- to 16-foot (3-5 m) jump ropes

Central Focus

To improve agility and cooperation while participating in a fitness jungle theme.

Objectives

- **Cognitive:** The child will differentiate between jumping for height and for distance and how to use specific body parts to complete these jumps.
- **Affective:** The child will be supportive as his or her partner attempts to jump for greater distance without falling into a make-believe swamp.
- **Psychomotor:** The child will fully participate in a series of creative jump rope learning tasks that progress from simple to more complex.

Component of Health-Related Fitness

Cardiorespiratory endurance

Learning Task 1: Preparing Our Bodies to Move

Class organization: Children are scattered throughout general space.

Challenge the children to perform the following actions:

- Can you *jump* high in the air to *catch* an imaginary jungle vine?
- Show me how you can *jump* forward for distance. Try to *swing* your arms forward and *land* with bent knees as if swinging on a vine.
- How many *jumps* would it take you to *move* from where you are standing to a different favorite spot in the playing area?

Learning Task 2: Partner Challenge

Class organization: Partners are scattered in self-spaces.

Present the following:

- Invent one way to *jump* with a partner and then give your partner a *high five*.
- Is it possible for you and your partner to *jump* over a swamp (i.e., two parallel lines on the floor approximately 2 feet [61 cm] apart) without getting your sneakers wet? Vary the width of the swamp depending on the physical abilities of the children.

Learning Task 3: Jungle Jump Challenges

Class organization: Children are scattered in identified groups.

Present the following:

Jump the vine: Explain to the children they will increase their fitness by playing a series of jump rope activities in which the jump rope remains close to the floor. Assign two children to be turners. The turners hold the rope stationary on the floor. All other children form a behind-line facing the rope several feet away and take turns jumping over the rope without touching it. The first child then goes around the turner and joins the back of the line. When the first child gets to the front of the line again, the children raise the rope a few inches. Older children can begin with the rope higher for an additional challenge. Change the turners frequently.

Super snake: The turners are on their knees and shake the rope back and forth across the floor. The children try to jump over the snake (i.e., rope) without touching it. The children create a continual flow as they jump over the rope and then return to the back of line. Change the turners frequently.

Jungle river is rising: The turners are on their knees and create small waves by shaking their wrists to move the rope up and down. Start with low waves and then gradually increase the intensity. The jumpers try to jump over the waves. Change the turners frequently.

Here comes the vine: The turners swing the rope low to the ground from side to side. A jumper can start in the middle and jump up as the rope approaches his or her body. The children who successfully jump over the vine can increase their number of jumps (e.g., first attempt, each child tries one time; second turn, each child tries to jump twice, and so on.) Change the turners frequently.

Run through the jungle: The turners continuously turn the rope clockwise a full rotation, and the jumper runs under the rope without touching it. Change the turners frequently.

Assessment Questions

1. Which parts of your body did you use to help you jump higher over the rope?
2. Which parts of your body are you making stronger when you jump rope?
3. Today we played jump rope jungle games. Does anyone have a favorite jump rope game that we could play? Show us.

Academic Language Demands

- **Language function:** Uses language to reinforce which body parts are used to complete a mature jump.
- **Vocabulary:** jump, swing, rotation, jungle, vine, swamp,   turner
- **Syntax or discourse:** A verbal interchange to discuss the difference in the skills needed to successfully complete a series of challenges.

ROCK FORMATIONS AND WATER

National Standards Addressed

- **Standard 1.** The physically literate individual demonstrates competency in a variety of motor skills and movement patterns.
- **Standard 4.** The physically literate individual exhibits responsible personal and social behavior that respects self and others.

Instructional Materials/Props

Nonslip carpet mats or rugs, movement spots or colored paper with tape, lively music

Central Focus

To improve balance skills while also demonstrating an understanding of spatial awareness.

Objectives

- **Cognitive:** The child will evaluate the challenges presented for the jump, leap, hop, and balance and adjust movements for each skill challenge.
- **Affective:** The child will brainstorm with a partner ways to create two balances that are different from the teacher's suggestion.
- **Psychomotor:** The child will make believe he or she is swimming and, when signaled, he or she will share a small space with a classmate.

Component of Health-Related Fitness

Muscular strength and endurance

Learning Task 1: Preparing Our Bodies to Move

Class organization: Children are scattered throughout general space.

Challenge the children to perform the following actions:

- Pretend you are *jumping* over small rocks.
- Show me how you can cross an imaginary stream by *leaping* from rock to rock.
- Who can *hop* from one foot to another?
- Can you *clap* your hands each time one foot lands on the floor?
- Is it possible to *balance* on one foot while *stretching* your arms out to the sides?
- Try to *balance* while *placing* your hands and arms elsewhere.
- See if you can *balance* while *standing* on your other foot.
- Who can *balance* on one foot while *bending* that knee?
- Find a way to *balance* with three body parts *touching* the floor.

Learning Task 2: Partner Challenge

Class organization: Partners are scattered in self-spaces.

Ask children to find a partner. One of the partners *balances* on one leg while the other partner offers a helping hand to maintain the balance. Partners exchange roles. Challenge the partners to work together and create two additional balances.

Learning Task 3: Rhythm Rocks

Class organization: Children are scattered throughout general space.

Present the following: *Algae are organisms that live in water or wet soil. Some algae are so small we need a microscope to see them. Algae help purify our air and water. Blue-green algae can coat rocks and make them slippery or slimy.*

Scatter river rocks (different sizes and shapes if possible) throughout general space. These river rocks can be formed using carpet squares or paper taped to the floor. Tell the children that in order to feel cool they can swim in the river. But, they must be careful because there are algae drifting in the river. As music plays, it is safe to swim around the river rocks.

When the music stops, all children must move to a rock so that no parts of their bodies are touching the water. The river rocks are varied in size to hold one or more children. If any part of the body, including shoes, is in the river, the floating blue-green algae will cover them. Instead of being eliminated, children use an imaginary hose to wash off algae. As the learning task continues, rocks can be removed one at a time, or made smaller for a greater challenge by removing some of the carpet squares or paper.

'Rithmetic river rocks: Give the children a simple math problem (e.g., 2 + 1 = 3; 5 – 3 = 2). The children provide the answer by placing that number of bodies on a river rock. If there are not enough children to create enough groups to equal the answer, they may raise hands and other body parts into the air to be counted.

Assessment Questions:

1. Which body parts did you use to balance on the rock?

2. Show me how you can run, stop, and balance on one foot quickly.

3. Math games are fun and we can play them in our class. Can anyone think of a movement if I ask other math problems? (e.g., wiggle 1 + 2 body parts)

Academic Language Demands

- **Language function:** Uses language to convince his or her classmate that two bodies can form a balance shape even when there is limited space to occupy.

- **Vocabulary:** algae, river rocks, organism, microscope, purify, slippery, slimy

- **Syntax or discourse:** A verbal interchange identifying the correct answer to a simple math equation and then responding by using that number of children in a physical challenge.

Math

JUMPING WITH WORDS AND NUMBERS THAT RHYME

National Standards Addressed

Standard 1. The physically literate individual demonstrates competency in a variety of motor skills and movement patterns.

Instructional Materials/Props

None required

Central Focus

To use auditory skills to identify the rhyming words that coincide with the number of times needed to jump.

Objectives

- **Cognitive:** The child will detect words that rhyme and respond when asked by the teacher to shout out the missing number in order to move correctly and complete the rhyme.
- **Affective:** The child will excitedly work with a partner and maintain vigorous movement for one minute.
- **Psychomotor:** The child will take part in a 12-stanza movement rhyme that requires active listening, performing a basic math skill, and demonstrating a mature jump a predetermined number of times.

Component of Health-Related Fitness

Cardiorespiratory endurance

Learning Task 1: Preparing Our Bodies to Move

Class organization: Children are scattered throughout general space.

Challenge the children to perform the following actions:

- Pretend you are a playground ball. How many different levels could you *bounce*?
- Follow me as I *jump* forward and create a large number 1.

Learning Task 2: Partner Challenge

Class organization: Partners are scattered in self-spaces.

Present the following: *Imagine you and a partner are a kernel of corn being heated. Show me how you can* grasp *hands and continuously* jump *like popcorn popping for one entire minute as I time you.*

Learning Task 3: Jumping Jellybean Numbers

Class organization: Children are scattered in general space.

Present the following: *I will read a rhyme slowly. At the end of each stanza, I will point to one side of the room (or a group of children) and those children will shout out the answer to the rhyme. All the children then* jump *the correct number of times and stop to listen carefully for the next rhyme.*

An old game, we have made new,

This is what you need to do.

   You will have fun while you learn,

   Words and numbers with each turn.

To play, you jump the number of a word that rhymes.

Like, when you hear the word "tree," you *jump* three times.

   If you *paddle* down a river in a canoe,

   Or *skip* to your neighborhood zoo,

   You *jump* _____ (two). (Children shout the correct number, and all jump two times.)

When you *shake* hands with someone,

Or *feel* the bones in your skeleton,

You only *jump* _____ (one).

   If you like *throwing* a ball with your friend Evan,

   Or imagine you are *cooking* in a giant oven,

   You *jump* _____ (seven).

Can you *buzz* about like a bee,

Or *swing* from a branch like a monkey?

You *jump* _____ (three).

   Who can *point* to an object that is alive,

   Or pretend to *leap* from an airplane and skydive?

   You *jump* _____ (five).

Can you pretend to use a broom to *sweep* a floor,

Or *stamp* and *stomp* like a heavy dinosaur?

You *jump* _____ (four).

   If you see ants *scurrying* at picnics,

   Or can pretend you are a magician doing *tricks*,

   You *jump* _____ (six).

If your body is strong and you *feel* great,

Or *bend* your knees and *lift* up a heavy weight,

You *jump* _____ (eight).

   If you can *balance* as you *walk* on a fine line,

   Or *reach* up high to *stretch* your spine,

   You *jump* _____ (nine).

If you take a *deep breath* of oxygen,

Or *visit* a bear at home in its den,

You *jump* _____ (ten).

   That's all. You are done.

   Yes, this game is easy and fun,

   Oops, you need to *jump* _____ (one).

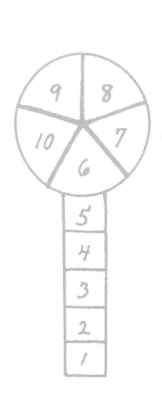

Assessment Questions

1. Who can think of two words that rhyme?

2. What if I said vine and gold mine. Who can jump _____?

3. Can you think of another movement instead of jumping for our math rhyme? Try your new movement when I read one part again.

Academic Language Demands

*   **Language function:** Uses language to identify specific numbers that correspond with words in a math rhyme.

*   **Vocabulary:** jump, skip, paddle, swing, point, leap, scurry, lift

*   **Syntax or discourse:** A verbal interchange aimed at finding a specific number because it rhymes with the words in the math stanza.

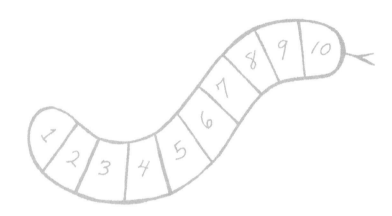

HOPPING WITH WORDS AND NUMBERS THAT RHYME

National Standards Addressed

Standard 1. The physically literate individual demonstrates competency in a variety of motor skills and movement patterns.

Instructional Materials/Props

None required

Central Focus

To use auditory skills to identify the rhyming words that coincide with the number of times needed to hop.

Objectives

- **Cognitive:** The child will detect words that rhyme and respond when asked by the teacher to shout out the missing number in order to move correctly and complete the rhyme.
- **Affective:** The child will excitedly work with a partner and maintain a vigorous movement for one minute.
- **Psychomotor:** The child will take part in a 12-stanza movement rhyme that requires active listening, performing a basic math skill, and demonstrating a mature hop a predetermined number of times.

Component of Health-Related Fitness

Cardiorespiratory endurance

Learning Task 1: Preparing Our Bodies to Move

Class organization: Children are scattered throughout general space.

Challenge the children to perform the following actions:

- What if your feet could draw on the floor? By *hopping*, can you create the first letter in your name?
- Copy me as I *hop* forward, backward, sideward, and in a zigzag line.
- Follow me as we *hop* on one foot and then the other.

Learning Task 2: Partner Challenge

Class organization: Partners are scattered in self-spaces.

Present the following:

- Follow your partner as you *hop* throughout the playing area. Exchange roles.
- Is it easier to hold a partner's hand while you *hop*?

Learning Task 3: Hip Hop Numbers

Class organization: Children are scattered in general space.

Present the following: *I will read a math rhyme slowly. At the end of each stanza, I will point to one side of the room (or a group of children) and those children will shout out the answer to the rhyme. All children then hop the correct number of times and stop to listen carefully for the next rhyme.*

An old game, we have made new,
This is what you need to do.

    You will have fun while you learn,

    Words and numbers with each turn.

To play, you *hop* the number of a word that rhymes.
Like, when you hear the word "glue," you *hop* two times.

    When you *rise* in the morning and *see* the sun,

    Have fun, taking your dog for a *run*,

    Keep *playing* a game until you have won,

    You only *hop* _____ (one). (Children shout the correct number, and all *hop* one time.)

If you *squeeze* a large yellow lemon,
Or share a drink with a boy named Kevin,
Try real hard in your movement lesson.
You *hop*_____ (seven).

    You don't need to keep score,

    If you *walk* through a door,

    Row a boat with an oar,

    You *hop*_____ (four).

If you can *tie* a knot from twine,
Or *draw* a line,
Make a design,
You *hop* _____ (nine).

    With your eyes you can *see*,

    You and I *become* we,

    Together we can make an important discovery,

    You *hop* _____ (three).

You *enter* a car and go for a *drive*,
Watch a swimmer take a *dive*,
Or a *swarm* of bees *buzzing* in a hive,
You *hop*_____ (five).

    If you can *cluck* and *peck* like a farmyard hen,

    Or *crawl* like a baby in a playpen,

    Write a letter to a friend,

    You *hop*_____ (ten).

If you can *point* to the color blue,
Wash your hair with shampoo,
Or have *played* peek-a-boo,
You *hop* _____ (two).

    If you *see* a building of bricks,

    Watch soccer players making kicks,

    See children *hopping* up and down on pogo sticks,

    You *hop*_____ (six).

If you *like* to skate,
Eat from a plate,
Shiver from cold until you *vibrate*,
You *hop* _____ (eight).

    That's all. You are done.

    Yes, this game is easy and fun,

    Oops, you need to *hop* _____ (one).

Assessment Questions

1. Which body parts do you use to help you hop?
2. Is it possible to hop and change your level from medium, to high, to low?
3. Can you describe how to perform a hop to a classmate who does not know what a hop looks like? Tell your classmate now.

Academic Language Demands

- **Language function:** Uses language to identify specific numbers that correspond with words in a math rhyme.
- **Vocabulary:** hop, run, squeeze, walk, row, tie, crawl, shiver, vibrate
- **Syntax or discourse:** A verbal interchange aimed at finding a specific number that rhymes with the words in the math stanza.

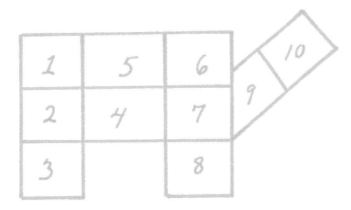

MOVING WITH WORDS AND NUMBERS THAT RHYME

National Standards Addressed

Standard 1. The physically literate individual demonstrates competency in a variety of motor skills and movement patterns.

Instructional Materials/Props

None required

Central Focus

To use auditory skills to identify the rhyming words that coincide with the number of times needed to move in a variety of ways.

Objectives

- **Cognitive:** The child will detect words that rhyme and respond when asked by the teacher to shout out the missing number in order to move correctly and complete the rhyme.
- **Affective:** The child will excitedly work with a partner and maintain vigorous movement for one minute.
- **Psychomotor:** The child will take part in a 12-stanza movement rhyme that requires active listening, performing a basic math skill, and demonstrating a mature locomotor skill a predetermined number of times.

Component of Health-Related Fitness

Cardiorespiratory endurance

Learning Task 1: Preparing Our Bodies to Move

Class organization: Children are scattered throughout general space.

Challenge the children to perform the following actions:

- Can you *skip* at a fast pace?
- Who can *skip* around the playing area while *waving* and *giving* their classmates huge smiles?

Learning Task 2: Partner Challenge

Class organization: Partners are scattered in self-spaces.

Present the following:

- Can you *slide* face to face, then back to back with your partner?
- Show how both of you can *slide* while facing each other throughout our playing area for one minute.

Learning Task 3: Nimble Numbers

Class organization: Children are scattered in general spaces.

Present the following: *I will read a math rhyme slowly. At the end of each stanza, I will point to one side of the room (or a group of children), and those children will shout out the answer to the rhyme. All children then move the correct number of times and stop to listen carefully for the next rhyme.*

An old game, we have made new,

This is what you need to do.

> You will have fun while you learn,
> Words and numbers with each turn.

To play, you move the number of a word that rhymes.

Like, when you hear the word "knee," you shuffle three times.

> If you like to *slide* on something slippery,
> And can *climb* like a chimpanzee,
> You *skip* _____ (three). (Children shout the correct number, and all *skip* three times.)

If you have *read* the *Little Red Hen*,

Touched a fuzzy peach's skin,

You *stamp*_____ (ten).

> If you have *seen* shells at the seashore,
> Or can *stomp* about like a dinosaur,
> You *tiptoe* _____ (four).

If monkeys *swing* on a vine,

And people *ask,* "Will you be mine?"

You *strut*_____ (nine).

> If you are nice to everyone,
> And *smile* and *laugh* when you have fun,
> You *slide* _____ (one).

If you *measure* something with yardsticks,

Hear peep, peep, peep from a brood of chicks,

You *march* _____ (six).

> If you can count to eleven,
> You *leap*_____ (seven).

If you like to go in a submarine for a deep-sea dive,

Or take a sports car for a test-drive,

You *gallop*_____ (five).

> If you *study* hard and *concentrate*,
> *Stop* what you are doing and *hesitate*,
> You *walk* _____ (eight).

If you *jump* up when someone says "Boo",

Or can *stick* something together with gooey glue,

You *crawl* _____ (two).

> That's all. You are done.
> Yes, this game is easy and fun.
> Here we go, let's start again with number _____ (one).

Assessment Questions

1. Can you name a movement that requires good balance?
2. How important was it to listen carefully when I was reading the rhyme? Why?
3. Who can combine three movements and move forward?

Academic Language Demands

- **Language function:** Uses language to identify specific numbers that correspond with words in a math rhyme.
- **Vocabulary:** slide, crawl, skip, stomp, kick, march, leap, stamp
- **Syntax or discourse:** A verbal interchange aimed at finding a specific number because it rhymes with the words in the math stanza.

GEOMETRIC SHAPES

National Standards Addressed

Standard 1. The physically literate individual demonstrates competency in a variety of motor skills and movement patterns.

Instructional Materials/Props

Construction paper to draw shapes on, marker or crayon

Central Focus

To increase the child's understanding of shapes and perform movements related to specific shapes.

Objectives

- **Cognitive:** The child will recognize similarities and differences within specific geometric shapes.
- **Affective:** The child will show an appreciation for the many shapes that are present in our environment and be able to create or move like several of these objects.
- **Psychomotor:** The child will successfully participate in moderate physical activity that encourages the identification of different shapes and action words associated with these shapes.

Component of Health-Related Fitness

Flexibility

Learning Task 1: Preparing Our Bodies to Move

Class organization: Children are scattered throughout general space.

Challenge the children to perform the following actions:

- *Walk* in different shapes: circle, square, triangle, the shape of the number eight.
- Follow me as we *jump* in the shape of a rectangle.

Learning Task 2: Partner Challenge

Class organization: Partners are scattered in self-spaces.

Present the following:

- Our world is filled with shapes. All objects have some form or shape. *Point* to your body parts that are round. Can you *move* one of these round body parts?
- People's faces can be square, round, oval, or heart shaped. The shape of a person's mouth can make him or her look happy or sad. Show me how to *form* a happy mouth, a sad mouth, and a surprised mouth.
- People build shapes. *Make* yourself into an airplane shape, a box shape, and a bridge shape.
- Animals have shapes that help them move. *Pretend* you are a dolphin moving through the water. Is it possible to have the wings of a bird *flying* in the sky?
- Long, narrow shapes stand tall or lie on the ground. See if you can *stand* tall and straight like a telephone pole. Now *lie* down like a log on the ground. *Shake* your two longest body parts.
- Nature produces some large shapes. Can you and your partner *form* a pointed mountain?
- What other shapes can you and your partner *create* together?

Learning Task 3: Super Shapes

Class organization: Children are scattered in identified groups in different areas of the playing area.

- Divide the children into groups of four or five.
- Explain to the children that you will name a specific shape. Draw this shape on construction paper for all in the class to see.
- Challenge the children to perform actions associated with the specific shape. For example, "This shape is a circle. Let's *bounce* like a ball." At the end of all groups participating in your suggested shape, encourage each group to brainstorm one additional object and perform that action to the class as a whole.

Examples are provided for the following shapes:

Triangle: A triangle has three sides and three corners.
- *Wave* a banner.
- *Cut* a pie into slices.
- *Eat* an ice cream cone.
- *Nail* shingles on a roof.
- *Dig* in the garden with a trowel.

Square: Squares have four sides the same length.
- *Open* a present.
- *Stack* five blocks.
- *Fold* a handkerchief.
- *Melt* like an ice cube.
- *Toss* and *catch* a bean bag.

Circle: Circles are round shapes.
- *Be round* like the letter O.
- *Roll* like a wheel.
- *Rise* like the sun.
- *Wind* a ball of yarn.
- *Throw* a baseball.
- *Move* like a yo-yo.
- *Crawl* through a hoop.
- *Grip* a steering wheel.
- *Burst* like a bubble.

Rectangle: Rectangles have four sides and four corners.
- *Open* and *read* a book.
- *Drive* a truck.
- *Close* a door.
- *Open* a window.

Star: Stars are symbols that have five or six points.
- *Wave* a magic wand.
- *Shine* a police badge.

Oval: Ovals are egg shapes.
- *Eat* a bunch of grapes.
- *Gather* eggs.
- *Squeeze* a lemon.
- *Look* in a mirror.

Diamond: A diamond shape looks like two triangles fitted together.
- *Fly* a kite.
- *Run* bases on a baseball diamond.

Assessment Questions

1. Which shape had the greatest number of objects?
2. What shape is your favorite toy? Can you make that shape with your body?
3. If you could invent a new shape, what would it look like? How might it move? Can you give it a name?

Academic Language Demands

- **Language function:** Uses language to identify familiar (and perhaps unfamiliar) shapes of different objects and things.
- **Vocabulary:** triangle, square, circle, rectangle, star, oval, diamond, shingle, trowel
- **Syntax or discourse:** A verbal interchange that assists in classifying objects according to their shape.

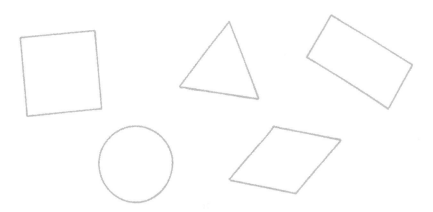

PUZZLE SHAPES

National Standards Addressed

- **Standard 1.** The physically literate individual demonstrates competency in a variety of motor skills and movement patterns.
- **Standard 4.** The physically literate individual exhibits responsible personal and social behavior that respects self and others.

Instructional Materials/Props

Two or more duplications of a simple puzzle containing 25 to 40 cardboard pieces (puzzles with fewer and larger pieces are suggested for preschool age children), containers for each puzzle.

Central Focus

To work collectively in a vigorous movement activity to construct a puzzle.

Objectives

- **Cognitive:** The child will point to different parts of the body that have bumps and rounded corners similar to some puzzle pieces.
- **Affective:** The child will strive to fit his or her body together with a partner's body to show how puzzle pieces fit together.
- **Psychomotor:** The child will demonstrate a variety of locomotor skills while participating in a vigorous physical activity that requires the cooperation of all group members to complete the final task.

Components of Health-Related Fitness

Cardiorespiratory endurance, flexibility

Learning Task 1: Preparing Our Bodies to Move

Class organization: Children are scattered throughout general space.

Challenge the children to perform the following actions:

- Puzzle pieces come in different shapes and sizes. Some pieces have bumps with rounded corners. *Point* to any part of your body that has a bump (e.g., elbow, knee, heel).
- Use your body to *create* a flat puzzle piece at a low level on the floor or ground.

Learning Task 2: Partner Challenge

Class organization: Partners are scattered in self-spaces.

Present the following:

- Can you *combine* your special puzzle shape with a classmate's shape? Try fitting the pieces together at a low level on the floor or ground.
- Try to *make* a different puzzle shape with your partner.
- Is it possible to work with two other partners and *make* a four-person puzzle?

Learning Task 3: Very Puzzling

Class organization: Children are scattered in identified groups.

- Divide the children into two to four groups depending on the number of available puzzles.
- Arrange the groups in behind-lines facing the container holding their puzzle pieces. Each line is the same distance from its container: 15 to 40 feet (4.6-12 m) depending on the group's age and stamina.
- On your signal, the first child in each line moves (e.g., runs, skips, hops, gallops, jumps) to the containers of pieces.
- Each child takes one piece of his or her group's puzzle and moves to the back of the line.
- Group members cooperate to complete their puzzle.
- After each puzzle is completed, challenge each group to create a giant group puzzle using their bodies.

Assessment Questions

1. Who can name a piece of clothing that must fit snugly over our bodies (e.g., socks, gloves, hat, shoes)?
2. Show me how your fingers can act like puzzle pieces.
3. Many objects are made up of parts of different sizes and shapes that fit together. How do they stay together (e.g., glue, tape, screws, nails)?

Academic Language Demands

- **Language function:** Uses language to compare the unique bumps on a human's body to the bumps found on puzzle pieces and discusses the best way to construct a simple puzzle.
- **Vocabulary:** flat shape, low level, run, skip, hop, gallop, jump
- **Syntax or discourse:** A verbal interchange aimed at the best way to complete a puzzle or some other simple structure.

BODY TRIANGLES

National Standards Addressed

- **Standard 1.** The physically literate individual demonstrates competency in a variety of motor skills and movement patterns.
- **Standard 4.** The physically literate individual exhibits responsible personal and social behavior that respects self and others.

Instructional Materials/Props

Lively music if possible, masking tape or chalk to make five to seven large triangle shapes on the floor

Central Focus

To recall concepts related to the triangle while participating in vigorous movement activities.

Objectives

- **Cognitive:** The child will locate triangle shapes that are part of the body and that can be created using different poses.
- **Affective:** The child will exhibit an eagerness to combine his or her body with a partner's body to create three different triangle shapes at varied levels.
- **Psychomotor:** The child will take part in group challenges that encourage vigorous jumping, running, and crawling and use his or her understanding of triangles as a primary focus in each task.

Component of Health-Related Fitness

Cardiorespiratory endurance

Learning Task 1: Preparing Our Bodies to Move

Class organization: Children are scattered throughout general space.

Present the following: *Many years ago a group of people known as the Greeks became interested in a shape called the triangle. A triangle is a shape that has three sides. The three sides meet at three points. The first triangle we will learn about has three sides of the same length (equilateral).* Challenge the children to perform the following actions:

- Let's find several triangles that are hidden in our bodies. The first triangle can be made with your hands. Can you *touch* your two pointer fingers together? Now *touch* your thumbs together. What shape do you see?
- Can you *trace* a line across your face from ear to ear? Now follow down to your chin and *move* from the chin to the other ear. You have three points on your face that make a triangle.
- Show me how you can make a triangle shape by *bending* forward and *touching* the floor with one hand.

Learning Task 2: **Partner Challenge**

Class organization: Partners are scattered in self-spaces.

Present the following:

- With a partner, see how many ways you can *create* a triangle with your bodies.
- Try to change the level of your body to *create* a triangle at a low, medium, and high level.

Learning Task 3: **Triangle Activities**

Class organization: Children are scattered in identified groups.

Present the following:

Triangle jumps: Use masking tape or chalk to make five to seven large triangle shapes on the floor. Leave adequate space between the triangles. Play lively music. The children perform locomotor skills until you give a signal (e.g., music stops). Children rush to the closest triangle and jump in and out three times. The learning task continues.

Triangle tunnels: Divide the children into two groups. One group consists of partners who grasp each other's hands. They stand side by side and touch the inside feet and stretch outward to make a giant triangle between them. The remaining children either move through the giant middle triangle or they may crawl under the triangle made from either of the two children's legs.

Three touches: Review the concept of three sides to a triangle. Play lively music for the children to dance or move in moderate to vigorous ways. When the music stops, the children tap three different body parts. The music continues with the children resuming their vigorous movements and concludes with all tapping three different body parts when the music stops.

Assessment Questions

1. What objects come to mind when you think of the triangle shape (e.g., roof, flag, slice of pie)?
2. Can you trace a triangle shape on the floor using one foot without losing your balance?
3. Let's see if you can combine a triangle with another triangle to form a different shape. What did you create?

Academic Language Demands

- **Language function:** Uses language to acquire information about the origin of triangles, their shape, and objects that are triangle shaped.
- **Vocabulary:** high, medium, low levels; crawl, tap, jump, balance, lean, triangle, equilateral
- **Syntax or discourse:** A verbal interchange focusing on the uniqueness of a triangle and the fact that more than one type of triangle exists.

MEASURING HORSES

National Standards Addressed

- **Standard 1.** The physically literate individual demonstrates competency in a variety of motor skills and movement patterns.
- **Standard 4.** The physically literate individual exhibits responsible personal and social behavior that respects self and others.

Instructional Materials/Props

Photographs of horses (optional)

Central Focus

To compare a horse's body parts and movements with the child's own body parts and movements.

Objectives

- **Cognitive:** The child will become familiar with the horse's anatomy, height, aspects of grooming, and locomotor skills specific to this particular animal.
- **Affective:** The child will give and receive feedback about the rocking horse that he or she creates for the partner and will cooperate when measured by his or her partner.
- **Psychomotor:** The child will participate with two other children to use their bodies to create an imaginary horse carriage that can maneuver throughout the playing area safely and while displaying control and swiftness.

Component of Health-Related Fitness

Cardiorespiratory endurance

Learning Task 1: Preparing Our Bodies to Move

Class organization: Children are scattered throughout general space.

Present the following and challenge the children to perform the actions:

- Horses have two oval eyes set at the sides of their head. Ask the children to explain where their eyes are located (e.g., in the front of the face, under the eyebrows, above the cheeks).
- Horses do not have feet. They have a single large toe called a hoof; therefore, they always walk on their tiptoes. Can you *move* throughout the playing area on your tiptoes?
- Horses need to be brushed to remove dirt from their bodies. Use your fingers and make believe you have a hair brush. *Brush* your fingers through your hair.
- Horses walk forward by first stepping with the right leg, followed by a step with the left leg, then another step forward with the left leg, and one more step using the right leg. See if you can try this movement several times.
- Prancing is a movement that horses perform by lifting each front leg upward as they walk. Is it possible to *lift* your knees high while you *prance* around a make-believe circus ring?
- Galloping is similar to a person's sliding movement. Show me how you can slide one foot away from the body, and bring the other foot to it.

Learning Task 2: Partner Challenge

Class organization: Partners are scattered in self-spaces.

Present the following:

- Who can form a rocking horse with a partner? One partner should stand and rock the body forward and backward while the second partner stands behind the first, and gently places his or her hands on the shoulder of the first partner.

- Tell the children that the height of a horse is measured from the ground to the highest point of a horse's shoulder. For many years people who owned horses, used the width of a hand to measure the horse's height. Ask the children to select a partner. The children take turns measuring each other's height from the floor to the shoulders by using their hands.

Learning Task 3: Horse and Carriage

Class organization: Children are scattered in identified groups.

Present the following: *The Morgan horse is known for its ability to pull carriages.* Ask the children to quickly form groups of three. Two children stand side by side and clasp hands. These two children are the Morgan horses. The third child stands behind the two horses and reaches forward to clasp their outside hands. This child is the carriage. All three children move forward throughout the playing area without colliding into other carriages.

Assessment Questions

1. Who can name animals that are taller than you are? Can you show me how they move?

2. What are the ways horses can move (e.g., gallop, prance, jump, trot)? Show me how you can gallop with a friend.

3. Horses and people have special and different abilities. If you could switch places with a horse for a day, what kinds of things would you like to do? Show me.

Academic Language Demands

- **Language function:** Uses language to recognize how our body parts are similar to that of a horse and indicate why the horse is such a special animal.

- **Vocabulary:** slide, lift, prance, trot, gallop, brush, hooves, carriage, width

- **Syntax or discourse:** A verbal interchange relating to the simplistic form of measurement that was once used to measure the height of horses.

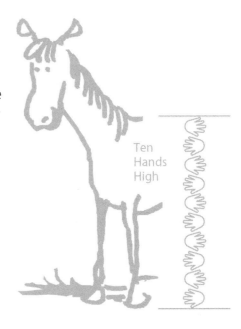

Ten Hands High

FIRST AND LAST

National Standards Addressed

- **Standard 1.** The physically literate individual demonstrates competency in a variety of motor skills and movement patterns.
- **Standard 4.** The physically literate individual exhibits responsible personal and social behavior that respects self and others.

Instructional Materials/Props

None required

Central Focus

To move consecutively from back to front while negotiating space.

Objectives

- **Cognitive:** The child will critique his or her methods of hopping when changing speeds, height, and distance.
- **Affective:** The child will maintain a high level of attentiveness while working with a partner to advance in a cooperative and creative manner.
- **Psychomotor:** The child will engage in a variety of locomotor skills while moving consecutively from the back to the front of a line.

Component of Health-Related Fitness

Cardiorespiratory endurance

Learning Task 1: Preparing Our Bodies to Move

Class organization: Children are scattered throughout general space.

Challenge the children to perform the following actions:

- Show me how fast you can *hop*. How slowly can you *hop*?
- Discover how far you can *hop*.
- How high can you *hop*?
- Is it possible to *hop* higher and higher each time you try? Try this five times to see how high off the ground you can *hop*.

Learning Task 2: Partner Challenge

Class organization: Partners are scattered in self-spaces.

Present the following:

- Can you quickly find a partner and form a behind-line?
- Let's see how quickly the person in the back can step in front of his or her partner.
- How else can the person in the back move in front of his or her partner (e.g., hop, jump)?
- Try it again using another way to move.
- Which set of partners can take turns moving to the front from the back until they have touched the opposite wall (or opposite end of the playing area)?

Learning Task 3: Moving Onward!

Class organization: Children are scattered in identified groups.

Present the following: Today you will use your bodies to play a group line activity.

- Divide the children into groups of five or six.
- Ask each group to form a long behind-line.
- The children in each line must place their hands either on the shoulders or on the waist of the person standing in front of them.
- On your signal, the child at the end of the line chooses how to move his or her body to the front of the line (e.g., jump, twirl, march, walk sideward or backward). The action continues with each child selecting new ways to move to the front until the entire line has moved to the opposite side of the playing area.
- For a greater challenge, substitute running with skipping, jumping, hopping, a favorite animal walk, or a tumbling skill if floor mats are available.
- Allow enough space for each child to have a turn to move from the back to the front of the line.

Assessment Questions

1. What actions did you use to move to the front of the line?
2. Can you name other ways to move to the front of the line?
3. Did it make any difference in the learning task Moving Onward! if you were standing at the front or at the back of the line? Why (i.e., everyone gets a turn)? This is called rotation when a person moves from the back of the line to the front.

Academic Language Demands

- **Language function:** Uses language to reflect how one feels when he or she is at the end of the line and why this placement is not important as long as everyone receives a turn.
- **Vocabulary:** hop, run, skip, jump, tumble, behind-line, back, front, rotation
- **Syntax or discourse:** A verbal interchange explaining one of the first natural forms of rotation and why it has worked for many years.

CREATIONS

National Standards Addressed

- **Standard 1.** The physically literate individual demonstrates competency in a variety of motor skills and movement patterns.
- **Standard 2.** The physically literate individual applies knowledge of concepts, principles, strategies and tactics related to movement and performance.

Instructional Materials/Props

Pictures of spacecraft for the partner learning task and large objects as listed in the whole-group learning task (optional)

Central Focus

To work collectively with classmates to create large shapes and critique all finished products.

Objectives

- **Cognitive:** The child will use his or her mathematical perception and collaborate with classmates to create a large structure using their bodies.
- **Affective:** The child will use imagination and brainstorm with a partner ways they can create a rocket ship with their bodies.
- **Psychomotor:** The child will move in a vigorous mode in order to avoid being tagged and, if tagged, will assist in the creation of a large object previously agreed on by other classmates.

Component of Health-Related Fitness

Cardiorespiratory endurance

Learning Task 1: Preparing Our Bodies to Move

Class organization: Children are scattered throughout general space.

Challenge the children to perform the following actions:

- Act as if you are very excited and happy while *running*.
- Can you *run* to (name a specific point in the playing area) and return to your original position?
- See if you can *walk* in a circle. Now try to slowly *rotate* (spin) your body as you *walk* in a circle shape.
- Show me what a rocket shape looks like.

Learning Task 2: **Partner Challenge**

Class organization: Partners are scattered in self-spaces.

Present the following:

- Try to build a large rocket using a friend's body.
- Is it possible to be astronauts and to move your spacecraft from one place in the playing area to another place? (One partner stands behind the first and places his or her hands on the first partner's shoulders.)
- Let's end our space travel by using our bodies to create an object we see in the sky (e.g., moon, sun, or star).

Learning Task 3: **Class Creations**

Class organization: Children are scattered in identified groups.

Present the following:

- Inform the children that today's task focuses on their ability to collectively use their bodies to create large shapes. Reinforce the need to work cooperatively and to use everyone's body.
- Select two or three children to be chasers. Before the action begins, the chasers must agree on a large object that they would like to see built (preschool children may require suggestions such as a train or a tunnel). The designated object is announced to the class (e.g., We would like a castle built.).
- The remainder of the children scatter throughout the playing area. When a child is tagged, he or she retreats to a designated area and assists the others in creating the object.
- After all the children are tagged, the chasers inspect the object by moving through, over, or around it.
- Additional shapes include an igloo, a fort, a school bus, a bridge, a race car, and a house.

Assessment Questions

1. In what ways did you need to change the shape as classmates joined you in the activity Class Creations?
2. Which object was the most difficult to make? Why?
3. If you could use magical powers to make tiny objects larger, what would you choose? Can we form this large shape?

Academic Language Demands

- **Language function:** Uses language to identify a variety of large objects or things that the children can make using everyone's body.
- **Vocabulary:** tag, chase, rotate, shapes, astronaut, spacecraft, inspect, igloo, fort
- **Syntax or discourse:** A verbal interchange centering on the act of inspecting to determine whether an object is appropriate.

CHAPTER 9

Moving With Words & Actions in Language Arts

Unlike many resources that reinforce academic concepts through movement activities, *Moving With Words & Actions* uses classroom content to expand the child's physical literacy. This use of academic concepts to enhance children's physical literacy should appeal to classroom teachers who want a fresh approach to meeting learning standards. This is especially true for teachers who have had to deemphasize the physical domain because of a lack of resources. Using academic concepts should also help to expand the child's movement vocabulary. From the child's perspective, he or she is simply using the information discussed in the classroom to participate in fun, physical activities.

The first series of learning tasks in this chapter is devoted to classroom concepts that focus on the alphabet. Children can expand their understanding of each letter in an exciting way (e.g., Alphabet Stretches). They also learn that they can use their bodies to form shapes and that these shapes coincide with specific letters in the alphabet (e.g., My Body Can Form Letters). Still other learning tasks in this section appeal to the child's love for rhyming words and active learning.

Shapes the Child's Body Can Make

- Angular
- Big
- Box
- Circle
- Crooked
- Curled
- Curved
- Diamond
- Flat
- Gigantic
- Little
- Long
- Narrow
- Oval
- Pointed

- Rectangle
- Round
- Sharp
- Short
- Skinny
- Small
- Square
- Straight
- Stretched
- Tall
- Thin
- Tiny
- Triangle
- Twisted
- Wide

Movement Narratives

The second series of learning tasks in this chapter focuses on increasing the child's language arts skills through the use of *movement narratives*. Movement narratives are a means by which you introduce fictional characters, settings, and events to enhance children's imagination and creativity, love for stories, and ultimately, their language arts skills. In the cognitive (or intellectual) domain, narratives increase children's movement vocabulary, language skills, and love for words that remind them of sounds.

In the affective (or social) domain, movement narratives have a beginning, middle, and end and include a variety of expressive feelings. They help children understand how family members and people react to situations and interact with each other. They also demonstrate that people like different things and can hold other viewpoints. Movement narratives also provide opportunities for children to portray the perspective of others in simple ways, such as acting very brave or frightened. These actions are one of the earliest steps toward developing empathy for other people and experimenting with adult roles of power and control.

Finally, within the psychomotor (or physical) domain, narratives offer numerous opportunities for the child to demonstrate a wide variety of physical literacy skills in an environment that encourages active responses. In short, movement narratives address all three domains of learning.

We have tried to present the narratives in a progressive order, beginning with the simplest and moving toward the most complex. The themes presented might be familiar to some young children and totally new to other children, depending on where they live. We also encourage you to read through the narratives while noting the complexity of the physical challenges. Select a narrative that is appropriate for your class's age and stage and proceed from there. Use the following information to implement movement narratives and, thereby, increase children's physical literacy and language arts skills.

- Foster the children's mental pictures of the story and setting by reading the narrative slowly and with enthusiasm. Some teachers and parents assume mistakenly that complex toys and elaborate costumes are needed to inspire children's imagination. They overlook the fact that imaginative qualities stem from children's ability to perform creative thinking and simple problem solving. Allow a moment for the children to visualize the desired physical literacy response.
- Help children learn to interact with peers in a social way. Discuss the interpersonal skills that they need: to take turns, lead and follow, share, and cooperate with one another or even a sibling at home.
- Use the imitative approach for young children who might find it difficult to interpret all of the action words. You can do that by demonstrating the correct way to perform a physical skill, narrowing the child's focus to one action or expression at a time. Then, allow each child to complete the skill or action before you move on to the next sentence.
- Adapt or modify your voice to create a unique voice for the characters presented in the narratives.
- Identify and praise the children who are expressing their feelings freely and are actively involved.
- Talk about the different locomotor and nonlocomotor skills demonstrated throughout the narrative. Which movements helped the character to accomplish the goal of the story? What actions showed how each body was moving?
- Suggest other ways that the narrative could have ended and ask the children to physically demonstrate how each might have looked.
- Always praise the children's efforts and creativity when they successfully complete the narrative.
- Assess the child's understanding of the action words and physical demonstrations to determine whether learning has taken place.
- Smile.

When to Use Movement Narratives

Depending on the length and the number of action words, you can use movement narratives as the initial activity to prepare the body for greater challenges or as a whole-group learning task. When the narrative is multifaceted and contains several characters and changes in the plot, some teachers create a lesson plan that identifies the more complex physical skills and uses them during the initial activity in a stretching or chase-and-flee activity, or they have partners practice the advanced skills to music and then implement the narrative.

Creative teachers review a narrative and incorporate three objectives, an appropriate initial learning task, and a partner learning task, and they take their time implementing the movement narrative to increase the child's movement vocabulary and language arts skills. This chapter offers three sample narratives containing all of these elements, followed by 15 additional narratives that you can use to enhance your repertoire.

Alphabet

ALPHABET STRETCHES A TO Z

National Standards Addressed

Standard 1. The physically literate individual demonstrates competency in a variety of motor skills and movement patterns.

Instructional Materials/Props

Letters of the alphabet on display (optional)

Central Focus

To identify specific letters of the alphabet and associate vigorous action words with those letters.

Objectives

- **Cognitive:** The child will recall which movement skills start with a specific letter of the alphabet.
- **Affective:** The child will exhibit a willingness to listen to the teacher and respond enthusiastically when participating in alphabet stretches.
- **Psychomotor:** The child will demonstrate the correct movement skill for each letter of the alphabet in the Alphabet Stretches A to Z.

Components of Health-Related Fitness

Cardiorespiratory endurance, flexibility

Learning Task 1: Preparing Our Bodies to Move

Class organization: Children are scattered throughout.

Present the following: *What if you could form the shape of letters by moving your body along the floor?* Challenge the children to perform the following actions:

- Can you *create* the shape of the letter J as you *jump*?
- See if you can *form* the letter Z as you *zip* back and forth in a *zigzag* pattern.
- *Waddle* like a penguin as you *form* the shape of the letter W.
- Show me how you can *hop* as you *create* the letter H.

Learning Task 2: Partner Challenge

Class organization: Partners are scattered throughout general space.

Challenge partners to take turns pointing to different body parts, identifying the letter of the alphabet that each body part starts with, and then moving that body part. Examples include A: arm, ankle, C: chest, E: elbow, eyes, eyelashes, ears, H: head, hips, F: feet, fingers, foot, K: knees, W: wrist, waist, L: legs, lips, N: neck.

Learning Task 3: Alphabet Stretches A to Z

Class organization: Children are scattered throughout general space.

Present the following: *Let's perform exciting movements for each letter of the alphabet.*

A is for the air. Who can take three deep breaths of air?

B is for bouncing. Can you *bounce* like a rubber ball?

C is for curling. See if you can *curl* your body into a round shape?

D is for dodging. Can you *dodge* to one side and then to the other side?

E is for exploring. Pretend to *explore* a long, dark cave.

F is for fun. Show me how your body *moves* when you are having fun.

G is for grip. Can you *curl* your fingers and *make* a tight grip?

H is for hug. *Give* yourself a great big hug.

I is for inflate. Let's pretend to *blow* and *inflate* a giant balloon.

J is for jump. Try to *jump* upward and *touch* the ceiling.

K is for kick. Show me how you can *kick* an imaginary ball with your foot.

L is for lower. How slowly can you *lower* your body to the floor?

M is for muscle. Try to *stretch* your arm muscles and *make* them long.

N is for narrow. Show me a tall, narrow shape.

O is for over. Pretend to *step* over a giant hole in the ground.

P is for plod. How would you *walk* while *plodding* through deep snow?

Q is for quick. Can you *move* your hands quickly at the sides of your body?

R is for roll. Is it possible to *create* a long shape and *roll* along the floor?

S is for swim. Show me how you can pretend to *swim* with your arms.

T is for tiptoe. *Stretch* high into the sky on your tiptoes.

U is for upward. Make believe you are a kite *soaring* upward.

V is for vibrate. Can you *rock, shake*, and *vibrate* like a giant machine?

W is for wiggle. In what ways can you *wiggle* your fingers?

X is for X-ray. Use your finger and *point* to a bone in your hand.

Y is for yank. Show me how you can *yank* an imaginary rope.

Z is for zigzag. Is it possible to *skip* in a zigzag pattern?

Assessment Questions

1. Which letters had actions that were the most fun to imitate? Can you show me?
2. Who can show me how you could move like the first letter in your name?
3. Can you identify a letter that had an action that was difficult to imitate? What can we do to make the action easier (e.g., T is for tiptoe: Stretch arms out at the sides of the body to improved balance.).

Academic Language Demands

- **Language function:** Uses language to verbally critique one's own performance of action words.
- **Vocabulary:** zigzag, curl, grip, plod, vibrate, yank
- **Syntax or discourse:** A verbal interchange concerning new vocabulary words and how to perform them.

ALPHABET LETTERS

National Standards Addressed

Standard 3. The physically literate individual demonstrates the knowledge and skills to achieve and maintain a health-enhancing level of physical activity and fitness.

Instructional Materials/Props

Photographs of objects or living creatures that move (optional), letters of the alphabet on display (optional), box, hat, or container (optional)

Central Focus

To manipulate the body in order to move like objects starting with a specific alphabet letter.

Objectives

- **Cognitive:** The child will name objects starting with specific letters of the alphabet and participate in the object's movement.
- **Affective:** The child will maintain a high level of attentiveness and desire to perform the movement of each object beginning with a specific alphabet letter.
- **Psychomotor:** The child will imitate the actions and movements of objects or things that begin with specific alphabet letters using the correct form in an appropriate and purposeful manner among his or her peers.

Component of Health-Related Fitness

Cardiorespiratory endurance

Learning Task 1: Preparing Our Bodies to Move

Class organization: Children are scattered throughout general space.

Challenge the children to perform movements of A, B, C, and D creatures at a farmyard pond: **a**nts *scurrying,* **b**ees *buzzing* from flower to flower, **c**rows *flying* overhead, **d**ucks *waddling.*

Learning Task 2: Partner Challenge

Class organization: Partners are scattered throughout general space.

Give partners a picture of an object or living creature that moves. You can also whisper the name of the object or creature if pictures are unavailable. Each set of partners takes turns acting out the movements of the object or creature while the other children guess what it is. Suggested pictures include airplanes *soaring,* balls *bouncing,* cars *racing,* drums *beating,* elephants *stomping,* frogs *jumping,* goats *kicking,* hands *clapping,* jellyfish *floating,* kites *soaring,* lions *pouncing.* Children can give verbal clues to assist their classmates in identifying the object or creature (e.g., Our letter is F.).

Learning Task 3: Alphabet Box

Class organization: Children are scattered in identified groups.

For very young children, reinforce that each letter of the alphabet can represent items or things. Encourage the children to use their bodies to create the movements of the objects beginning with alphabet letters. Whenever possible, use photographs or drawings of the objects or things because some ELL children may not know the English names of the objects. For slightly older children, write each letter of the alphabet on a small piece of paper or index card and place the cards in an envelope, hat, or plastic container. This container becomes the alphabet box. Organize the children into four or five groups. One child from each group picks a card from the container and reads the alphabet letter aloud to the entire class. Read aloud the list of objects associated with that letter and ask the children to perform the corresponding actions.

A

Astronauts *floating*

Apes *swinging*

B

Balloons *inflating*

Butterflies *fluttering*

Bubbles *bursting*

Birds *flying*

Baseball bats *swinging*

Buffalo *stampeding*

C

Clocks *ticking*

Cats *arching*

Chicks *chirping*

Crabs *walking*

Camels *plodding*

Crocodiles *crawling* alongside the swamp

D

Dancers *twirling*

Dolphins *leaping*

Deer *running*

Donkeys *plodding*

E

Elbows *bending*

Eagles *soaring*

F

Fans *spinning*

Fish *swimming*

Feet *stamping*

G

Gerbils *scurrying*

Geese *flying*

Goldfish *swimming*

Gophers *digging*

H

Hammers *pounding*

Hippopotami *splashing*

Helicopters *hovering*

I

Ice skates *sliding*

Ice *melting*

J

Jets *soaring*

Jump ropes *turning*

Jaguars *stalking*

K

Kittens *stretching*

Keys *turning*

Knots *twisting*

L

Leopards *pouncing*

Lambs *prancing*

Lungs *expanding*

M

Mice *scampering*

Mops *swishing*

Motorcycles *speeding*

Machines *vibrating*

Mighty muscles *stretching*

N

Neon lights *flashing*

Nightingales *flying*

O

Owls *hooting*

Oak trees *swaying*

P

Pigs *rolling*

Pinwheels *twirling*

Penguins *waddling*

People *hugging*

Popcorn *popping*

Q

Quails *cooing*

Quadriceps muscles *stretching*

R

Rabbits *jumping*

Roosters *strutting*

Rhinoceroses *charging*

Reindeer *prancing*

S

Snails *slithering*

Sleds *dashing*

Sailors *scrubbing*

Squirrels *scampering*

Spiders *crawling*

Seals *clapping*

Scorpions *stinging*

T

Tigers *charging*

Tails *wagging*

Trains *trudging*

Trees *swaying*

Turkeys *trotting*

Trout *swimming*

U

Umbrellas *opening*

Ukulele strings *vibrating*

V

Vehicles *zooming*

Vines *climbing*

Vultures *circling*

W

Water *dripping*

Whales *diving*

Woodcutters *chopping*

Wolves *howling*

Woodpeckers *pecking*

Worms *wiggling*

Wheels *turning*

XYZ

Yo-yos *rising* and *lowering*

Yachts *sailing*

Zebras *galloping*

Zippers *zipping* up and down

Assessment Questions

1. Can you trace your favorite letter in the air?
2. Show me how you can move like an object or creature that begins with that letter.
3. If you could bring a make-believe object to school, what would it be? What letter does your object start with? Show me how you could move like that object.

Academic Language Demands

- **Language function:** Uses language to describe how to move like the object or thing.
- **Vocabulary:** stampede, hover, stalk, sway, coo, strut, slither, scamper
- **Syntax or discourse:** A verbal interchange focusing on experiences the children have had related to specific objects or living creatures.

ALPHABET TREASURES

National Standards Addressed

Standard 2. The physically literate individual applies knowledge of concepts, principles, strategies and tactics related to movement and performance.

Instructional Materials/Props

Letters of the alphabet on display (optional), pictures of alphabet treasures (optional)

Central Focus

To imitate movements common to objects and things that begin with each letter of the alphabet.

Objectives

- **Cognitive:** The child will differentiate between a variety of directions, levels, and speeds in preparation for an imaginary search for alphabet treasures.
- **Affective:** The child will strive to follow his or her partner and imitate the movements demonstrated while searching for the imaginary buried treasure.
- **Psychomotor:** The child will display the correct movements and actions of the letter being presented in each alphabet letter challenge.

Component of Health-Related Fitness

Muscular strength and endurance

Learning Task 1: Preparing Our Bodies to Move

Class organization: Children are scattered throughout general space.

Challenge the children to perform the following actions:

- Can you *walk* and change your direction? Level? Speed?
- Is it possible to *run* while your body is close to the floor and then rise to your highest running position?

Learning Task 2: Partner Challenge

Class organization: Partners are scattered throughout general space.

Partners take turns being the leader *searching* for a buried treasure while the other partner follows. Encourage partners to change direction, level, and speed while they travel over various imaginary terrains (e.g., high mountains, low valleys, narrow pathways, and rocky stepping stones) until you shout, "I see the alphabet treasure over there," and point to a space in the playing area. The learning task continues until both partners have had a turn at being the leader.

Learning Task 3: Searching for Alphabet Treasures

Class organization: Children are scattered in self-spaces.

Present the following: *Today is the day we search for alphabet treasures. This search takes place every fall (or winter, spring or summer). Your task is to use your imaginations to move with each letter of the alphabet. Some of the objects are very large, and some are very small. Each imaginary object must be placed into a magic sack. This magic sack will let you carry all the objects at the same time.*

A is for apple. Because the apple tree is tall, you will need to reach up as high as you can. Now *stretch* up on your tiptoes and *grab* for an apple. When you *reach* the apple, *pull* it down, and *place* it in your sack.

B is for bicycle. A bicycle needs to be pedaled. Lie on your back and use your legs to *pedal* a bicycle before you put it in the sack.

C is for cow. To get a cow's attention you need to sound like a cow. Can you do that?

D is for dinosaur. Dinosaurs are very large and heavy animals. To catch a dinosaur, try sneaking up quietly and slowly to surprise it.

E is for egg. Eggs break very easily. You need to carefully lift them from a nest so they do not break. Pretend you are *protecting* the eggs with your arms.

F is for frog. Frogs live in ponds and jump from lily pad to lily pad. To catch a frog, make believe that you are *following* it across the pond.

G is for guitar. Guitars have strings to make music. Can you *strum* a tune? We can all play together. Ready? One, two, three.

H is for horse. When horses move very quickly, we call the action galloping. See if you can *gallop* in a circle.

I is for ice cream. Ice cream is very cold until it begins to melt. Can you make your body *shiver* because it's cold like ice cream? Slowly *melt* to the floor.

J is for Jell-O. Jell-O wiggles and jiggles. Show me that you can *wiggle* and *jiggle*.

K is for kangaroo. Kangaroos carry their babies in pouches, and they jump using their back legs. How high can you *jump*?

L is for lasso. Lassos are special ropes that cowboys and cowgirls use. They twirl them high over their heads and at the side of their bodies. What kinds of things can you do with a lasso?

M is for monkey. Monkeys climb, swing on vines, and jump from tree to tree. How would you *act* if you were a monkey?

N is for noodle. Before noodles are cooked, they are stiff. After they are cooked, they are limp and wiggly. Who can show me what happens to a noodle when it is cooked?

O is for octopus. An octopus lives in the water and has eight tentacles. Tentacles are like our arms and legs. Make believe your legs and arms are tentacles.

P is for parachute. People use parachutes when they jump out of planes. Parachutes help them to float to the ground safely. Show me how you can *jump* and then *float* to the ground.

Q is for quack. Ducks quack as they waddle. Show me how you can quack and *waddle*.

R is for robot. Robots are made of metal and use stiff and jerky motions when they walk. Who can show me how a robot *walks*?

S is for snake. Snakes do not have arms or legs so they must slither on the ground by wiggling their body. Make believe you are a snake and *slither*.

T is for top. Tops spin around and around. Let's all *spin* like a top without falling down.

U is for umbrella. Umbrellas help to keep us dry when it rains. Please *pick* up one umbrella, *open* and *close* it, and *put* it in your sack.

V is for volcano. Volcanoes are mountains that contain a very hot liquid. When this liquid gets too hot, it suddenly shoots up from the top of the volcano. Is it possible to *explode* like a volcano?

W is for worm. Worms look like very small snakes, and they live in the dirt. To find a worm, show me how you would *dig* a hole.

X is for xylophone. Xylophones are musical instruments that you play by striking it with two sticks. Before you place it in the sack, let's try to *play* a song.

Y is for yo-yo. Yo-yos move up and down on a string. Imagine you are a yo-yo *rising* up and then *lowering* down toward the floor.

Z is for zipper. Zippers help us to close our coats, pants, and shirts. Zippers also move up and down. Show me how you can *close* an imaginary coat.

Wonderful! You have completed the search for alphabet treasures.

Assessment Questions

1. Who can move like their favorite object or living thing?

2. I hope you remembered to place the objects in your magic sack. Next year, the search for alphabet treasures will begin again with new objects to find. Before we leave, please empty your sack into the box in the center of the play area so that others will find these special objects someday when they search for alphabet treasures.

3. Before we finish, who can move like an object that was not in our sack? Share your ideas.

Academic Language Demands

- **Language function:** Uses language to interpret instructions for a successful imaginary treasure hunt.
- **Vocabulary:** stretch, pedal, strum, shiver, twirl, waddle, explode, protect, treasure
- **Syntax or discourse:** A verbal interchange between children concerning how to respond to the second part of the movement task in each sentence.

ALPHABET RHYTHM

National Standards Addressed

- **Standard 2.** The physically literate individual applies knowledge of concepts, principles, strategies and tactics related to movement and performance.
- **Standard 4.** The physically literate individual exhibits responsible personal and social behavior that respects self and others.

Instructional Materials/Props

Lively music

Central Focus

To perform actions that coincide with words that represents each letter of the alphabet.

Objectives

- **Cognitive:** The child will discuss objects representing letters of the alphabet and the way in which these objects move.
- **Affective:** The child will continue to participate actively with enthusiasm even when fatigued in the partner task.
- **Psychomotor:** The child will exhibit the correct action verb in the poem and move appropriately as the teacher recites the poem for each letter of the alphabet.

Component of Health-Related Fitness

Cardiorespiratory endurance

Learning Task 1: Preparing Our Bodies to Move

Class organization: Children are scattered throughout general space.

Challenge the children to perform the following actions: Begin by playing music with all children dancing and moving about. When the music stops, the children freeze. Call out a letter and an action word that coincides with the letter, as in J for jumping. When the music resumes, the children jump. The learning task continues as you change the locomotor or nonlocomotor skill each time the music stops (e.g., M for marching, W for wiggling, S for shaking).

Learning Task 2: Partner Challenge

Class organization: Partners are scattered throughout general space.

Play lively music and challenge partners to hold hands and *shake*, *wiggle*, and *move* around while continuing to hold one or both hands.

Learning Task 3: Alphabet Rock and Roll

Class organization: Children are scattered in self-spaces.

Explain that the alphabet has been used in many lively songs. Then present the following rhyme and challenge the children to respond in creative, musical ways:

We got the moves from A to Z,
Clap your hands and *stomp* your feet.
We got the moves from A to Z,
Come and make some moves with me.
A is for alligator, *chomp, chomp, chomp,*
B is for bear, *stomping* with a thump.
C is for a cat, *chasing* a mouse,
D is for dog, *scampering* into his house.
E is for elephant, *stomping* and *eating* peanuts from my hand,
F is for fish, *plunging* toward the sand.
G is for ghost that makes us *tremble* and *shake,*
H is for *happy* faces we can make.
I is for inchworm, *creeping* along my arm,
J is for jolly, *rolling* pigs on the farm.
K is for kite, *flying* in the sky,
L is for lizards, *leaping* high.
M is for mouse, *sitting still* as can be,
N is for bird, *chirping* in a nest in a tree.
O is for octopus, *wrapped* in a ball,
P is for peacock, *strutting* proud and tall.
Q is for the quickness of a *jumping* kangaroo,
R is for rooster, *crowing* cock-a-doodle-do.
S is for a long, *slithering* snake,
T is for tortoise, taking a *stroll* by the lake.
U is for *looking* up to find a shooting star,
V is for the vroom, vroom, vroom of a *speeding* race car.
W is for the *whirling* winds of a cyclone,
X is for the circus horses, *prancing* to the xylophone.
Y is for yaks, *plodding* two by two,
Z is for zebra, *galloping* at the outdoor zoo.

Assessment Questions

1. What object or thing challenged you to move the most?
2. Can you think of another way to move to your favorite letter?
3. Let's create another alphabet sentence about an object. What letter does it start with? How would this object move?

Academic Language Demands

- **Language function:** Uses language to explain the movement of the object or thing that the body can make when asked.
- **Vocabulary:** stomp, plunge, tremble, creep, strut, stroll, whirl, plod
- **Syntax or discourse:** A verbal interchange focusing on the rhyming alphabet objects and how each object moves.

MY BODY CAN FORM LETTERS

National Standards Addressed

- **Standard 1.** The physically literate individual demonstrates competency in a variety of motor skills and movement patterns.
- **Standard 4.** The physically literate individual exhibits responsible personal and social behavior that respects self and others.

Instructional Materials/Props

One large poster containing the letters of the alphabet displayed at a height that permits all children to see the letters clearly. The dots on each letter indicate where each child's head can be positioned.

Central Focus

To challenge children to create alphabet letters by using their bodies to form lines and half circles.

Objectives

- **Cognitive:** The child will make comparisons of the letters of the alphabet to those being created by the body.
- **Affective:** The child will listen to the suggestions of his or her partner when creating alphabet letters.
- **Psychomotor:** The child will explore a variety of circles and lines the body can make to create several letters as indicated on a poster.

Component of Health-Related Fitness

Flexibility

Learning Task 1: Preparing Our Bodies to Move

Class organization: Children are scattered throughout general space.

Present the following: *Let's start by finding different ways to write letters without using a pen or pencil.* Challenge the children to perform the following actions:

- Pretend you are a giant paint brush and *brush* the letter L as you *slide* your feet along the floor.
- Find three ways to use your body to *write* the letter S.
- Can you *draw* in the air a large letter O? Show me that you can add eyes, a nose, and a smile to your large circle and *create* a smiley face.

Learning Task 2: Partner Challenge

Class organization: Partners are scattered throughout general space.

Present the following: *People learn to print alphabet letters by drawing straight lines and half circles.* Challenge the children to perform the following actions:

- Who can *demonstrate* a long, thin, narrow shape at a low level? See whether you can curl your body into a curved shape. These shapes are needed to make the lines in alphabet letters.
- Select a partner, buddy, or pal and *form* three alphabet letters at a low level.

Learning Task 3: **Word of the Week**

Class organization: Children are scattered in identified groups.

- Organize the children into trios. Ask each set of three to form two letters.
- Reorganize the children into groups of four. Ask each group of four to select and form one alphabet letter.
- Complete the learning task by asking the class, as a whole, to use their bodies to spell out the word of the week (e.g., fun, joy, eye, leg, ear, head, nose, food, face, move, smile, alphabet, muscle, healthy). Write the word in large letters for all to see, and review what the word means.

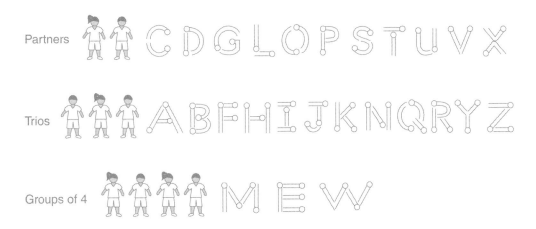

Assessment Questions

1. Who can recall the shapes our bodies made to form alphabet letters (e.g., long, thin, narrow shapes; curves)?
2. Which letters were the most difficult to create with your bodies? Why?
3. Can you think of a three-letter word that you could create with a trio that means to be happy (joy or fun)?

Academic Language Demands

- **Language function:** Uses language to describe and model a letter that is needed to create a word.
- **Vocabulary:** muscle, healthy, (any word that serves as the word of the week)
- **Syntax or discourse:** A verbal interchange focusing on how to combine everyone's body to create a large word on the floor.

BRAIN-AND-BODY CONNECTION

National Standards Addressed

- **Standard 1.** The physically literate individual demonstrates competency in a variety of motor skills and movement patterns.
- **Standard 3.** The physically literate individual demonstrates the knowledge and skills to achieve and maintain a health-enhancing level of physical activity and fitness.

Instructional Materials/Props

None required

Central Focus

To complete a verbal challenge sentence with a logical answer and respond by physically acting out the sentence.

Objectives

- **Cognitive:** The child will match an object to a specific movement vocabulary word to logically complete a sentence.
- **Affective:** The child will listen to his or her partner's creative word and respond in a supportive way.
- **Psychomotor:** The child will perform the correct response in the movement sentence and move in a manner that is recognizable throughout the series of challenges.

Component of Health-Related Fitness

Cardiorespiratory endurance

Learning Task 1: Preparing Our Bodies to Move

Class organization: Children are scattered throughout general space.
Challenge the children to perform the following actions:

- Discover the smallest *leap* you can make; now the largest.
- Show me how you can *leap* as high in the air as possible.
- Try *leaping* over an imaginary pile of leaves.

Learning Task 2: Partner Challenge

Class organization: Partners are scattered throughout general space.
Present the following:

- Invent a crazy word with your partner and *move* like that word.
- Can you think of another way of *moving* for your word?

Learning Task 3: Think and Move

Class organization: Children are scattered throughout general space.
Present the following: *The names of objects and actions are words. In this active guessing game, you will read a sentence that has one word missing, fill in the blank, and demonstrate the action of the sentence.*

Use the following example: I can *throw* a _____ (e.g., ball). In this example, the children should orally reply "ball" followed by a brief demonstration of a throwing action. (*Note*: You may also point to one child or ask one child to shout out an answer followed by all children demonstrating the action.)

I can *hide* under a _____ (e.g., bed, table).

I can *climb* a tall _____ (e.g., tree, hill, mountain).

I can *walk* down _____ (e.g., stairs, steps).

I can *open* a _____ (e.g., present, door).

I *sleep* in a _____ (e.g., bed, cot).

I *sit* on a _____ (e.g., chair, couch).

I *ride* in a _____ (e.g., car, bus, truck).

I can *stack* _____ (e.g., blocks, books, boxes).

I can *pull* a _____ (e.g., wagon, toy).

I can *leap* over a _____ (e.g., puddle).

I can *prance* like a _____ (e.g., horse).

I can *skate* on _____ (e.g., ice).

I can *march* like a _____ (e.g., robot, soldier).

I can *slither* like a _____ (e.g., snake).

I can *spin* like a _____ (e.g., helicopter, top).

I can *waddle* like a _____ (e.g., duck, penguin).

I can *wiggle* like a _____ (e.g., worm).

I can *burst* like a _____ (e.g., bubble).

I can *melt* like _____ (e.g., ice cream, snow, ice).

I can *jump* _____ (e.g., rope).

I can *trudge* through the _____ (e.g., snow, mud).

I can *sway* like a _____ (e.g., flower, tree).

I can *flutter* like a _____ (e.g., butterfly, leaf).

I can *float* like a _____ (e.g., cloud, bubble, boat).

I can *sing* like a _____ (e.g., bird, sparrow, robin, parakeet).

Assessment Questions

1. Who can tell the class about their favorite guessing game?
2. When we guess an answer we have to use our thinking skills. Show me how your body moves when you are thinking.
3. Can you and a partner think of another creative way to move?

Academic Language Demands

- **Language function:** Uses language to give reasons for an action when asked.
- **Vocabulary:** climb, stack, leap, prance, skate, burst, trudge, sway, flutter, float
- **Syntax or discourse:** A verbal interchange concerning which object or thing to select when asked.

BODY LANGUAGE

National Standards Addressed

Standard 4. The physically literate individual exhibits responsible personal and social behavior that respects self and others.

Instructional Materials/Props

Lively music

Central Focus

To use various body parts and gestures to communicate through movement.

Objectives

- **Cognitive:** The child will recall that body language and facial expressions are a form of communication and he or she can match these movements to their verbal counterparts.
- **Affective:** The child will exhibit an eagerness to participate in the silent partner activity.
- **Psychomotor:** The child will demonstrate a variety of facial expressions and use gestures to urge classmates to follow and repeat a desired movement.

Component of Health-Related Fitness

Flexibility

Learning Task 1: Preparing Our Bodies to Move

Class organization: Children are scattered throughout general space.

Challenge the children to perform the following actions:

- *Run* lightly on your toes throughout the playing area, and please be careful not to bump a classmate.
- Follow me as I *run* using different steps (e.g., tiny, long, light, heavy, crisscross, wide).

Learning Task 2: Partner Challenge

Class organization: Partners are scattered throughout general space.

Ask the children to quickly select a partner and then present the following: *We can use our body parts to tell people things or to communicate how we are feeling without saying a word. Show me how you use your hands to say hello to your partner (e.g., wave, shake hands).* Challenge the children to perform the following actions:

- *Wave* both arms high into the air to get your partner's attention.
- Can your shoulders say to your partner you feel tired?
- How would you show that you are very strong?
- Use your hands to say good job (e.g., thumbs up, clap).
- How do you use your hands to tell your partner to follow you?
- Find a way to show your partner that your legs are stiff, now floppy, now happy.

Learning Task 3: Body Language Follow the Leader

Class organization: Children are scattered throughout general space.

Present the following: *Use body gestures and movements to "talk" or communicate with each other while performing specific tasks.* Use the following examples:

- The first child stoops in a small shape and indicates by a wave of the hand that the second child is to move over his or her body.
- The second child motions for the first child to follow and skip to a particular side of the room by pointing to the space.
- Encourage small groups of children to play follow the leader without talking.

Assessment Questions

1. Which body parts do we most often use to communicate?
2. What do you think are the best ways to communicate?
3. Can anyone tell me what sign language is and who uses it?

Academic Language Demands

- **Language function:** Uses language to sequence movements when necessary.
- **Vocabulary:** communicate, body gestures
- **Syntax or discourse:** A verbal interchange aimed at specific follow-the-leader actions.

TWISTING AND TWIRLING ACTIONS

National Standards Addressed

Standard 2. The physically literate individual applies knowledge of concepts, principles, strategies and tactics related to movement and performance.

Instructional Materials/Props

Four to six bean bags, floor spots, or similar small objects

Central Focus

To differentiate between twisting and twirling movements while performing individual and group movement tasks.

Objectives

- **Cognitive:** The child will indicate the importance of safely navigating through general space.
- **Affective:** The child will show a sense of responsibility by assisting the group's effort to twirl around a circular shape.
- **Psychomotor:** As part of a group of four, the child grasps hands or wrists and twirls in a circular shape in a controlled manner.

Component of Health-Related Fitness

Muscular strength and endurance

Learning Task 1: Preparing Our Bodies to Move

Class organization: Children are scattered throughout general space.

Challenge the children to perform the following actions:

- See if you can *run* fast and stop suddenly on my signal.
- Suppose you pick an imaginary spot on the floor away from you. Now *run* to it, and return without bumping into anyone.

Learning Task 2: Partner Challenge

Class organization: Partners scattered throughout general space. Partners collaborate to problem-solve the challenges listed as you present the following:

- Show your partner how many body parts can you *twist* (e.g., ankles, wrists, and hips).
- Can you show your partner how you can *twist* your whole body into a new shape?
- See if you and your partner can *twist* your hips to dance back and forth.
- With your partner, find a way to *twirl* your bodies around and around without losing your balance. Try again, only this time begin with your arms close to your chest and then slowly *twirl* around while *extending* your arms outward.
- Discover a way for you and your partner to *twirl* your bodies around several times and stop in a *twisted* narrow shape.
- Is it possible to hold your partner's hands and see if you can *twirl* each other safely in a circular shape?

Learning Task 3: Flying Spaceships

Class organization: Children are scattered in identified groups.

- Create groups of four. Challenge the groups to grasp hands or wrists and to twirl in a circular shape.
- Encourage the groups to change from a medium level to a low level while slowly raising their hands to a high level.
- Challenge the groups to twirl and move forward like a flying spaceship.
- Explain that you have scattered several small objects throughout the activity area. They are called landing pads.
- Challenge the groups of four to twirl while moving to each landing pad.
- The groups should hover over a marker for three seconds before moving on to a second marker.

Assessment Questions

1. What body parts can you easily twist without injuring the body (e.g., ankles, wrists, and hips)? Twist those body parts.
2. What body parts did you use most to keep your balance when you were twirling in a group circle?
3. Why do you think it is necessary for all group members to cooperate when twirling in a circle as a group?

Academic Language Demands

- **Language function:** Uses language to signal group members' twirling movement so that it is controlled.
- **Vocabulary:** twirl, twist
- **Syntax or discourse:** A verbal interchange focusing on why it is necessary to have the cooperation of all group members in order to twirl in a circular shape.

HALLOWEEN OBJECTS

National Standards Addressed

Standard 2. The physically literate individual applies knowledge of concepts, principles, strategies and tactics related to movement and performance.

Instructional Materials/Props

Pictures or objects associated with Halloween (optional)

Central Focus

To use different body parts to create make-believe objects associated with Halloween.

Objectives

- **Cognitive:** The child will describe how objects associated with Halloween move.
- **Affective:** The child will show a willingness to change partners and combine bodies when asked to create larger Halloween objects.
- **Psychomotor:** The child will move in a manner associated with a variety of Halloween objects and recognize expressions and gestures that coincide with those objects.

Components of Health-Related Fitness

Cardiorespiratory endurance, flexibility

Learning Task 1: Preparing Our Bodies to Move

Class organization: Children are scattered throughout general space.

Challenge the children to perform the following actions:

- Imagine you are wearing a Halloween mask. Show me what it looks like.
- How many different ways can you *stretch* your monster muscles?
- *Shake* your bony arms and legs as you *move* like a skeleton.
- Show me how you can *walk on your tiptoes* like black cats *balancing* along a narrow fence.
- *Swing* your long tail, roar, and *breathe* fire as you *stomp* loudly like a dragon.
- Can you be a large round jack-o'-lantern or pumpkin shape?
- *Skip* along with your friends and make believe you are *carrying* a large bag of Halloween treats.

Learning Task 2: Partner Challenge

Class organization: Partners are scattered in self-spaces.

Present the following:

- How would you *move* if one partner pretended to be a broom and the other pretended to be a witch?
- Spiders have many legs. Can you and a partner *move* like a spider?
- Is it possible to *join* another set of partners and *create* a four-person monster?

Learning Task 3: **Haunted House**

Class organization: Children are scattered in identified groups.

- Divide the children into two groups. One group constructs the walls of a house by forming two side-by-side lines facing each other. Children in the second group make believe they are trick-or-treaters and merrily skip throughout the playing area.

- When you signal that it is nightfall, the walls of the house can reach out, move, and shake in their self-spaces to scare children. Remind the children that the walls should not grab at the trick-or-treaters, only stretch and try to scare the children while remaining in a stationary line. Exchange roles.

Assessment Questions

1. Halloween is a time when children can dress up in costumes and pretend to be objects, animals, cartoon characters, and people. What kinds of faces might a jack-o'-lantern have? Show me.

2. Use your imagination to show me how a spook moves through a haunted house.

3. Name three things we should do to be safe on Halloween.

Academic Language Demands

- **Language function:** Uses language to discuss the movements of different objects or things associated with Halloween.

- **Vocabulary:** shake, stretch, walk on tiptoes, scary, nightfall

- **Syntax or discourse:** A verbal interchange concerning how Halloween objects and things most commonly move according to one's interpretation.

Movement Narratives

PLACES IN OUR COMMUNITY

National Standards Addressed

- **Standard 1.** The physically literate individual demonstrates competency in a variety of motor skills and movement patterns.
- **Standard 4.** The physically literate individual exhibits responsible personal and social behavior that respects self and others.

Instructional Materials/Props

Pictures of different types of communities (e.g., located near water, in the desert, on a mountaintop, urban, small town) (optional)

Central Focus

To explore a series of physical skills while making believe he or she is traveling within a community and to faraway destinations.

Objectives

- **Cognitive:** The child will distinguish a variety of physical actions associated with traveling locally and outside of the community using both the body and imaginary modes of transportation.
- **Affective:** The child will express enjoyment while imitating the movements and varying speeds set by his or her partner.
- **Psychomotor:** The child will perform numerous locomotor skills as each action word is verbally conveyed to the class as a whole while also exhibiting appropriate behaviors and emotions that naturally coincide with the key characters in the narrative.

Component of Health-Related Fitness

Cardiorespiratory endurance

Learning Task 1: Preparing Our Bodies to Move

Class organization: Children are scattered throughout general space.

Challenge the children to perform the following actions:

- Our feet contain muscles for moving on many surfaces. Show me how you are *walking* up, up, up a hill and now imagine the hill has become a steep mountain and *stretch* upward on your toes.
- Can you make believe you are at the beach, barefoot and *walking* on hot sand? Take three *hops* on one foot saying "Ouch! Ouch! Ouch!" and then *hop* on the other foot saying, "Hot, hot, hot." Try this three times.

Learning Task 2: Partner Challenge

Class organization: Partners are scattered in self-spaces.

Present the following:

- Is it possible to *run* side by side with a partner at the same speed, such as fast, slow, and medium?
- Play follow the leader with one partner showing how to *step* over or *move* around large rocks. Follow your partner's pathway. Exchange roles.

Learning Task 3: Means of Transportation

Class organization: Children are scattered in general space.

Present the following: *I will read a story aloud to the class, and it is your task to imitate the action words and behavior in the story.*

> Aisha *stretched* upward on her toes to look out the window. She liked school, and she loved riding on the long, yellow school bus. While waiting for the school bus, Aisha began to imagine that she was . . .
>
> *Walking* to the movie theater,
>
> *Jogging* to the park,
>
> *Running* to the playground,
>
> *Galloping* on horseback at the farm,
>
> *Pedaling* her bicycle to the grocery store and *roller skating* or *ice skating* at the rink.
>
> "Someday I will travel to faraway places," thought Aisha. She imagined . . .
>
> *Driving* a motorcycle along twisting roads,
>
> *Swinging* on long vines in the jungle,
>
> *Chugging* along railroad tracks,
>
> *Sprinting* across the lake in a speedboat,
>
> *Trudging* up a hill in a large tank,
>
> *Rocking* back and forth on a sailboat,
>
> *Plodding* across the desert on a tall camel,
>
> *Blasting* upward in a rocket to the moon and *parachuting* down from a plane.
>
> At that moment, the school bus arrived at Aisha's house. "Today, I will *ride* the elevator down, down, down and happily travel on the bus to school," she said.

Assessment Questions

1. Who can name a place they would like to visit?
2. What activity would you perform there? Show me.
3. Is it possible to show me your parents' or grandparents' favorite way of traveling?

Academic Language Demands

- **Language function:** Uses language to identify different ways that we can use our body to move as well as describing different forms of transportation.
- **Vocabulary:** chug, trudge, rock, pedal, parachute
- **Syntax or discourse:** A verbal interchange focusing on how to best demonstrate some of the more advanced forms of transportation and how to best show the emotions that most often coincide with each form of transportation.

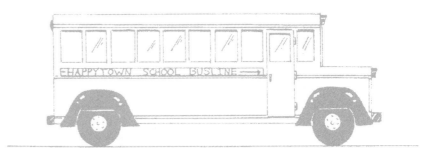

SUPER BODIES

National Standards Addressed

- **Standard 1.** The physically literate individual demonstrates competency in a variety of motor skills and movement patterns.
- **Standard 4.** The physically literate individual exhibits responsible personal and social behavior that respects self and others.

Instructional Materials/Props

Lively music, photographs or posters of superheroes on display (optional), scarves as superhero capes (optional)

Central Focus

To increase the child's language arts skills while imitating actions and expressive feelings of the characters in the fictional narrative.

Objectives

- **Cognitive:** The child will respond to verbal directions associated with fictional and real superheroes.
- **Affective:** The child will express an interest in moving in a lively manner and imitating the actions and behaviors of superheroes.
- **Psychomotor:** The child will display the actions and movements of imaginary fictional characters directly after they are read and respond in an orderly way in the task reflecting superheroes.

Component of Health-Related Fitness

Cardiorespiratory endurance

Learning Task 1: Preparing Our Bodies to Move

Class organization: Children are scattered in self-spaces.

Challenge the children to perform the following actions:

- Superheroes have many special powers. To be one of the fastest-running superheroes, stand in your self-space and show me how you can *run* fast by *pumping* your arms at your side.
- See if you can *jump* in the air and *land* lightly and quietly. Try this three times.

Learning Task 2: Partner Challenge

Class organization: Partners are scattered in general spaces.

Present the following: *Make-believe superheroes help people throughout our cities.* Organize the children into partners.

- One partner uses his or her body and becomes a superhero and moves with the other superheroes to an area in the corner of the room.
- The other partner works with his or her side of the class to create city buildings that are scattered throughout the playing area.
- When you play lively music, the superheroes leave their area and fly between the scattered buildings. When the music stops, the partners exchange roles and the buildings become the new superheroes.

Learning Task 3: Heroes on the Move

Class organization: Children are scattered in general spaces.

Present the following: *I will read a story aloud to the class, and it is your task to imitate the action words and behavior in the story.*

Clifford left the movie theater feeling very excited. The movie had shown brave men and women performing many daring deeds. "If I were a superhero, I could move in many different ways," thought Clifford. "I would be able to . . .

Run and *jump* into the air,

Leap over tall buildings,

Gallop along on a large white horse,

Crawl up the sides of buildings,

Grab a vine and *swing* from tree to tree,

Burst through a wall without being scratched,

Change my body into rubber and *bounce* like a ball,

Stretch my body as if it is a ginormous rubber band,

Soar through the air like an eagle,

Crawl low to the ground using my arms and legs,

Stoop and *lift* large, heavy objects,

Tiptoe quietly like an invisible person,

Melt into a liquid state on the ground,

Swim like a shark,

Stamp out forest fires without burning my feet,

Transform my body into a giant bulldozer and *push* the land,

And *run* faster than a steaming locomotive,

All on the same day."

Assessment Questions

1. Who can demonstrate the movements of their favorite superhero?
2. There are also heroes in our community who don't wear masks. They perform courageous acts every day. Can you name any?
3. If you could choose a super power, what would it be? Why?

Academic Language Demands

- **Language function:** Uses language to recall their favorite superhero's actions and movements.
- **Vocabulary:** fly, burst, bounce, soar, melt, stamp, transform
- **Syntax or discourse:** A verbal interchange identifying common superhero behaviors and their movements.

FAIRY TALE ACTIONS

National Standards Addressed

- **Standard 1.** The physically literate individual demonstrates competency in a variety of motor skills and movement patterns.
- **Standard 4.** The physically literate individual exhibits responsible personal and social behavior that respects self and others.

Instructional Materials/Props

Lively music (optional), photographs of fairy tale characters (optional)

Central Focus

To increase the child's language arts skills while imitating actions and expressive feelings of the characters within the fictional narrative.

Objectives:

- **Cognitive:** The child will recognize that the characters he or she is portraying are performing unique movements and actions unlike those in the original fairy tale.
- **Affective:** The child will cooperate with a partner in order to skip together without disruption.
- **Psychomotor:** The child will perform creative and imaginative physical skills of well-known fairy tale characters in scenarios that are unlike their original story and will listen carefully in order to exhibit the expression or perform the action called for in the narrative.

Component of Health-Related Fitness

Cardiorespiratory endurance

Learning Task 1: Preparing Our Bodies to Move

Class organization: Children are scattered in self-spaces.

Challenge the children to perform the following actions:

- Imagine you are *walking* through gooey mud, on slippery ice, on the moon.
- Create different ways to *jump* over a puddle of water without getting wet.
- Pretend you are a frog. Show me how you can move like a frog *jumping* from one lily pad to the next. Remember to land on all fours.
- Make believe you are *running* in a deep forest and *dashing* from side to side to avoid the low branches.

Learning Task 2: Partner Challenge

Class organization: Partners are scattered throughout general space,

Challenge partners to *grasp* hands and *skip* down an imaginary long, winding forest path. Use music whenever possible.

Learning Task 3: Fearless Fairytale

Class organization: Children are scattered throughout general space.

Present the following: *I will read a story aloud to the class and it is your task to imitate the action words and behavior in the story.*

Each night, Arlene's father asked her the same question, "Which fairy tale would you like to hear this evening?"

Each night, Arlene replied by saying, "All of them, Daddy." One evening, Arlene's father decided to grant his daughter's request. He began the task by asking her to make believe she was a character in the fairy tale. Feeling *fearless,* she *stretched* her body into a strong shape as her father began the story.

He said, "Once upon a time a little girl named Gretel began *searching* to find her brother Hansel. She started her journey by *galloping* down a narrow, twisted road to the shoemaker's house. "Have you seen my brother, Mr. Elf?" asked Gretel.

"No, but please help us *stretch* this leather, and *hammer* a pair of shoes," said the elves. Gretel helped *stretch* and *hammer* before *sneaking* over to see the Big Bad Wolf.

"Help me *huff* and *puff* and *blow* down this house, and we will learn whether Hansel is inside," said the Wolf. Gretel *tried* three times until she *collapsed* to the ground. Hansel was not inside. "If you move quickly, Little Red Riding Hood will be skipping through the forest," said the Wolf. Gretel *tramped* through the deep forest.

She *climbed* a large tree to locate Little Red Riding Hood. "Come *skip* with me and we might see Hansel," said Little Red Riding Hood.

After *skipping* down a dark path, Gretel decided to stop and ask Cinderella. "I'm certain Hansel will be at the ball," said Cinderella. Gretel joined Cinderella and other people on the dance floor. She *shuffled* her feet quickly for one dance, *spun* around in a circle for a second dance, and *clapped* and *kicked* up her heels on the third dance.

"This is wonderful," thought Gretel, "But it is 12 o'clock and I must leave because Hansel is not here."

Gretel was becoming *sad.* Her body *drooped* forward when Cinderella said, "I know where Hansel might be. He must be visiting Snow White."

Gretel *trudged* up the hill to the castle door. She *tiptoed* past the wicked queen. "Maybe one of the Seven Dwarfs can help me," thought Gretel. Grumpy *stomped* both feet and was no help at all. Sleepy *curled* his body into a tiny ball and *closed* his eyes. Bashful *hid* his face while talking to Gretel, and Sneezy could not stop *sneezing.* Happy *pranced* and *strutted* along, but he had not seen Hansel.

Night began to fall. Gretel's body was feeling very *heavy.* She *strolled* slowly to her gingerbread home. Just then Hansel *jumped* out from behind a large rock. "Where have you been, my brother?" asked Gretel.

"First," said Hansel, "I used my strong arms to *climb* a large beanstalk with Jack. Then, I helped three bears *mix* and *stir* a large pot of porridge. Finally, I *pushed* a mean, old, wicked witch into the oven and *fastened* the bolt."

"Oh, Hansel," said Gretel, "You did make my body *tremble* with worry. I'm so glad you had a quiet day."

"Daddy!" exclaimed Arlene, "That is a silly ending to the fairy tale."

"Yes," said Arlene's father, "I should have added that Hansel and Gretel lived happily ever after." With this ending, Arlene *placed* her hands at the side of her face and fell fast *asleep.*

Assessment Questions

1. Which movements were the most difficult to perform and why?
2. Can you and a partner think of another ending for our story?
3. What are other stories that you would like to act out at home with your friends? Name them.

Academic Language Demands

- **Language function:** Uses language to justify a new ending for the whole-group movement task.
- **Vocabulary:** stretch, hammer, huff and puff, blow, skip, shuffle, stomp, hide, curl
- **Syntax or discourse:** A verbal interchange identifying the specific movements of well-known storybook characters.

SO VERY SMALL

National Standards Addressed

- **Standard 1.** The physically literate individual demonstrates competency in a variety of motor skills and movement patterns.
- **Standard 4.** The physically literate individual exhibits responsible personal and social behavior that respects self and others.

Central Focus

To increase the child's language arts skills by imitating actions and expressive feelings of the character in the fictional narrative.

Learning Task

Class organization: Children are scattered in general spaces.

Present the following: *I will read a story aloud to the class, and it is your task to imitate the action words and behavior.*

Ronen watched the tiny insect *curl* its body into a small ball shape. "Being small might be great fun," thought Ronen. "If I were very small, I could . . .

Ski down my bedroom pillow,

Sit in a peanut shell and *paddle* a canoe,

Swim in a teacup swimming pool,

Jump rope with a shoestring,

Hit a home run with a toothpick,

Drive a toy car,

Jump up and down on a kitchen sponge,

Squeeze through cracks in the wall,

Climb a hair comb ladder,

Skate on an ice cube,

Hide in a bottle cap and never be found,

Roll a marble bowling ball,

Float to the ground using a tissue paper parachute,

Touch my toes three times on a potholder exercise mat,

Fly on the back of a buzzing bee,

Or, I could *curl* into a small ball shape like the tiny insect and *sleep* in a slipper."

THE LETTER S

National Standards Addressed

- **Standard 1.** The physically literate individual demonstrates competency in a variety of motor skills and movement patterns.
- **Standard 4.** The physically literate individual exhibits responsible personal and social behavior that respects self and others.

Central Focus

To increase the child's language arts skills by associating and performing actions related to the letter S.

Learning Task

Class organization: Children are scattered in general space.

Present the following:

Time can be measured by minutes and hours in a day. Time is also a word that indicates the moment when something should be started or completed. Listen to the story about a young boy who is learning about time. Your task is to imitate the action words and behaviors as I read aloud.

"What time is it, mother?" asked Sergio from his bedroom door. Sergio didn't wait for his mother's answer.

With a sly *grin*, Sergio decided it was time to move like the letter S so he . . .

Stamped one foot up and down,

Strolled throughout this room,

Sank low to the floor in a flat shape,

And, *shook* his body from head to toe.

"Maybe," thought Sergio, "it's time to . . .

Shrink into a tiny shape,

Stretch into a long shape,

Sway my body from side to side,

And, *spin* around and around in a circle."

"Of course," thought Sergio, "it could be time to . . .

Strut around my room feeling very proud,

Slither like a snake along the floor,

Scuffle my feet as I walk, or

Swim in my bathtub."

Sergio's mother decided to *sneak* upstairs and surprise Sergio. "I think it is time to tidy your room," said Sergio's mother. With that suggestion, Sergio gave a big *smile*, *squeezed* his toys, and knew it was time to clean his room.

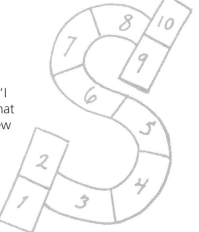

SMALL TO TALL

National Standards Addressed

- **Standard 1.** The physically literate individual demonstrates competency in a variety of motor skills and movement patterns.
- **Standard 4.** The physically literate individual exhibits responsible personal and social behavior that respects self and others.

Central Focus

To increase the child's ability to identify and demonstrate actions that coincide with several occupations.

Learning Task

Class organization: Children are scattered in general space.

Present the following: *I will read a story aloud to the class, and it is your task to imitate the action words and behaviors.*

Sophia *stood* very still as Isabella measured her height. She was 3 feet and 3 inches (99 cm) tall. A *frown* came across Sophia's face as she *dropped* her chin to her chest. Her greatest dream was to be tall and strong and a very special person. "What will I grow up to be?" she wondered.

Maybe one day, I'll be a baker,

Mixing bread, cookies, and cakes.

I'll *shake* and *stir* and *measure*.

Until the batter is ready to bake!

Maybe one day, I'll be an astronaut,

Flying among the stars.

I'll *zoom* by all the planets,

Saturn, Jupiter, and even Mars!

Maybe one day, I'll be a gardener.

I'll *pull* and *yank* every weed in sight.

My peas and beans will *stretch* upward,

As I *water* the plants with great delight!

Or, maybe one day, I'll be a dancer,

Twirling and *spinning* around.

Sounds of lively music will thrill me,

As I *leap* forward and *land* without a sound!

Sophia was continuing the daydream when she heard the sound of her grandmother's car. She decided, "Maybe today I'll be Sophia at 3 feet, 3 inches (99 cm) tall, and I'll *skip* to the door to greet my grandmother, because I can have fun being small!

OBJECTS IN OUR HOUSE

National Standards Addressed

- **Standard 1.** The physically literate individual demonstrates competency in a variety of motor skills and movement patterns.
- **Standard 4.** The physically literate individual exhibits responsible personal and social behavior that respects self and others.

Central Focus

To increase the child's language arts skills by imitating actions and expressive feelings of the character in this fictional movement narrative about appliances found in the home.

Learning Task

Class organization: Children scattered in general space.

Present the following: *I will read a story aloud to the class, and it is your task to imitate the action words and behaviors.*

Ella *tiptoed* quietly down the stairs so she wouldn't wake her parents. She had just started to *open* the refrigerator door for a snack when the refrigerator said, "Hello, Ella. Would you like to join a kitchen party?" "Okay, what do I do?" Ella asked.

The frying pan told Ella to make believe she was *breaking* two eggs and *scrambling* them with a fork.

The stove asked Ella to show how fast she could *run* and how *hot* she could become.

The toaster challenged Ella to *stoop* down low and *shoot* upward like a slice of toast.

The hand mixer told Ella to use her arms and *whip* the pancake batter.

The juicer asked Ella to *squeeze* three oranges to make orange juice.

Ella was beginning to feel *tired* when the blender exclaimed, "Ella, we can make a fruit smoothie!"

She *stretched* and *reached* for the milk in the refrigerator and carefully *poured* it into the blender. Next, she added blueberries and strawberries. The blender said, "Now *dig* deep into the yogurt container and *scoop* out large round balls of frozen yogurt." Ella *screwed* the lid on the blender so she wouldn't spill the fruit smoothie. With a *push* of one button, she began to *race* around in a circle while *waving* her arms to *mix* all the ingredients together.

"Time to clean the kitchen," said the refrigerator. With that suggestion, the dishwasher challenged Ella to *wave* her hands in a *splashing* motion.

The vacuum cleaner asked to be *pushed* forward and *pulled* back and to the side and in a zigzag direction.

"Wait, I seem to be doing all the work for this party," said Ella as she *collapsed* into a chair.

"Wake up, sleepy head," whispered her mother, "It's time to help me prepare a large, healthy breakfast."

"Thank you, Mother. A small bowl of cereal and a glass of milk would do nicely," Ella said as she thought back on her midnight visit to the kitchen.

AMUSEMENT PARK

National Standards Addressed

- **Standard 1.** The physically literate individual demonstrates competency in a variety of motor skills and movement patterns.
- **Standard 4.** The physically literate individual exhibits responsible personal and social behavior that respects self and others.

Central Focus

To increase the child's language arts skills by imitating actions and expressive feelings of the character in the fictional movement narrative related to a visit to the amusement park.

Learning Task

Class organization: Children are scattered in general space.

Present the following: *I will read a story aloud to the class, and it is your task to imitate the action words and behaviors.*

> Yosi's heart was beating quickly as he entered the amusement park with his uncle.
>
> On the Ferris wheel, Yosi *moved* in a large circular shape.
>
> He *bobbed* up and down on the merry-go-round's moving horse and,
>
> He *zoomed* to the top of a steel mountain on the giant roller coaster.
>
> The mirrors in the funhouse made Yosi look very *tall* and *skinny*, *short* and *wide*, and even *crooked*.
>
> His body *whirled* around and around on the spinning-cup ride.
>
> He was *jerked* from side to side while *steering* a bumper car.
>
> The haunted house made Yosi *shake* and *tremble* with fear.
>
> He *floated* in the clouds in the balloon ride.
>
> He *dangled* over a cliff in the daredevil ride,
>
> And he ended the day by *sliding* down a long, steep water slide.
>
> "That was great. My heart has been beating fast all day," said Yosi.
>
> "Your heart is very fit," replied his uncle. "Let's see if it can pump faster," Yosi's uncle said as he challenged Yosi to a *race* home.

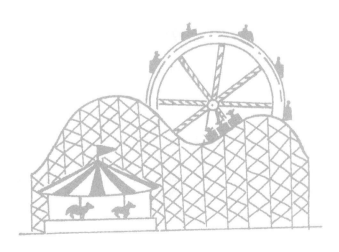

ICE RINK

National Standards Addressed

- **Standard 1.** The physically literate individual demonstrates competency in a variety of motor skills and movement patterns.
- **Standard 4.** The physically literate individual exhibits responsible personal and social behavior that respects self and others.

Central Focus

To increase the child's language arts skills by focusing on the letters W, S, and P and by imitating actions and expressive feelings of fictional characters at an ice skating rink.

Learning Task

Class organization: Children are scattered in general space.

Present the following: *I will read a story aloud to the class, and it is your task to imitate the action words and behaviors.*

Will *reached* and *stretched* for his ice skates. He *ran* to his school's hockey rink called the Frosty Forum. He arrived just in time to *find* his own self-space for the team's daily stretches.

He *stretched* his body to *create* a wide shape and a twisted shape, followed by a narrow shape, and then he *curled* his body into a tiny snowball shape. Coach Wally Walrus told the team it was important to warm the leg muscles. Everyone began to *run* and *pump* their arms while staying in their self-space. Will could feel his heart pump faster.

Will *stooped* down and *laced* his skates. On the ice, he *skated* faster and faster, his little legs taking long strides. Soon Will spied his two teammates Peter Polar Bear and Sasha Seal. The three teammates *dashed* and *darted* throughout the ice rink without touching each other.

"I know!" said Will, "We can also make paths on the ice to get in shape!" The three friends *skated* in the shape of a triangle, a rectangle, a circle, and a figure eight.

"Let's try to *skate* in the shapes of the letters of our first names," said Sasha Seal. Will *wobbled* along and made a letter W on the ice. Sasha *skated* smoothly over the ice while making the letter S, and Peter Polar Bear *plodded* along in the shape of a letter P.

Coach Wally Walrus *blew* the whistle to gather his team. Will was feeling very happy and knew it was going to be a good season.

SPORTS STADIUM

National Standards Addressed

- **Standard 1.** The physically literate individual demonstrates competency in a variety of motor skills and movement patterns.
- **Standard 4.** The physically literate individual exhibits responsible personal and social behavior that respects self and others.

Central Focus

To increase the child's language arts skills while imitating actions and expressive feelings of the characters in this fictional movement narrative about a variety of physical activities that take place at a sports stadium.

Learning Task

Class organization: Children are scattered in general space.

Present the following: *I will read a story aloud to the class, and it is your task to imitate the action words and behaviors.*

Andre and Alexis waited quietly in line to pay for the tickets to the sporting event. The sports stadium was a giant round shape that contained many seats. People came to the stadium to watch players do these things:

Jump high to shoot a basketball,

Kick a soccer ball down the field,

Swing a tennis racket at the side of the body,

Skate gracefully in the shape of the number eight,

Run and *catch* a football with *outstretched* hands,

Leap in the air and then *roll* on a gymnastics mat,

Sprint in an oval shape quickly in a track race.

Andre and Alexis liked to watch the players *jump* up and *slap* hands and give each other *handshakes* at the end of the game.

Today, the two children *wave* their arms, and *clap* their hands for their favorite team.

Tomorrow, they will practice *running, hopping, jumping,* and all the physical skills in their favorite sport so that someday people will come to watch them play in the sports stadium.

HARDWARE STORE

National Standards Addressed

- **Standard 1.** The physically literate individual demonstrates competency in a variety of motor skills and movement patterns.
- **Standard 4.** The physically literate individual exhibits responsible personal and social behavior that respects self and others.

Central Focus

To increase the child's language arts skills by imitating actions associated with tools found at a hardware store.

Learning Task

Class organization: Children are scattered in general space.

Present the following: *I will read a story aloud to the class, and it is your task to imitate the action words and behaviors.*

Zach was fascinated with tools. As Zach and his father entered the hardware store, his father turned toward Zach and said, "Let's play a game to help you learn about each tool."

Zach's father *stretched* up to *reach* for the handsaw. Handsaws have very sharp teeth to cut lumber. "*Show* me your sharp teeth," he said.

"Now pretend to *saw* lumber by *pushing* one arm out in front of the body and *pulling* it back in. Do this five times."

"Drills are used for boring holes. *Spin* your body around three times like the movement of the drill."

"Pretend your arms are pliers and *squeeze* them together to *grip* the wood."

"Can you *twist* your whole body around and make believe you are a screwdriver?"

"What movement would your arm make if you were using a hammer?" asked Zach's father (*pounding*).

"Is it possible to *tighten* a nut and bolt with a wrench? Keep *twisting* the nut toward you."

"Now we need to *rub* sandpaper back and forth to make the wood smooth."

"If you can make the shape of a hook, I will buy one for home," Zach's father said.

With that, Zach *curled* both arms to form the shape of a hook. "Why do we need a hook?" asked Zach.

"To hang this special bird house in our backyard," replied Zach's father.

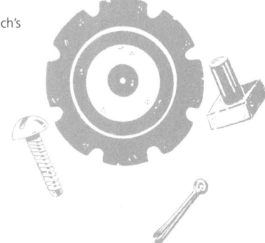

RACETRACK

National Standards Addressed

- **Standard 1.** The physically literate individual demonstrates competency in a variety of motor skills and movement patterns.
- **Standard 4.** The physically literate individual exhibits responsible personal and social behavior that respects self and others.

Central Focus

To increase the child's language arts skills by imitating actions and expressive feelings of the characters in the fictional movement narrative related to car racing at the racetrack.

Learning Task

Class organization: Children are scattered in general space.

Present the following: *I will read a story aloud to the class, and it is your task to imitate the action words and behaviors.*

Hiroshi took the white paper napkin that protected his ice cream cone and *crinkled* it in his hands. This would make a perfect cloth to *rub* water on the windshield of the bright-red race car. "I want to be a race car driver when I grow up," thought Hiroshi.

Hiroshi's sister, Yoko, was frantically *waving* and *jumping* up with excitement. She yelled, "Hurry, Hiroshi, we need to find a seat in the bleachers."

Hiroshi *dodged* and *darted* through the crowd. He *climbed* up 10 steps to sit with his sister. As he watched the cars drive closer to the starting line, he *closed* his eyes and thought what it would be like to be a world-famous race car driver.

He thought about *strapping on* his helmet and safety belt, *turning* the key, and hearing the engine firing. The *trembling* of the car made his hands *shake* on the *vibrating* steering wheel. Suddenly, the light turned green and the man *waved* the start flag. Hiroshi *extended* his leg and *slammed* on the gas pedal as the car *accelerated* to a high speed.

Weaving in and out, he began to *pass* other drivers. As he approached the lead car, he heard the crowd *cheering* and *clapping*. He wanted to finish in first place, so he *squeezed* the wheel and made an abrupt *turn* without touching any of the other cars. The car's tires *spun* as he *grabbed* the gear shift and *moved* it forward with one hand. The car *shook* as he moved closer to the finish line and *zipped* past all the other drivers. "I won! I won!" yelled Hiroshi, as he *waved* one hand in the air.

"What are you shouting about?" asked Yoko, "The race hasn't even begun." The two children *sat* motionless, waiting for the start of the race. Feeling carefree, Yoko *closed* her eyes and wondered what it would be like to be a famous race car driver.

SHOE STORE

National Standards Addressed

- **Standard 1.** The physically literate individual demonstrates competency in a variety of motor skills and movement patterns.
- **Standard 4.** The physically literate individual exhibits responsible personal and social behavior that respects self and others.

Central Focus

To increase the child's language arts skills by imitating actions and expressive feelings associated with the use of various forms of footwear found in a community shoe store.

Learning Task

Class organization: Children are scattered in general space.

Present the following: *I will read a story aloud to the class, and it is your task to imitate the action words and behaviors.*

A trip to the community shoe store was a special event, and Malika and Rashid's mother had promised the children they could each purchase one new pair of shoes. Malika considered buying a pair of ballerina slippers so she could *twirl* and *whirl* around and around.

"Perhaps I'll try on a pair of running shoes," said Malika. The salesman quickly *stretched* his arms over his head and *climbed* 10 rungs of the tall ladder to locate the shoes. He handed each child a pair of shoes. The children noticed that these shoes made them feel as light as a feather as they *sprinted* forward in the store's aisles.

"May we try on a pair of basketball shoes?" asked Malika. The salesperson *climbed* nine rungs of the ladder. Rashid began to *dribble* imaginary basketballs in zigzag patterns and take fancy *shots* over his head. Malika showed the salesperson how to *run* in place and *lift* her knees to get in shape for basketball.

"I'm really more interested in buying tennis shoes," said Rashid. So the salesperson *climbed* eight rungs of the ladder. Malika and Rashid pretended to *swing* tennis rackets beside their bodies and *hit* the tennis ball forcefully over the net.

The salesperson suggested buying soccer shoes because the boys and girls in the neighborhood were beginning to form teams. The children imagined themselves *dribbling* a soccer ball using the inside of each foot.

"May we try on football shoes?" asked Rashid. The salesperson then *climbed* seven rungs of the ladder. "*Run* backward for a long pass," yelled Malika, "A little more, a little more, *stop* and *catch* the football." Both children *jumped* up and down because they had scored a touchdown!

"Can you please show us a pair of hiking boots?" Malika asked sweetly as the salesperson *climbed* six rungs of the ladder. Malika and Rashid *pulled* on the heavily padded boots. The children pretended to *throw* safety ropes and *climb* jagged rocks along wooded trails.

"These shoes *make* me feel heavy," said Malika, "I would like to try a pair of swim flippers." The salesperson watched the children *sit* on the floor and quickly *flutter* their legs up and down to test the flippers.

Suddenly, Rashid *pointed* to a soft pair of slippers with bunny ears and a fluffy tail. "Yes, yes, if that is what you want, but you must promise to *jump* like a bunny when you leave," said the salesperson as he *climbed* up five rungs for his final trip up the ladder.

The two children *scuffled* around the footstool, *scampered* on their hands and feet, *sprang* high into the air, and finally pretended to *jump* like a bunny as they agreed to buy the warm and fuzzy slippers.

The children *jumped* seven times to exit the store. The salesperson *looked* at the large pile of opened boxes, "I wonder whether those soft, fluffy slippers would fit me?" he asked with a *smile* and a long sigh.

MAGICAL POWERS

National Standards Addressed

- **Standard 1.** The physically literate individual demonstrates competency in a variety of motor skills and movement patterns.
- **Standard 4.** The physically literate individual exhibits responsible personal and social behavior that respects self and others.

Central Focus

To increase the child's language arts skills by imitating actions and expressive feelings of the characters within a fictional narrative.

Learning Task

Class organization: Children are scattered in general space.

Present the following: *I will read a story aloud to the class, and it is your task to imitate the action words and behaviors.*

A long time ago in a neighborhood far away lived a small boy named Tyrell. It was Tyrell's dream to become a fearless knight and to slay mean dragons with his sword. Every day, Tyrell would *tiptoe* to the garden to watch the knights train for this job. Tyrell liked to *grab* a long stick and pretend it was a mighty sword. He *charged* forward and *plunged* the sword into the air.

He knew that knights needed to be very strong and quick on their feet. He practiced *marching* in circles, *shuffling* his feet very quickly, *crouching* down, and *hiding* behind rocks. He learned how to *spring* up, *pointing* his stick into the air.

One day, the tallest knight spied Tyrell *skipping* back and forth to make his leg muscles stronger. "Would you like to join the other knights in hunting for a dragon?" the tall knight asked. Tyrell *jumped* up three times with excitement. He *ran* to *snatch* his stick, and with one big *leap*, he *landed* on the knight's white horse.

The two riders *galloped* along on the horse *searching* and *exploring* the deep forest with the other knights. Finally, one knight began to *wave* a large flag. All the knights *bounded* off their horses. Tyrell *smacked* the ground with a big kerplunk!

Suddenly Tyrell began to feel *timid* and *small.* He *coiled* his body into a tiny shape. His shoulders *shivered* with fear, "What am I doing here?" he thought.

Tyrell *felt* a tap on his shoulder. He *hid* his head in his hands, fearing that it might be a fire-breathing dragon *stomping* through the forest. He slowly *lifted* his head. It was the Great Wizard *looking* down at him. "Tyrell, do you really want to slay a dragon?" asked the wizard.

"No," replied Tyrell. "I want to return to the castle where I am safe from dragons and swords." "Very well," said the wizard as he *waved* a wand over Tyrell's head.

Tyrell felt his body *twirling* and *spinning* around and around until he heard a *thump.* He was *sitting* quietly in his mother's large wooden chair. "There's my brave boy," said Tyrell's mother. "What do you have in your hand, a make-believe sword?"

"Oh, no," said Tyrell, "That could be dangerous. My stick is a make-believe wand so I can practice *flying* through the sky like the Great Wizard who rescues little boys and girls from wicked dragons."

"Very well," said Tyrell's mother, "But first you must *wash* your hands for dinner." "Yes," said Tyrell as he *tossed* the stick into the fireplace and *smiled.*

RAINBOW MAGIC

National Standards Addressed

- **Standard 1.** The physically literate individual demonstrates competency in a variety of motor skills and movement patterns.
- **Standard 4.** The physically literate individual exhibits responsible personal and social behavior that respects self and others.

Central Focus

To increase the child's language arts skills by imitating actions of the characters, natural objects, and living creatures found outdoors depicted in a fictional movement narrative.

Learning Task

Class organization: Children are scattered in general space.

Present the following: *I will read a story aloud to the class, and it is your task to imitate the action words and behaviors.*

Hans *skipped* to the window. It was no longer raining. He said, "*Look*, Jules, a giant rainbow has formed in the sky and it ends in our backyard!" The two children *rushed* outside. They began to *hunt* and *search* for the pot of gold that is supposed to be at the end of every rainbow. After *crawling* around the bushes, *leaping* over mud puddles, and *searching* under every rock, the children *plunked* their bodies down. "I do not understand," said Hans. "There should be a pot of gold."

Suddenly a tiny green man appeared. He was only 6 inches (15 cm) tall. "Perhaps children, I can help you find gold." The children *jumped* up with excitement. They *watched* the little man *pick* up a stick and *point* to the grass. The little man said, "Show me how your body can be long and narrow like a tall, green blade of grass." Then he *pointed* to a green grasshopper and a green frog. "Can you *rub* your legs together and *jump* from flower to flower like the grasshopper?" "*Stoop* down on your hands and feet and use all of your muscles to *jump* like a frog."

The little green man *pointed* his stick at the colorful treasures in the fruit and vegetable garden. He said, "See if you can *make* the shape of a large orange pumpkin. *Bend* carefully and *pull* the orange carrot from the ground. Who can *stretch* up on their toes toward the blue sky to *pick* red apples? Try to be as tiny as the red cherries hanging from the tree. Can you *combine* your bodies to form a bunch of purple grapes?"

The little man motioned the children to *gallop* to the oak tree. "Wonderful," thought Hans, "Maybe the gold is hidden in the tree."

The little man asked the children to *place* their hands on their heads and to *stoop* low to the ground. "Hee hee, you've made the cap and the shape of a brown acorn!" laughed the little man. The children continued by *scurrying* along on their hands and feet pretending to be black ants. "You may *stand* now," said the little man. "It is time for me to go."

The two children had just begun to *stretch* their bodies into a tall shape when they both shouted, "No, wait! We did not find the gold!"

"Oh, yes, you did children," said the little man as he started to *float* away. "You found the gold when you first entered your backyard. *Stretch* up and look in the sky."

"Oh," said the children as they *glanced* up. The sun's golden rays shone brightly into their eyes.

MACHINES

National Standards Addressed

- **Standard 1.** The physically literate individual demonstrates competency in a variety of motor skills and movement patterns.
- **Standard 4.** The physically literate individual exhibits responsible personal and social behavior that respects self and others.

Central Focus

To increase the child's language arts skills by imitating actions of the objects and machines depicted in a fictional movement narrative.

Learning Task

Class organization: Children are scattered in general space.

Present the following: *I will read a story aloud to the class, and it is your task to imitate the action words and behaviors.*

Chen and Tao were *excited* to visit the Machine Factory. They knew that each object in the factory challenged visitors to move in a special way. The trip through the factory would end when the two children found the world's greatest machine.

The first learning center was called the Wonder Wheel. Here the children were encouraged to *make* the shape of a wheel and to *roll* forward. Some children were even able to *roll* backward.

The Pastel Pendulum Center challenged the children to *raise* their arms over their heads and to *sway* their bodies to one side as far as possible and then to *sway* their bodies in the opposite direction. The next *swaying* action was slightly smaller and then smaller until their bodies were *still*.

The sign at the Expanding Escalator said, "Walk to the Stars." To perform this challenge, the children pretended to *walk* up stairs for one minute.

The Exercise Elevator encouraged the children to *stoop* into a small shape and then slowly *rise* into a *stretched* shape. Tao liked the feeling of traveling upward.

The next learning center was the Wacky Windmill. In this center, the children pretended their arms were large windmill sails being *turned* by the wind. Chen said, "This is how we cool our home with fans!"

The guide at the Machine Factory said, "Now that our journey is almost completed, who would like to guess what the world's greatest machine is?" Chen *raised* his hand and said, "It's a supersonic jet," as he quickly *zoomed* throughout the activity area. Tao said, "It's a giant submarine," as she pretended to *dive* and *speed* through the water. Other children guessed the movement of a rocket *blasting* upward, a helicopter with *twirling* blades, a giant cruise ship *moving* through the ocean, and an underground railway *following* curvy tunnels.

"These are wonderful machines," said the guide, "but the world's greatest machine is the heart inside your body. The heart muscle continually *pumps* blood around the body." She told the children that they had the power to make the machine pump faster by *running* quickly, *jumping* up, *galloping* in a circle, *leaping* over imaginary objects, and by performing other fun movements.

"You also have the ability to slow this machine by *lying* quietly at a low level." With that suggestion, Chen and Tao decided to *rest* the World's Greatest Machine.

SPACE TRAVEL

National Standards Addressed

- **Standard 1.** The physically literate individual demonstrates competency in a variety of motor skills and movement patterns.
- **Standard 4.** The physically literate individual exhibits responsible personal and social behavior that respects self and others.

Central Focus

To increase the child's language arts skills by imitating actions of the characters in a movement narrative when taking a journey through our solar system.

Learning Task

Class organization: Children are scattered in general space.

Present the following: *I will read a story aloud to the class, and it is your task to imitate the action words and behaviors.*

One sunny afternoon Aaron and Shira decided to take a trip to Space World. Their adventures began at the Moon Walk, where they were encouraged to *step* over five large moon craters. Real craters are formed when stray pieces of rock collide with the moon. This exciting walk led the children to the Space Maze, where they *dashed* and *darted* along narrow pathways and then *crawled* through a black hole.

As the children *raised* their bodies, they saw a sign for Meteor Magic. Meteors, or shooting stars, burn up as they streak into the Earth's atmosphere. At this station the ground was hot, so the two children *walked* on their *tiptoes.* At the Milky Way Mystery, the children *stretched* up to *touch* 10 bright stars that were sparkling in the sky.

In Planet Play, the children traveled through the solar system where they . . .

Marched in a circle around Mercury,

Vibrated back and forth and made *shaking* movements to visit Venus,

Skipped in an oval shape to reach Saturn,

Jumped high with two feet to reach Jupiter, and
They *advanced* bravely forward while *ducking* and *dodging* through the meteor shower.

They also . . .

Leaped over hot lava pits on Mars,

Plodded along to Pluto,

Soared to the Sun,

Strutted to Neptune, and
They *charged* through the comet's long tale.

The last space station was the most challenging. It was called Save Our Planet. At this station the children *collected* a bag filled with cans and bottles, *stacked* newspaper into piles, *painted* garbage cans, and learned the importance of keeping the Earth clean and safe.

With this important message, Aaron and Shira *stooped* low, *blasted off,* and *soared* at full speed until they landed at home.

SCIENCE MUSEUM

National Standards Addressed

- **Standard 1.** The physically literate individual demonstrates competency in a variety of motor skills and movement patterns.
- **Standard 4.** The physically literate individual exhibits responsible personal and social behavior that respects self and others.

Central Focus

To increase the child's language arts skills by imitating actions and comparing the movements of several living creatures from prehistoric times to those today.

Learning Task

Class organization: Children are scattered in general space.

Present the following: *I will read a story aloud to the class, and it is your task to imitate the action words and behaviors.*

"Just think, all life began in the water!" Lars said, as he *stretched* up to *set* the plastic glass container in the sink. "I wish I had been born when the giant dinosaurs roamed the earth."

"Not me," said Eva. "Some of the first fish were sharks with pointed snouts, frightening jaws, and razor-sharp teeth. I like my goldfish." The two children *grabbed* their dinosaur backpacks and *sprinted* to Dinosaur Kingdom, a favorite community attraction.

At the first learning center, a guide told the children that the largest dinosaur was called the Brachiosaurus. It was taller than a four-story building. Its nose was a bump on the top of its head. Lars and Eva were challenged to *move* like several large animals that still exist today. They pretended to *dive* through the water like the huge blue whale, which can weigh as much as 30 elephants, and they *splashed* in make-believe water like a hippopotamus, and they *pounded* on their chests like a gorilla.

At the second learning center, the children viewed the next-largest dinosaur, the Apatosaurus. This dinosaur was 80 feet (24 m) long with legs as thick as tree trunks. It used to be called the Brontosaurus, which means thunder reptile. The children were challenged to *walk* and *stomp* so that their footsteps sounded like thunder.

"The Apatosaurus liked to eat the leaves from the tallest trees," said the guide. "We have animals today that stand very tall. Giraffes can eat more than 65 pounds (29.5 kg) of leaves in one day." "Gee, that's how much I weigh," said Eva. Who can *gallop, stop*, and *stretch* up to *snatch* an imaginary acacia leaf like the 16-foot (5 m) giraffe we see in the African savanna?

In the third learning center, the children watched a movie about the Stegosaurus. This name means "roofed reptile." This 30-foot-long (9 m) creature had large bony plates on its back and tail. It had four sharp spikes at the end of its tail to swing at other dinosaurs. The guide reminded the children of the porcupine. Porcupines are the size of small dogs, but if you get too close it may strike you with its tail, which is covered with sharp quills. Can you pretend to be a porcupine by *turning* your back on your attacker, *rattling* your quills, *grunting*, and *stamping* your feet?

At learning center four, the children learned that some dinosaurs could fly, but they didn't have feathers. One of these was called the Rhamphorhynchus. It had skin that stretched from its front legs to its back claws. It flapped this skin to glide in the air and used its long tail to help it steer. Lars *jumped* up and said, "I can move like several large birds." So he *soared* like an eagle, *swooped* down to the water like a brown pelican spotting fish near the surface, and imagined he could *stretch* his arms to be like the 9-foot (3 m) wings of the California condor.

At learning center five, the children marveled at the statue of the Styracosaurus. This dinosaur had huge horns on its head and a bony frill made of six sharp spikes around its neck. The frill was heavy and caused it to *clomp* along slowly on four thick legs. Today's black rhinoceros has two large horns and charges if it is attacked by a lion. Lars showed the group how to *scuff* at the ground and *charge* like a raging rhino.

In learning center six, the guide showed the children a large stuffed Archelon and said, "This dinosaur looked like the turtles we see today, except that it was as large as a car!" At this center, the children were asked to move like the animals we see today that live on the land and that swim in the water. Lars used his arms and *dragged* his body along the floor like a walrus. Eva chose to *slip* and *slide* like a seal, which can stay under water for an hour before coming up for air.

At learning center seven, the children saw a make-believe skeleton of the Tyrannosaurus Rex. The guide said, "This dinosaur was the largest of the meat-eating reptiles. It walked on two legs and could lift more than 400 pounds (181 kg) with its arms. It was the most feared by all the dinosaurs. It was feared like the lion, the king of beasts in the jungle. Did you know that rex is a Latin word meaning king? So the lion and Tyrannosaurus Rex are king in their own worlds. " Lars pretended to *stalk* prey like a Tyrannosaurus Rex. "That's correct," said the guide.

The children began to feel tired when the guide said, "There were more than 350 types of dinosaurs, but you can return tomorrow and we'll continue." Lars and Eva were leaving Dinosaur Kingdom when Eva spotted a water fountain. "Do you want a refreshing drink of water, Lars?" she asked. "No thank you," he replied as both children *leaped* over stone pebbles on their way home, "I think I'll switch to milk."

References

Bandura, A. (1977). *Social learning theory.* Englewood Cliffs, NJ: Prentice Hall.

Beaty, J. J. (2014). *Observing development of the young child* (8th ed.). Boston: Pearson Education.

Bloom, B., Englehart, M. Furst, E., Hill, W., & Krathwohl, D. (1956). *Taxonomy of educational objectives: The classification of educational goals. Handbook I: Cognitive domain.* New York, NY: Longmans, Green & Co.

Clements, R. (2016). Physical education. In D. Couchenour & J. K. Chrisman (Eds.), *Encyclopedia of contemporary early childhood education* (pp. 998-1000). Thousand Oaks, CA: Sage Reference Publication.

Clements, R. (1998). "Integrating Physical Play Throughout the Prekindergarten Program." Illinois Resource Center Summer Institute, 1998.

Clements, R. (1988). A multi-case study of the implementation of movement education in selected schools. Ann Arbor: MI : UMI: Dissertation Service.

Copple, C. & Bredekamp, S. (Eds.) (2010). *Developmentally appropriate practice in early childhood programs serving children from birth through age 8* (3rd ed.). Washington, D.C.: National Association for the Education of Young Children.

Dewey, J. (1916). *Democracy and education: An introduction to the philosophy of education.* New York, NY: Macmillan.

Erikson, E., (1993). *Childhood and society.* New York, NY: Norton. (Original work published in 1963)

Froebel, F. W. A. (1887). *The education of man.* (W. N. Hailmann, Trans.) New York, NY: Appleton. (Original work published 1826)

Graham, G., Holt/Hale, S., & Parker, M. (2012). *Children moving: A reflective approach to teaching physical education with movement analysis wheel* (9th ed.). New York, NY: McGraw-Hill Education.

Mandigo, J., Francis, N., Lodewyk, K., & Lopez, R. (2012). Physical literacy for educators. *Physical Education and Health Journal,* 75(3): 27–30.

McAfee, O., Leong, D., & Bodrova, E. (2015). *Assessing and guiding young children's development and learning* (6th ed.). Boston: Pearson Education.

National Association for Sport and Physical Education, now known as SHAPE America - Society of Health and Physical Educators. (2009). *Active start: A statement of physical activity guidelines for children from birth to age 5* (2nd ed.). Reston, VA: Author.

Office of Head Start. (2015). *Head Start early learning outcomes framework: Ages birth to five.* Washington, DC: Office of Head Start.

Piaget, J. (1962). *Play, dreams, and imitation in childhood.* New York, NY: Norton.

Roetert, E. P., Jefferies, S.C. (2014). Embracing physical literacy. *Journal of Physical Education, Recreation and Dance, 85*(8) 38-40.

SHAPE America – Society of Health and Physical Educators. (2013). *National Standards for K-12 physical education.* Reston, VA: Author.

SHAPE America – Society of Health and Physical Educators. (2013). *Grade-level outcomes for K-12 physical education.* Reston, VA: Author.

SHAPE America – Society of Health and Physical Educators. (2014). *National Standards & Grade-Level Outcomes for K-12 physical education.* Champaign, IL: Human Kinetics.

Singer, J. L. (1973). *The child's world of make-believe. Experimental studies of imaginative play.* New York, NY: Academic Press.

Skinner, B. F. (1974). *About behaviorism*. New York, NY: Knopf.

Stanford Center for Assessment, Learning, & Equity (SCALE). (2016). *edTPA early childhood assessment handbook*. Stanford, CA: SCALE.

The National Association for the Education of Young Children (2003). *Early-childhood curriculum, assessment, and program evaluation: Building an effective accountable system in programs for children birth through age eight*. (Joint Position Statement of the National Association for the Education of Young Children and the National Association of Early-Childhood Specialists in State Departments of Education NAECS/SDE).Washington, DC: Author.

Van Horn, J., Nourot, P. M., Scales, B., & Alward, K. R. (2015). *Play at the center of the curriculum* (6th ed.). Boston, MA: Pearson Higher Education.

Warner, L., & Sower, J. (2005). *Educating young children from preschool through primary grades*. Boston, MA: Allyn & Bacon.

Whitehead, M. (2001). The concept of physical literacy. *European Journal of Physical Education*, 6, 127–138.

Suggested Resources for Teachers

Casbergue, R. M., & Strickland, D. S. (2015). *Reading and writing in preschool*. New York, NY: Guilford Press.

Graves, M. F. (2016). *The vocabulary book: Learning and instruction*. (2nd ed.). New York, NY: Teachers College Press.

Hayes, L. & Flanigan, K. (2014). *Developing word recognition*. New York, NY: Guilford Press.

Helman, L. (Ed.) (2016). *Literacy development with English learners: Research-based instruction in grades K-4*. New York, NY: Guilford Press.

Hodgson, J. (2001). *Mastering movement: The life and work of Rudolf Laban*. New York, NY: Routledge and Kegan Paul Ltd.

James, A., & Manson, M. (2015). *Physical education: A literacy based approach*. Urbana, IL: Sagamore.

Koster, J. B. (2015). *Growing artists: Teaching the arts to young children* (6th ed.). Stamford, CT: Cengage Learning.

Lange, R. (Ed.). (1975). *Laban's principles of dance and movement notation*. London, England: MacDonald & Evans. (Original work published in 1956)

Lehn, B. (2002). *What is an artist?* Brookfield, CT: Millbrook Press.

Muybridge, E. (1957). *Animals in motion*. Mineola, NY: Dover.

About the Authors

Rhonda L. Clements, EdD, is a professor and the director of the master's of arts in teaching (MAT) program in physical education and sport pedagogy at Manhattanville College in Purchase, New York. At Manhattanville College, she collects data regarding early childhood play activities and teaches about historical and sociocultural issues in sport and physical education.

Clements is the author of 10 books on movement, play, and games. She is past president of the American Association for the Child's Right to Play, a United Nations–recognized association composed of experts in play, games, and sports from 49 countries. The association's primary purpose is to protect, preserve, and promote play and leisure activities throughout the world.

Clements has written numerous articles related to physical education, including 20 on sport and play factors. She is also a consultant for several manufacturers of sport equipment and playthings and has been interviewed by more than 300 journalists regarding children's right to leisure and physical play. She has presented at 40 international or national conferences and more than 60 state or local conferences on topics related to cultural understanding through play and sport. Clements lives in New York City.

Sharon L. Schneider, MS, is an early childhood adjunct assistant professor at Hofstra University in Long Island, New York. At Hofstra University, she teaches all the required courses for undergraduate and graduate students pertaining to child movement, music, rhythm, and play and their integration into academics for early childhood and elementary educators. In addition, she has been a keynote speaker, a consultant for numerous groups, and a visiting scholar at the University of Wisconsin–Madison.

Schneider has served as a national physical activity consultant for Head Start Body Start and the National Center for Physical Development and Outdoor Play, and she has served as a facilitator for I Am Moving, I Am Learning. She has been an officer and member of the executive board of the American Association for the Child's Right to Play, for which she also served as an alternate representative to UNICEF and the United Nations Early Childhood Care and Development in Emergencies Working Group.

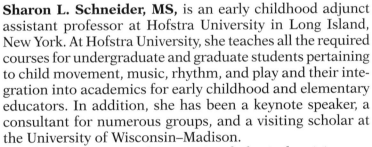

Schneider enjoys family adventures, her grandchildren, and the bragging rights she earns playing in her family's fantasy football league.

About SHAPE America

SHAPE America – Society of Health and Physical Educators is committed to ensuring that all children have the opportunity to lead healthy, physically active lives. As the nation's largest membership organization of health and physical education professionals, SHAPE America works with its 50 state affiliates and is a founding partner of national initiatives including the Presidential Youth Fitness Program, Active Schools, and the Jump Rope For Heart and Hoops For Heart programs.

Since its founding in 1885, the organization has defined excellence in physical education, most recently creating *National Standards & Grade-Level Outcomes for K-12 Physical Education* (2014), National Standards for Initial Physical Education Teacher Education (2016), National Standards for Health Education Teacher Education (2017) and *National Standards for Sport Coaches* (2006). Also, SHAPE America participated as a member of the Joint Committee on National Health Education Standards, which published *National Health Education Standards, Second Edition: Achieving Excellence* (2007). Our programs, products and services provide the leadership, professional development and advocacy that support health and physical educators at every level, from preschool through university graduate programs.

The SHAPE America website, www.shapeamerica.org, holds a treasure trove of free resources for health and physical educators, adapted physical education teachers, teacher trainers and coaches, including activity calendars, curriculum resources, tools and templates, assessments and more. Visit www.shapeamerica.org and search for Teacher's Toolbox.

Every spring, SHAPE America hosts its National Convention & Expo, the premier national professional-development event for health and physical educators.

Advocacy is an essential element in the fulfillment of our mission. By speaking out for the school health and physical education professions, SHAPE America strives to make an impact on the national policy landscape.

Our Vision: A nation in which all children are prepared to lead healthy, physically active lives.

Our Mission: To advance professional practice and promote research related to health and physical education, physical activity, dance and sport.

Our Commitment: 50 Million Strong by 2029

Approximately 50 million students are enrolled currently in America's elementary and secondary schools (grades preK through 12). SHAPE America wants to ensure that by the time today's youngest students graduate from high school in 2029, all of America's young people are empowered to lead healthy and active lives through effective health and physical education programs. To learn more about 50 Million Strong by 2029, visit www.shapeamerica.org.

With one step, you'll join a national movement.

Membership will advance your career — and connect you to a national movement of educators who are preparing students to lead healthy, physically active lives.

Joining SHAPE America Is Your First Step Toward:

- **Improving your instructional practices.** Membership is your direct connection to the classroom resources, webinars, workshops, books, and all the professional development you need. **Members save up to 30%!**

- **Staying current on trends in education.** We will deliver the news to you through our weekly e-newsletter *Et Cetera,* our quarterly member newsletter *Momentum,* and peer-reviewed journals such as *Strategies: A Journal for Physical and Sport Educators,* the *American Journal of Health Education, Journal of Physical Education, Recreation & Dance,* and *Research Quarterly for Exercise and Sport.*

- **Earning recognition for you and your program.** Showcase your school's achievements and gain funding through grant and award opportunities.

- **Growing your professional network.** Whether it's a face-to-face event or online through the member-exclusive community—*Exchange*—you'll gain access to a diverse group of peers who can help you respond to daily challenges.

Join Today. shapeamerica.org/membership